EDUCATIONAL REFORM

A Self-Scrutinizing Memoir

EDUCATIONAL REFORM

A Self-Scrutinizing Memoir

Seymour B. Sarason

Teachers College, Columbia University
New York and London

Published by Teachers College Press, 1234 Amsterdam Avenue, New York, NY 10027

Library of Congress Cataloging-in-Publication Data

Sarason, Seymour Bernard, 1919–
   Educational reform : a self-scrutinizing memoir / Seymour B. Sarason.
     p. cm.
   Includes bibliographical references and index.
   ISBN 0-8077-4243-0 (pbk. : alk. paper)—ISBN 0-8077-4244-9 (cloth : alk. paper)
   1. Educational change—United States. 2. Education—United States—Evaluation.
   I. Title.
LA217.2 .S26 2002
370'.973—dc21   2001060376

ISBN 0-8077-4243-0 (paper)
ISBN 0-8077-4244-9 (cloth)

Printed on acid-free paper
Manufactured in the United States of America

09 08 07 06 05 04 03 02   8 7 6 5 4 3 2 1

To

Kenneth Wilson for intellectual stimulation

Robert Echter for unfailing friendship

Lisa Pagliaro whose graciousness and friendship
made writing for me a practical possibility

Contents

Preface

By titling this book as I have, it tells the reader that it is a personal book, an attempt to look back and judge ideas and actions I have come to see as regrettable for one or another reason. I have made mistakes and errors of omission and commission, misplaced emphases, and watered down the depth and scope of my criticisms of the reform arena. Also, the self-scrutiny revealed how I failed to see connections between that arena and other arenas of national policy, on the surface seemingly unrelated conceptually to educational reform. That does not mean that I was wrong in my basic arguments but that I did not do them the justice they deserve. That, I would like to believe, is not surprising if only because I witnessed, participated in, and wrote about educational reform for over 4 decades, a period of dizzying social and institutional change.

From the nature of the goal of this book it should be expected that themes in my previous book reappear here. I have tried to keep from going over old ground in any detail. And yet, precisely because this book by its very nature or purpose was to reexamine some of that ground, I have concentrated on what I consider a handful of ideas central to my professional development. I have learned a lot, unlearned a lot, about myself as a person and thinker; and I hope that comes through to the reader. I can assure the reader that I have always been painfully aware that my best efforts as a thinker, activist, and writer fell short of the mark I had set for myself. This book is a form of archeology of how I thought and wrote in the past. This book made me more aware of the discrepancy between what I think I wanted to do and what I did not accomplish. So what else is new in human affairs?

Seymour B. Sarason
Stratford, CT

Chapter 1

Why Not Fold My Tent and Depart?

Over 45 years I have been involved in educational reform as participant, observer, and writer. After writing my book *Teaching as a Performing Art* in 1999, I concluded that I had no more to say about educational reform. Coinciding as that decision did with the fact that I was in my eighties, I felt regret and relief. Regret because I had nothing more to say; the springs of creativity were but a trickle. Relief because I could now turn to write a second draft of a novel I wrote 10 years ago. That would not be as much of a change as one might think. Writing has always been the way I could make sense of what I had experienced, and the novel was an attempt to make sense of what I had experienced over 50 years as a faculty member at Yale. Strangely, to me, I encountered resistance to changing, revising that first draft. I say strangely because what I found so fascinating and enlivening about writing the novel was that I did not have to deal with the "real world" but with the one I was creating. It was then that I realized that I did not want to go through the *sturm und drang* of changing and reshaping what I had written; I would be operating under the constraints of what already existed, what to me was a real world with a definite form, theme, and direction.

What flashed through my mind was the question: Was my belief that I had no more to say about educational reform determined by a feeling—sometimes vague, sometimes not—that what I had written or would write had or would have no discernible, positive consequences on the arena of reform? Yes, I knew that more than a few people responded positively to what I had written, but it was also true that nothing I had written had been taken seriously for the purpose of improving education. To add insult to injury, so to speak, I did not want to admit that I truly believed that not only was there no improvement—the usual minuscule number of exceptions aside—but that the situation would inexorably slowly get worse, a belief that I stated early on in a somewhat muted form in a 1965 paper. All that I have subsequently written was an elaboration of that belief, *but I never stated it as boldly as I have here*. Why not? Was it because I did not want to be seen as a depressed pessimist or nihilist, or destructive critic? Did I harbor doubts about whether I was right?

I had no doubt that I was right. On that score I should note that I have had occasion to talk with officials in teacher unions and members of professional organizations of school administrators. I have also had opportunities to talk with scores of individuals who are faculty members of schools of education. They told me several things. The first had already begun to be publicly reported in the mass media: Over the next several years a million or more teachers as well as a significant percentage of school administrators would leave the field or retire. The second was that a significant number of retirees were leaving because they were burned out; they had no reason to believe that improving schools would ever happen. The third was that many teachers and administrators were planning to retire at the earliest time state regulations made them eligible for retirement. "They are fed up"; "They are burned out"; "They have had it"—these were the most frequent explanations. What they said was not new to me. There are data indicating that the number of new teachers who leave the field after 3–5 years of teaching is not small. Apparently, I am by no means the only person who sees school improvement as hopeless.

Why did it take so long for me to own up to the substance and depth of my belief? Why did I avoid stating and discussing it in my writings? What permitted me to ignore the obvious? Wherein was my thinking faulty? To what had I not been paying attention? These and kindred questions plagued me. If I came to the belief late in the game, I could not, should not, assume that the way I had been thinking over the years did not deserve scrutiny and criticism. The corpus of my writings contained a lot of evidence that should have forced me to recognize that what I had been experiencing and observing over the years led to the unhappy but logical conclusion that the educational reform movement as we have known it was doomed.

I did a lot of soul searching. I began to review my history of involvement in educational reform. I started with this question: When I got into the game of educational reform, what conceptual baggage was I unknowingly carrying that would render me over time blind to a belief that I only came to over decades? That led to a second question: What are the limitations of abstract knowledge when it is applied in practice? And there was a third question: Why is it so difficult to apply experience and knowledge gained in one arena of life to another which on the surface has a different label, appearance, and organization? And, finally, there is the most troubling question of all: Since it is a glimpse of the obvious that we live in a society in which different individuals and groups have different values— the *shoulds* and *oughts* that govern behavior and relationships—how do we justify saying that one value is better than another?

Pursuing these and similar questions was a humbling intellectual eye-opener. Each of my past books had two major purposes. The first was to identify relatively discrete aspects of the educational enterprise, the ways in which we ordinarily think about and engage in them, and why these ways tend to defeat our stated objective to improve the educational process and outcomes. So, for example, I wrote about the school as a social organization, the selection and preparation of educators, the role of parents, the role of the political system and its leaders, the formulation of standards and the use of tests, issues of governance, how students come to regard school learning, and more. The second purpose was to suggest alternative ways we might think about these aspects.

In the pages that follow I do not go over ground I have covered in the past. What I have said I have said, and I see no reason to change substance and thrust. But as a result of a good deal of self-examination I have come to see that the overall picture I had painted—it would be better to say mosaic than painting—was more a series of sketches than a final product or a final solution to the problem with which I was struggling. I should have known that because I have always been fascinated when I have had the opportunity to see a painting I very much liked and then to see and study the sketches—and they can be many—the artist drew before deciding to do the painting the viewer will see. It may sound oxymoronic to say that for the artist, sketching is a serious way of "playing around." The artist knows what the theme, content, and thrust of the painting will be, but he or she also knows, often from bitter experience, that there are thorny problems of spatial composition and color which will have to be confronted and resolved in a way that will do justice to theme, content, and thrust. The process of sketching is more than technical; it is more than a how-to-do-it process, a process involving more than sheer craftsmanship. It is a process of viewing and reviewing solely in the service of an already known goal: to attain that degree of technical and perceptual understanding that confirms the artist in the belief that he or she can begin to paint the final product, and to do it in a way that is satisfying to him or her. That does not mean that the artist has concluded that there is only one way best to illuminate the theme, content, and thrust; as often as not, that is not the case, which is why so many artists will, over time, produce a series of paintings having similar and even identical content. It is as if they engaged in a process of reviewing what they had done in the quest to illuminate better the artistic problem that has gripped them. It would be fair to say that it was as if they were unable or reluctant to let go of the problem, as if there was more to the problem they wanted to understand, as if the understanding they had already achieved was incomplete in one or another way. It was not that the previously achieved understanding was wrong but that it was incomplete.

I said that I regard my books as a series of sketches, each of which dealt with one or two problems of education which had not received the close scrutiny they deserved and, as a consequence, could not be a positive factor in furthering reform. But sketches for what overarching goal? What was the final picture in which these sketches were to be related to each other in ways that gave added meaning to each at the same time that each was an indispensable building block for a larger picture. The process of self-scrutiny forced me to admit several things. The first was that the conceptual picture I was trying to construct had been, to say the least, vague and murky. Second, because it was vague and murky, the sketches or building blocks would be incomplete and their potential for a larger picture unrecognized. Where you want to arrive determines how you see and judge where you are. Third, the call for reform is a call for action which in the social arena, any social arena, requires you to have a comprehensive conception of why and when people willingly change their outlooks, actions, and relationships; in addition, the conception of change should be no less relevant to the reformer than to those whom the reformer seeks to change. Just as war changes everything and everyone, ourselves as well as the enemy, the same is the case in institutional reform. I dealt very inadequately with that crucial point in my sketches; although the word *change* probably has the highest word count in my writings, my conception of change was too simplistic. Fourth, the process of self-scrutiny revealed that there is a built-in tension, even conflict, between the desire to understand social phenomena and the desire in some way to influence, change the dynamics of those phenomena. There need not, in principle at least, be a tension or conflict between the two; indeed, understanding which does not have its origins in personal experience with those phenomena is likely to be empty rhetoric or an organized set of abstractions which deserve the quip that "deep down he is shallow." But the fact is that far more often than not the desire to understand is trumped by the desire to bring about change. Finally, the desire to understand educational reform in any of its aspects, vicissitudes, and history will be woefully incomplete if that understanding is sought only in the American context.

The process of self-scrutiny is neither linear nor rational, especially if you are aware that you are engaging in the process because you have come to question whether you are justified in the way you feel about the adequacy of your past thinking, actions, formulation, and explanations. For example, I said I had concluded that I had said all I could say about educational reform. But self-scrutiny almost immediately revealed that what I had said about educational reform did not add up to a conceptually broad understanding or picture, a picture satisfying to me. It is one thing to say that you have no more to say, it is quite another thing to imply that there is not more you need to understand. That implication was at best self-serving and at worst an indulgence of arrogance. Having confronted the fact that I had not cornered the market on the understanding of educational reform, I was faced with the question: So how do I pursue achieving more understanding? Where do I start? Where do I want to end up? It has always been the case that when I start to write a book I have a pretty good idea (a kind of road map) of how I will go "from here to there." In this instance I had no road map; I had no confidence that the self-scrutiny process would ever justify writing another book. I am not here foisting my personal dilemmas on the reader but rather as a way of indicating that if there is a dividing line between the personal and the intellectual, it is very faint indeed. That is an obvious point but, as later pages of this book indicate, that point has hardly been taken seriously in educational reform on the level of thinking, acting, and writing.

The reader will inevitably judge whether the fruits of my self-scrutiny contribute to an understanding of the goals and strategies of educational reform, whether I have produced another sketch that adds little or nothing to the reader's understanding of the conceptual and practical dimensions of educational reform. It is my hope that the reader will not be passive in reacting to what I have written.

Chapter 2

The Phenomenology of the Reformer

What tends to happen to your thinking and actions when you switch from your accustomed field of work to one which is quite different in many ways? How much of your previous knowledge, skills, and experience can be utilized in what you know will be unfamiliar territory? When a person makes such a switch, it is usually because an employer has concluded that aspects of what you have previously done are transferable to the company's needs; and because you have sought to make a switch, you have made a similar decision; there is a meeting of minds, so to speak. That kind of switching or changing of career directions is very frequent, but I am not aware of any systematic studies of the phenomenology of those who make such a personally important change or how they come to judge the wisdom or adequacy of the change. I made such a change over 30 years ago, and I devote this chapter to what the self-scrutiny process revealed to me. In my case there was no employer who was seeking my services. I was a Yale professor, fully tenured, who in the traditions of the university could pretty much decide to move in any direction his interests dictated. In that sense Yale was not the conventional employer. I was on my own. My livelihood was not at stake. If it turned out that the change was unproductive or even a complete failure, I had no one to blame but myself, and the dynamics of that fact have their pluses and minuses. The major plus is that it galvanizes, stirs, and excites you because you have the opportunity to realize your ideas, hopes, dreams. It is a rejuvenating dynamic. You feel like a juvenile eager to display his adulthood, to change and conquer the world, at least a part of it. It is not unlike what happens to parents at the birth of their first child: Their dreams, hopes, expectations about what that neonate will or should become take on a strength and immediacy they did not have during the pregnancy period. (The best example of this is the song "My Boy Bill" in the musical *Carousel*, the longest solo ever in a musical.) Of course these parents "know" there will be problems ahead, predictable and unpredictable, but it is abstract knowledge, psychologically unusable knowledge.

The major minus is that it has the major defects of the plus: What galvanizes, stirs, and excites you is so compelling, magnetic, and alluring that it can—I would say always does—limit to a small or large extent how you apply the knowledge you have gained in past experience. You may have learned a great deal, but your enthusiasm and vision inherent in your goals prevent recognition of or sensitivity to factors which one part of you knows should not be downplayed, let alone ignored. Keep in mind that I am talking of switches or changes where the personal stakes are high, where your self-regard, competence, and ambitions are involved. This is not an instance of penny-ante poker; the personal stakes are high because you know that you will have to live with the consequences. And there is everything in you to want those consequences to be positive by your lights. It is not a dynamic calculated to alert you to the possibility that you are not doing justice to knowledge previously gained, whether that knowledge derives from your personal experience or that reported by others.

Let me now illustrate and elaborate on the above with my own personal switch. Here are some background factors to that switch.

1. Although I had been in and around schools from 1942 to 1960, the bulk of that involvement involved me as a researcher on test anxiety in elementary school children. I was not part of the school culture; I was an external agent. There was much I learned, a lot that puzzled me, and a good deal that disheartened.

2. I had been a clinical psychologist who had spent time diagnosing and treating individuals who asked me for help in coping with their personal problems. From 1945 until the switch I was a director of the graduate training program in clinical psychology.

3. I became dissatisfied with clinical psychology's riveting on individuals and its unrelatedness to the societal contexts in which many of the problems that individuals experienced were either caused or exacerbated. Clinical work is one of repair, not prevention. I was more interested in how you prevent disabling personal problems. Aware as I was that schools had a surfeit of problems, that they had neither the resources of knowledge and personnel to deal with these problems, let alone to prevent them, and given my longstanding interest in institutional and social change, I decided to devote myself to understanding the school as a social organization which had a distinctive culture and traditions. And this at a time that schools were the objects of a cascade of criticisms from many sources. School change was in the air, it was in the mass media, the corridors of politics, and community controversy.

4. I decided to create a vehicle, the Yale Psycho-Educational Clinic, by means of which we could be of service to teachers with the problems for which we might be helpful. It would not be a clinic to which schools would send their problem students. We would be in the schools, in classrooms,

trying to be helpful, and only in local ghetto schools where the need was greatest.

5. I would have to garner funding to attract a staff, and my expectation was that if the schools came to value our services, the school system would be one source of support.

So where should I start? What would be our port of entry into the schools? As a clinical psychologist I was used to dealing with troubled people who came to me. But no one was asking for our services. No one in the schools knew or heard about the new clinic. So how do we get our foot in the door? It came about in the most serendipitous way. At a wedding of a mutual friend I met and talked with the activist head of the local Ford Foundation–sponsored community action program, one that antedated the War on Poverty program. In the course of conversation I told him my plans for the new clinic. His opinion of the New Haven schools was that they were scandalous, intractable messes. But he was taken with the idea that we wanted to work only in ghetto schools. He said two things: If we worked in those schools, he would give us a modest sum of money ($10,000) to help us get started, and he would arrange for me to meet with the new school superintendent who, he said, also took a dim view of the city's schools.

I met with the superintendent. He was a very bright, articulate, decisive, no-nonsense, likeable individual. I was taken with him. Yes, he said, there were two schools near the clinic that were at the bottom of the list of the worst schools where he would like us to start. He would arrange for them to be receptive to our services. The port of entry problem was solved!

Why was I so satisfied and relieved? Why did I "screen out" what in the abstract I knew was an instance of problem creation through problem solution: The two schools were not asking for any services, the superintendent was; and I knew from my clinical work, especially with children, that who does the asking is a difference that makes a very big difference. But I screened out that knowledge and previous experience, for several reasons. First, I was, appearances to the contrary, anxious. I had never started a new setting from scratch; I had a good deal of experience with clinics but that was not helpful for the task of creating and directing one.

Second, the clinic had an explicit rationale about where, how, and why services would be provided to teachers in their classrooms. But if the rationale was explicit, it was untested, it did not derive from past personal experience. What if that rationale turned out to be unproductive and impractical? What would we do? Fold our tents and fade away? Would I react to failure as just one of those things and move on, chalking it up to experience? I did not want to face up to how deeply committed I was to the fulfillment of my ideas and the clinic. I spent little or no time coming up with scenarios of failure, partial or complete.

Third, I was a product of the Great Depression: I know what it is when a family does not know where the next meal is coming from. I have to feel certain that I am not in a position where I do not have the money to meet whatever obligations I may have. So, one of my goals for the clinic was that over 5 years we would have enough money "in the bank" so that if the world collapsed, we would have funds enough to function for at least a year. That explains why I was so happy to get the relatively small grant from the local community action program. And it also explains why I came to quick agreement with the superintendent. If things went well, there might be more money given to us, significantly more. I also need to tell the reader that to start the clinic I applied twice for grants and they were not approved. Although the department of psychology allocated some money to start the clinic, it was far from sufficient for what I wanted the clinic to be. The result was that I was confronted with what was for me a very anxiety-arousing problem: How do I get financial help from agencies of any kind for a new clinic with a new, untested rationale? That is why I left the superintendent's office with a sense of welcome relief.

Fourth, there was time pressure. Some of it, not a small part, was internal. By temperament I am the kind of person who, when he decides to do something that he considers important (like starting the clinic), wants to proceed as quickly as possible. I have to feel that I am active and moving to the goal. But there was also external pressure. Faced as he was with a plethora of inadequate schools, the superintendent wanted us to start 2 months hence at the beginning of the new school year. During that interval I gave little thought to anything except how I would approach the schools, how many days in a week I could be in the school, and steeling myself for a role I had never been in before. I gave little thought to the possibility that precisely because our port of entry had been the superintendent, not the schools, there could be problems ahead. Again in the abstract I knew there had to be problems, but what I knew in the abstract stayed in the abstract; it did not cause me to review and reflect on the wisdom of or the alternatives to how we got into the schools.

I was influenced by two things I had learned in my clinical work. The first was that anything a teacher said to me or I observed a teacher do would be considered confidential. That is to say, if a teacher sought my help, that teacher should know that I would not relate whatever went on between us to any other person in the school system. Without such assurance why should any person reveal anything about himself that may convey inadequacy, guilt, and so forth? The second thing I brought from my clinical role to the new one was not to raise unrealistic expectations about what could be accomplished in the relationship. However insecure, anxious, pressured the clinician may feel, he or she—be it for psychological, social, economic reasons—must avoid arousing unrealistic expectations in the client in regard to outcomes. In starting the clinic I experienced all those feelings, but one decision I made acted as a control over them: I made it clear that we were venturing into what was for us a new role and that we would learn as much, if not more, than the school personnel with whom we would work. That message, of course, has its own dangers. The major danger is that, depending on how you came to be in the school, that message can be interpreted as proof positive that the powers that be wield power foolishly and insensitively.

I have described aspects of my phenomenology in starting the clinic in order to make several crucial points. The first, the most important, and one ordinarily ignored or downplayed, is that I was not dealing with one problem but several, all interrelated. *The problem was not how do we get into the schools, but rather what was the universe of alternatives I should consider in getting into schools, and what were the pros and cons of each alternative?* For reasons I gave earlier we used the superintendent as our port of entry not because I had thought through that approach but rather because of financial considerations and certain of my temperamental-psychological characteristics: I like to get started quickly, I have to feel I am moving ahead, I do not take kindly to a state of continuous insecurity about the future, especially if it is economic insecurity. So, when serendipitous circumstances presented the opportunity it did, I went into action. As a result, I blotted out what I knew about gaining port of entry through the superintendent's office, the top-down mode which can be quick in terms of approval but which also opens a can of worms once you approach the site which is the object of help or change. (I take this up in detail in the next chapter.) There was another alternative. I knew a fair number of teachers and midline New Haven administrators with whom I could have discussed what the clinic stood for and wanted to do. I could have arranged meetings with groups of them and asked for their reactions and advice for how we might informally try out our rationale for being helpful, a trial run, so to speak. I truly believe that more than a few of them would have been receptive, given their candid advice, and come up with ideas about which schools (their principals and teachers) would be open to further discussion about a relationship with the clinic. In other words, the goal would be to be invited by those "on the firing line," not the superintendent. That is a difference that makes a big difference. Given my psychological makeup, that alternative had clear drawbacks: It would take a lot of time; I would not know where, when, or if we would hit pay dirt territory; the receptive schools might not be ghetto schools; and there would be no money involved. The virtues of this alternative would be that the schools who wanted a relationship would feel they had some ownership of the project, they could help shape it; they would not feel they were objects of change but willing participants in change. I made short schrift of that alternative, and I regret it.

The fact is that despite its drawbacks we could have spent the year pursuing that alternative. Although it would have introduced a variety of complications, we could have managed, albeit with difficulty. But the fact remains that I did not allow myself to give it anything resembling serious thought; I was too eager to get started.

What I have just related I have observed time and again when I have served as consultant to school reform projects. The change agents begin with a rationale and then unreflectively (like me) go through higher power administrative echelons; the port of entry is opened for them; then they approach the schools to explain what the change effort is about, all the while assuming that verbal explanations and assurances are sufficient to elicit enthusiasm and other than surface cooperation in those who are the objects of change, as if the words we use to convey our ideas, hopes, and plans can be truly embraced by others who have not experienced what we experienced in arriving at our plan for change. Loving as we do and wedded as we are to our ideas, there is everything in us to want to believe that others will respond similarly to the way we pursue our vision.

There was another alternative which in some ultimate sense involved a method and a goal I believed was the most important of all. It would not be enough for me for the clinic to demonstrate that it could render demonstrably productive help in two schools. The problem was how that demonstration over time would be seen by the school system as desirable and *transferable* to its other schools. That could never happen if other schools did not know what we had done (except, of course, through the rumor mill). That kind of expansion requires a variety of methods which would allow school administrators (including the superintendent) and teachers in other schools to become knowledgeable about what we were doing in the two schools *as we were doing it*. At the very least, it requires forums which could or might elicit interest in our efforts on the part of others in the system. I am sure that readers, especially if they work in schools, know that doing even some justice to that goal would be extremely difficult. Just as changing one classroom in one school, or one school in one school system, is not to be derogated, educational reform which does not spread has to be judged as a wasted opportunity.

The description of my phenomenology at that time is incomplete. The more I have replayed the problems I had to deal with, *beginning with the decision to start the clinic*, the longer became the list of the problems which I had to confront. More correctly, each problem created new problems: the relation of the clinic to the department and the university, explaining the clinic to community agencies who might see the clinic as unnecessary duplication and competition, obtaining the pros and cons in regard to where the clinic would (could) be housed, who I could attract to join me there as colleagues, and more, much more. I said that I had to confront these problems. That does not mean that I "solved" them in the sense that $4 \div 2$ is a solution. Some of those problems had consequences after the clinic got off the ground, instances of problem creation through problem solution. I tell this to the reader to make a point that is as obvious as it is unreported and undiscussed in the educational reform literature: The phenomenology of those who seek to change schools has the characteristics of a crazy quilt. The difference is that the person who designs a crazy quilt is far more in control of the process—its colors, juxtapositions, materials, size—than the educational reformer who quickly learns that his or her external world has unpredictable, uncontrollable features which push and pull you. If, when I conceived the clinic, I assumed that I would be master of my fate and captain of my soul, I quickly learned otherwise.

Neither by training, experience, or my readings was I prepared for the complexities of the process. Let me hasten to say that those complexities are not preventable. They are not. I have no doubt that under two conditions they can be less stressful or destabilizing, or downright painful. The first condition hardly exists, and by that I mean that there is pitifully little in the literature to sensitize you to the fact that you are undertaking a task that will, to indulge understatement, *test and change* you and there is no way around that. I am, of course, in no way suggesting that we need a manual to tell us what steps A, B, and C should be and how to handle them, or a manual containing bromides which like clichés contain small nuggets of truth. What is needed are concrete instances of why and how the experience is inevitably so fraught with pitfalls for thinking and action; why from beginning to end your ideas, you as a person, and those you seek to change will experience the *sturm und drang* of change. The key word here is *experience* of a very personal nature, the stuff we are reluctant to reveal or write about because such revelations will demonstrate the obvious: The process of planning and acting is emotionally and cognitively rough stuff, and we are imperfect organisms. I say *is* rather than *may* or *might* because there is everything in us to want to believe that we will be the exception, that we will not be faced with thorny means-ends problems that can bring out our less desirable characteristics and personal vulnerabilities; for example, barreling ahead on the assumption that your status, charisma, and (of course) your good ideas and intentions will allow you to dilute the doubts, resistance, and misgivings others may have. This could be called the "Mama or Papa knows best" syndrome. Leaders of a change effort, like leaders generally, tend to be self-confident and ambitious, and I am not in any way suggesting that those characteristics are not necessary. But far more often than not, they contribute to the loneliness of the leader, as if he or she cannot or should not put out on the table for examination the means-ends dilemmas he or she is mulling over. If Mama or Papa knows best, what is there to be gained by seeking the advice of others? What I am describing here is a subtle process for which there is no self-correcting mechanism or forum. And, I should emphasize, that subtle process gains strength when there is time pressure to plan and act. In schools there is the undergirding assumption that children can learn by a calendar-driven curriculum; this is known as the "page 52 syndrome." By the end of October we should or must be on page 52. Similarly, given the ways in which and the sources from which change efforts are funded, the leaders of such efforts screen out from their thinking any self-correcting mechanism or forum which will add pressure on and complications for the precious resource of *time*. One of the major reasons educational reform efforts fail or fall far short of the mark is the pressure to plan and act according to a predetermined time schedule. That, among other things, is why I wrote *Charter Schools: Another Flawed Educational Reform?* (1998a).

The book *Redesigning Education* by Wilson and Daviss (1994) is relevant here. They make a number of important points among which the following need to be mentioned. First, the research and development necessary to come up with a commercial product that people will want to purchase is from beginning to end a design process in which numerous technological problems have to be identified, overcome, and integrated. Edison's electric light bulbs and the Wright brothers' airplane are obvious examples. Today we are witnessing thousands of companies who are seeking to design a product that will fill a need in some aspect of the computer, internet, or web site arenas. They all start with what they consider innovative and marketable ideas. But they know that the road ahead will not be an easy one because the technical problems of design, manufacture, and marketing are many and thorny. There is no surfeit of good ideas; the goal is to put it all together in a way that will meet customer needs and be profitable to the company. During that process they are highly vigilant to factors that they may not have anticipated and that then require alteration in design. This is a self-correcting process. Second, even though they may come up with a satisfactory Model A and they market it, they are again vigilant to what customers report about the pros and cons of the product and how the product may be improved. And they use these reports to begin redesign and develop an improved Model B, a process which takes into account similar products of other companies. The self-correction process can give rise to many subsequent models. That is the process which over a 50-year period describes the change in airplanes from the initial Wright brothers' plane to a supersonic one.

A school or school system change effort is a design process. The word *design* ordinarily conjures up imagery of lines, drawings, charts about things, inanimate things; or we think of the artist as he or she is painting a picture involving relationships among people, for example, some of the paintings of Brueghel or Tintoretto; or a choreographer who has to inter-relate the movements of many dancers; or an architect who has to be concerned not only with a physical structure but how that structure has to meet the kinds of needs of the kinds of people who will work or live in it.

Conceiving and implementing an educational change rationale is a design process in which your starting point is how and why school personnel do what they do and interrelate or interact with each other with consequences you and others deem ineffectual. It is a starting point at which you literally have imagery about how different things will be after your ideas have been assimilated into practice. In between the starting and end points you employ what can legitimately be called a social-psychological technology intended to change the thinking and behavior of individuals and groups and their interrelationships. You do not proceed in a random manner; you know you are kin to choreographer or theater director whose task it is to coordinate role and movement to achieve an end result that will impact positively on audiences. That is why, for example, a Broadway theatrical production will not open there but in another city where "bugs" can be identified and rectified. And they do this after weeks of prior re-hearsals, after everybody has already experienced change. It is not infre-quent that this self-correcting process is negatively affected by the pres-sures of money and, therefore, time. What I am describing is more than a self-correcting process, it is also a problem-anticipating process.

What I have just said is second nature to those in theatrical, operatic, and ballet productions. It is not second nature to almost all of those who spearhead educational change, which is a far more complicated process, one that is captured in Murphy's law: If anything untoward can happen, it will. It is my definite impression that educational reformers learn little, if anything, from reading what other reformers have done. In the conven-tional performing arts directors and actors zealously make it their busi-ness to go and observe what and how artists elsewhere are doing; reading what critics say is one thing, observing and inquiring is another. In large part that is because the reform effort is written up in a very incomplete way, leaving out or playing down the vicissitudes of the planning process; the problem-anticipating, problem-solving content and stances; the uni-verse of alternatives considered and why this and not that alternative was chosen; the inadequacies of the conceptual rationale; why the direction, strategies, and tactics were or were not changed; the embarrassing mistakes that were made; and how much the reformers changed as thinkers and actors at different points in the experience.

Self-correction is both a process and attitude, and by attitude I mean a stance which allows you to recognize when and if you should rethink in some way roles in the design of the reform effort. And that recognition can happen in circumstances in which you have little or no time to be reflective. You are required to act at the same time that you feel that you are between a rock and a hard place; that is to say, you have two options for action, and both will negatively affect how you are perceived by those you seek to help. Let me give you an example. As background, the reader needs to know the following:

1. It was 4 months after I began to work in this century-old ghetto school in New Haven.

2. The principal was a constricted, authoritarian, middle-aged woman who viewed me as a Yale professor whom she would prefer to stay in his university office. I was an uninvited character intruding into classrooms. To me she was the opposite of spontaneous, friendly, warm, let alone gracious. (In the next chapter I indicate why today I see her somewhat differently. Why should I have expected her psychologically to embrace me?)

3. I had made it clear at the outset that my role in the school was to try to be helpful in the classroom with students a teacher deemed to have learning and/or behavior problems. We were not there to work with children but with teachers who could accept or reject any advice we would offer. We did not possess, nor wanted to possess, power to require anybody to do anything.

I was observing in a classroom on the third floor of the school. A student came into the room, said something to the teacher, who immediately came to where I was sitting in the back of the room and told me that the principal, Miss Z., wanted to see me *immediately* in her office on the first floor. I was puzzled and anxious. I did not look forward to a confrontation with Miss Z. even though I had no inkling that I had done anything to arouse her ire. I entered her office and she told me that a student, Tom, who had been an intractable behavior problem to his teacher, had been acting up all morning. She told the boy to go to the principal's office, he refused, the teacher tried to take his hand to take him to the principal. Tom became both resistant and violent, a struggle took place. Tom ended up lying on the floor, his legs flailing each time the teacher approached. He responded similarly when Miss Z. approached him. Would I go in and see if I could remove him before the other students became more upset than they were? I went with her to the classroom, expecting that I might be able by words to get him to come with me to a place where we could talk and I could try to help him. When I started to approach, he slithered away from me, his legs and arms flailing away.

What to do? I was very much aware of the traumatic facial expressions in the faces of the other students who were like onlookers at a crime scene where the criminal was on the ground physically resisting arrest. I was also aware that Miss Z., the teacher, and the students were staring at me and wondering what I would do. I was acutely aware of three things. First, this was an unhealthy situation for the other students. Second, because I had very limited use of my right arm because of childhood polio, I was by no means certain I could manage physically to get hold of him and remove him from the classroom. Third, by virtue of the agreement about my role I was between a rock and a hard place. If I could remove him, I would be viewed by teachers and students alike as one who could play the role of disciplinarian, in flagrant contradiction to our self-assigned role to work only with teachers; I was not a policeman and I did not want to do anything that would make it easy for Miss Z. and teachers to put me in that role. Fourth, if I could not or would not get Tom out of the classroom, it was likely that Miss Z. and the teachers would probably conclude: "When we asked him to deal with a problem that was really upsetting, he copped out, he was of no help to us when we *really* needed help." If I helped in the way they defined help, our rationale for being in the school would be endangered; the school did not, of course, lack behavior problems.

I was in the classroom no more than 4 or 5 minutes. No one likes to make snap decisions, least of all in a situation where issues of time and the future of your role are racing through your head, and, I should add, when in my case I was in a new role in a school and very much committed to testing a particular helping rationale. What made me decide to try physically to remove the boy was the frightened expressions on the faces of the other third-grade students. It was not easy, but I was able to remove him after which he seemed to relax, but I was unable to get him to talk to me. The rest of the story is not relevant to the point of the tale, which was my strong reluctance to depart from the way I had "designed" my role. I wanted to be "pure." I had not anticipated I would be in the situation I had described. The consequences of my action were not negative. Indeed, they were positive because Miss Z. and the teachers began to see me not as a head-in-the-clouds professor from ivied Yale but as someone willing to be helpful in ways school personnel defined help.

After the incident I neglected to do one thing I later realized I should have done. I should have asked for a meeting with Miss Z. and the teachers to explain to them why I felt bewildered by what I should do. It could have been a means by which school personnel came better to understand why I was in the school as I was. In any event, the incident set me to begin to rethink and redesign our rationale. I was learning. So let me tell you about a later example in that same school when I departed again from the way I defined my role.

In the classroom of a fourth-grade teacher I saw a boy climb the walls. In this ancient school that was possible because steam pipes were exposed. The teacher was a well-intentioned, dedicated, friendly, early-middle-aged woman, Mrs. X., who also was immature, dependent, mammothly insecure, and disorganized. Teachers in the school never said anything to me that was critical of another teacher, except about Mrs. X. In subtle but unmistakable ways they conveyed misgivings about her. They felt sorry for her, she simply did not comprehend that the students in this school were not the children she knew in her sheltered, middle-class background. She was always glad to see me come into the room, would always tell me about kids who were not learning or were a disruptive influence on what she was trying to teach them. Her stance with me was "What should I do? Tell me." She seemed incapable of thinking for herself. She wanted advice, direction, and support. She would listen to what I would say (after I had observed the child on at least three different times), never disagreed with anything I said, and would act on my advice in inappropriate, ineffective ways. I never looked forward to our interactions. I had to conclude that even if I were a more skilled, understanding, and creative person, Mrs. X. was hopeless. She did not belong in that ghetto school, not in any school.

So what do I do in a situation where students are being scandalously shortchanged? What do you do with a teacher who sincerely wants help but cannot benefit from it? My relationship with the teachers was a confidential one. I could not discuss her with the principal, let alone anyone higher up in the pyramid of power. I struggled for several months with an ethical, personal problem: Should I take up with her the advisability of her seeking a transfer to another school containing the kinds of students who would not play into her vulnerabilities? If I did, I would be going well beyond my agreed-upon role. Also, if I did, I could not by any means be sure that she would not tell others that it was my idea and she is not at all happy that I had been critical. Furthermore, if she took this up with the principal, would she look upon it as criticism of her inaction? I knew Mrs. X. wanted out, but I also knew that what she would say about why she was seeking a transfer could make problems for me in that school and in the system's central office.

Again I decided that the welfare of her students was more important and urgent than my staying in my agreed-upon role. As I predicted, Mrs. X. greeted my suggestion enthusiastically. But I was careful to say that if indeed she would seek a transfer, I wanted her permission to talk to the principal and tell her that Mrs. X. would better serve the needs of students in a white, middle-class school. Initially, for about 10 seconds, I wondered if I should tell the principal what and why I was going to suggest to Mrs. X. that she seek a transfer, that I knew I was going beyond my role. But I had been in the school long enough to know that Miss Z. might well tell me to mind my own damned business. Mrs. X. said I could go to the principal, and when I did, Miss Z. said she would support the request for transfer. I was surprised and, needless to say, relieved. At the beginning of the new school year Mrs. X. was transferred. When in subsequent years I would be asked how many children benefitted from what I did in that school, I would say, "After my first year in that school I prevented 25–30 children from being exposed to a blatantly unproductive context of learning and living."

The two instances I have described illustrate more than the fact that I planned/designed a role I was prepared to stick with come what may. A more honest and revealing way to put it is that I gave no thought to possible situations which would pose or challenge the rationale. That could have been a crucial omission because in the following year the clinic was to have two new staff as well as several advanced graduate students who would be working in schools. As a result of my baptismal year in the new role, I changed the rationale in two respects. The first was less a change than an addition. We would keep in mind that there might well be times, usually unpredictable, when we might decide to go beyond the confines of the basic rationale. I used examples from my first year, and there were more than the two I have discussed here, plus others that although dreamed up by me could well occur in schools. The other change was truly a change. The rationale was crystal clear that the initiative for anything we did came from, and only from, the teacher. In the future we should not overlook possibilities where we would take the initiative provided that we had good reason to believe that the initiative (1) stood a chance of helping a child and (2) it had the support of the relevant school personnel. These exceptions would or should be infrequent because we do not want to be perceived as outsiders who want to "take over." We would not shy away from such an initiative when, but only when, the responsibility for action was a shared one. That is to say, we should not be in a situation where if our initiative and actions were ineffective, we and we alone would be blamed. We *and* school personnel were going to learn together from successes and failures. What all this could mean in practice is illustrated in an example from the third year of the clinic.

A school principal asked us to look into and do what we could to bring back to the school two students, a boy and a girl, who were school phobic and had not been to school for weeks. The graduate student working in that school discussed the matter with me because it was obvious that the students and the parents would have to be seen both at home and at the clinic. It was rare for us to see children for psychotherapeutic purposes at the clinic unless, and only unless, that child had been observed over weeks and that those observations could be the focus of a short-term psychotherapy that would change the child's behavior in the classroom. Our approach required the permission of but not the participation of parents. Both the student and the teacher were told and agreed with our focus: to understand and change behavior in the classroom. But the school-phobic students had not been in a classroom since the beginning of the school year, and neither was known to the graduate student.

To make a long story short, the school-phobic boy was fragile, vulnerable, passive, and no candidate for short-term, classroom-focused psychotherapy. (I was to supervise the graduate student in psychotherapy.) The girl was a very different character. From therapeutic sessions, talks with parents, and home visits one could not avoid the conclusion that this 10-year-old girl was bright, assertive, articulate, willful, and domineering. As the graduate student put it, "She is a tyrant. Her parents simply cannot stand up to her. They quickly retreat when she says no to them about going to school." The principal found none of this surprising.

What to do? I suggested to the graduate student that he get the parents to tell the girl that on a specific date they would send her to school, whether she liked it or not, whether she screamed or resisted or not; the graduate student would be at her home, the principal would meet her at the entrance of the school. (The principal had told me that if we got her to the entrance, he would take care of the rest. The principal, Mr. Barbaresi, whom I knew well, was known for doing what he said he would do.)

The graduate student, who was not an assertive person, was aghast at my plan. He thought it was punitive, perhaps unethical, manipulative, counterproductive, nontherapeutic. Even if the graduate student was not an assertive person, he could be very stubborn. Besides, he said, if he was present when the parents were going to take her to school, what would he do if, as he expected, the girl would act up and refuse to go? As the supervisor of graduate students, I did not have the right to foist, require, or demand that he do as I say. That would have destroyed the plan and my relationship with him, especially if it failed. So for several weeks our supervisory hours consisted largely of his telling me that he was not getting to first base with this willful girl. Toward an end of a session I would ask if he felt differently about my plan. He did not. Then came a session when on his own he said that he should stop seeing her because it was a waste of time and he now felt that drastic measures should be taken to get the girl back to school. He said he would implement the plan even though he had no confidence that the parents could act forcefully.

He arrived at the family's home a half hour before school was to open. The war had already begun. The mother was crying and wailing, the father stood by helplessly, the graduate student could do nothing. The father had told his brother about the plan, and lo and behold he showed up. He sized up the scene and took charge. He told the girl he was going to take her to school, like it or not, even if that meant physically subduing her, tying her up, putting her into his car, and driving to the school where the principal would meet her and take her to her classroom. Her entire demeanor changed, and she put on a jacket and went off with her uncle. The principal greeted her and, taking her by the hand, brought her to the classroom. She never stayed away from school again. She was an excellent student.

A critic could say that this girl and her parents needed intensive, long-term therapy. But she also needed to be in school, which she would not be, at best, for many months because such therapy is the opposite of a quick fix. And it was likely that she would not be promoted and that would bring in its wake new problems.

I do not want to convey the impression that I was 100% certain the plan would work. (It would not have worked if the uncle had not come on the scene.) I knew we and the principal were taking chances because the stakes were so high for this girl. But given all that I knew about the girl, her parents, and the principal, I felt we should take the chance, we should take the initiative. Doing it was the last thing that would have occurred to me in my first year in a new role.

Let me go back for a moment to the wall-climbing boy because he said something to me that I have never forgotten, something that may well have been in the back of my mind when I came up with my plan to get the girl back to school. I had taken him from the classroom out to the hall to talk with him. (There was no room in the ancient, crowded building for a one-on-one conversation.) At one point I asked him, "Next year you are going to have Mrs. A. as your teacher. Are you going to behave in her classroom as you are behaving in your present classroom?" He looked at me with something akin to staring disbelief and replied, "Of course not, she would kick the shit out of me." He was right. I never saw Mrs. A. put a hand on a child. She was a very big woman with a semigruff voice. But she gave her all for her students, she respected, knew, and loved them. They could trust her to be fair and trustworthy. But she would not countenance misbehavior. She did not have to because her students loved and respected her. Misbehavior was very rare in her classroom.

I have been discussing one of the two conditions which can dilute (not eliminate) the destabilizing, painful, self-defeating consequences of how the planning, designing, and implementation of a reform effort are ordinarily experienced. The second condition concerns the psychological characteristics of the planner or leader. To assume such a role is not for everyone. Good ideas, good intentions, elevated status, and previous accomplishments in other arenas with different goals and problems are necessary but very far from sufficient. You may be, or at least have the reputation of being, warm, likeable, smart, but if that reputation was not earned in contexts where your goal was not only to change how *individuals* thought, acted and interacted, but also to effect an *institutional* change, the road ahead can be very rocky and destabilizing.

Let me elaborate on this point by analogy. Conventional psychotherapies involve two people: patient and therapist. To become a skillful therapist requires both long, supervised training and more than a few years of subsequent experience to develop sensitivity, to learn from mistakes, to be realistic about limits and power of psychotherapy, to learn with which clients and problems you are most comfortable and successful, to learn when you should seek advice of colleagues, and more, much more. But what about family therapy where you literally face the entire family? You do not seek to change one member of the family but to change the psychological web in which all members interrelate and impact on each other. It is a very complicated web, and it takes a good deal of knowledge, skill, and experience to understand that web and to adapt one's approach in response to your understanding of how this family differs from previous ones you have encountered. It is not that family therapy is more complicated than the one-on-one types but rather that they are very different ball games, most of all for the therapists. Because you have been a successful therapist with individuals does not justify expecting to be equally successful with families. I have had the opportunity to observe (through a one-way mirror setup) competent psychotherapists who wanted to learn to do family therapy anxiously struggle to appear to be competent at the same time they would later tell me they knew that they were making every mistake in the book. They agreed on two points. First, although their experience in individual psychotherapy was not totally irrelevant, their experience simply did not prepare them to deal with a complicated family. Second, they had a lot to unlearn and learn. Some of them had already decided that they were not cut out to be family therapists.

So what characteristics should a designer and implementer of a school change effort have? There is a prior question: What sense of obligation should you have to determine what others have done and experienced, and this before your own plans are crystallized? When I started out, the literature contained few accounts of educational reform efforts. Many of those efforts were in the works, so to speak, and did not get reported until several years later. I was aware of such efforts in New Haven and other local school districts, I had occasion to talk with some of their initiators, but what I essentially heard and was told about were great expectations. My own thinking was too incomplete and unsophisticated to alert me to ask questions about the nitty-gritty details which have caused me to write this book. Today the reform literature is vast, but in my opinion what we are given are largely sanitized accounts, by which, I should hasten to add, I do not mean they are in any way fabrications, deliberate efforts to mislead the reader. And I certainly do not mean they are without value. What I do mean is that they do not contain accounts of how, for example, the port of entry was accomplished and the problems that it caused in its wake in regard to those who were the objects of change; nor do we learn what "second thoughts" the initiators had about how they had conceived and implemented their design for action, or how issues of time and resources affected their actions and results, or how the changers were themselves changed in the process, or the small and not so small ways they or others by their actions changed tactics and even expectations, or the role that serendipitous factors or the whims of Lady Luck played. And let us not overlook the fact that in writing up the account the authors understandably are reluctant to be critical of themselves and others, or both. Considerations about maintaining relationships are, of course, not immune from what may legitimately be called political, diplomatic, interpersonal, and future consequences. What we get, again understandably, are relatively impersonal accounts in which the irrational is an absent ingredient in the cauldron of change. I am, of course, also talking about myself, and I do not excuse myself when I say that I have never talked to a reformer who in private conversation disagreed with what I have just said. It is necessary, but not sufficient, to read the literature. Wherever possible, you should talk to those who have been through the ringer. And I include here those whose efforts were aborted or failed and who saw no justification for publishing their experiences; they are far greater in number than those who have published their experience.

One characteristic the reformer should possess is what I can only call common knowledge or common sense. I am referring here to those reform efforts which are ambitious in goal and require employment of a staff who will be responsible for implementation; the port of entry problem is over, sites are selected, and the newly hired staff has been trained—educated in the overall rationale, design, and implementation role. What if the designer-reformer has not experienced the personal, practical, thorny issues and problems that implementation, to small or large degree, inevitably presents, and I use the word *inevitably* advisedly? There is much for which Freud can be criticized, but one of them is not his insistence that in order to become a psychoanalyst you have to be willing to undergo a personal analysis and, therefore, experience what your patients will experience. He called it a training analysis; you learn by personal experience. Similarly, the reformer should be willing to experience the implementation process in all of its complexities, to be in and not above the fray for a reasonable amount of time, sufficient time to justify calling such an experience an instance of the self-correcting process. It is one thing to have designed the project, to have set the stage for implementing staff to "go." It is quite a different thing to do all that after you have already "gone"; you are now talking from direct experience.

A personal example is relevant here. Pursuing school change was only one of the reasons I started the clinic. As I have discussed in my autobiography, *The Making of an American Psychologist* (1988), a more personally compelling reason was a question that occupied me in the 1930s when I was in college and a member of a radical left-wing party vociferously opposed to how Stalin had corrupted the Russian revolution. How could the creation of a new state fail so miserably, so inhumanely? Then, my first job after graduate school was in a spanking new institution for the mentally retarded based on a very innovative educational rationale. In the few years I was there I was witness to another instance of a new setting that was and would continue to fall very short of the mark. It was then that I came up with the phrase "the creation of settings" as a way of labeling the fact that new settings seemed to have problematic futures. I defined a new setting as when two or more people get together in new and sustained relationships to achieve agreed-upon goals. Marriage was the smallest instance, and a national revolution was the largest. Then, when I went to Yale and started the test-anxiety-research project, I became immersed in schools among which were several new ones, that being a time when the post–World War II baby explosion forced communities to build new schools as fast as possible, like yesterday. And that provided more instances of new settings whose goals were subverted.

How do or could I study the creation of settings? An existing relevant literature virtually did not exist. What did exist was always written many years after the setting had been created and then had either been utterly transformed beyond recognition or, more frequently, had withered away (e.g., the communes of the nineteenth century). The above explains why when the idea of a clinic began to germinate in my head, I realized that such an endeavor was an opportunity to experience what was involved in creating a setting. The more I thought about it, the more my previous experience began to be more understandable, especially my observations of new public schools.

The years between creating the clinic and stepping down from being its director were the peak experience of my professional life. I learned about myself, the anxieties and problems of being a leader, the pressures of time and limited resources, how hard it is to tolerate frustration, that like it or not you had to deal with external individuals and agencies who had different agendas and values, that you had to know the difference between compromise and caving in, that having around you two dozen staff of articulate, ambitious characters who are as smart as you are can be both comedy and melodrama (sometimes at the same time), that the name of the game was mutuality, respect, and trust.

In 1972 I wrote *The Creation of Settings and the Future Societies*, in which I conceptualized and described the predictable problems and stages that new settings confront. In the decades after its publication I received many letters from people who had started new settings—most had disappeared or had been radically transformed—and later had read my book and now were writing to tell me that it made their past experience comprehensible. The fact is that I included surprisingly little of my phenomenology. Although I was generalizing from my experience, I had left out some of the truly personal, more than could be justified if the reader was to understand the personal complexities inherent in creating a new setting. I sought to include those omissions when in 1988 I wrote my autobiography, *The Making of an American Psychologist*.

I have related this fragment of personal history in order to emphasize how crucial it is personally to experience an encompassing process which you have conceived but which others will implement. I realize that reformers tend to be those who have more than a few professional responsibilities and are unable to take off that amount of time truly to experience the process of implementation. (Besides, funding agencies do not take kindly to a budget in which there is an item for one year of the initiator's salary.) The problem is exacerbated when the plan is year by year to increase the number of sites, near and far. *Absentee direction, like absentee ownership, is problem producing.*

When I wrote *The Creation of Settings*, charter schools, a quintessentially clear example of creating new settings, were not on the horizon. But when they did appear in the early 1990s and I began to talk to some of those who were going to start a charter school or to apply for charter school status, it was obvious to me that they had no personal-experiential road map to alert them to predictable problems. So, even though there really were no data on their accomplishments, I concluded that, generally speaking, they would fall far short of their mark. And I reached that conclusion on two grounds. First, I had experienced the process in spades, and, second, since the clinic had been created, I had spent 3 decades in and around schools and educators. I never met an educator who heard about my book. I did not feel it was premature or unfair to write *Charter Schools: Another Flawed Educational Reform*? (1998a).

Another characteristic an initiator should possess is a degree of self-confidence which in no way dilutes or interferes with a true respect for ideas, feelings, and needs of his or her colleagues. The person should never forget the difference between leadership as a means for embarking on an ego trip and as an opportunity to further the development of others as well as of himself. I am talking of a self-confidence which prevents you from responding to challenges or criticisms of your ideas or actions by impulsive action, overt anger, or an eye-for-an-eye response. And self-confidence should be no inhibitor of the admission either that you are wrong or you need time to think, to reflect. But self-confidence also means that you are able to put your cards on the table not in a "Here is what you (or we) will do" manner but rather "Here is what you (or we) will do, *what do you think?*"

The leader of a reform effort is almost always self-selected, which means that he was not selected by others who by their criteria chose him or her as leader. The match between leader, on the one hand, and the demands and obligations of implementation, on the other hand, is crucially important. I would say decisive. (The leadership-governance variable has turned out to be the most frequent source of divisiveness and conflict in charter schools.)

Another characteristic the reformer should possess is less a psychological characteristic than it is a brute fact of institutional reform and, perhaps, even social living generally. Strangely, it is a fact we want very much to ignore, i.e., not think about it. And when we are forced to recognize it, the future takes on a dysphoric hue. I refer to the fact that educational reform has no final solutions as in mathematical solutions. One problem supplants another; the same problems recur; unwanted, unpredictable surprises occur; there are no still, smooth seas. If by temperament or for other reasons you cannot accept that fact, you will, knowingly or not, psychologically distance yourself from your setting, be less responsive to its problems, and settle into a routine of superficial thinking and relationships with colleagues.

Why did I step down as director of the Psycho-Educational Clinic after 8 years? There were two reasons. The first is that by the 5th year I realized that I had already experienced and learned more than I had ever expected. I began to feel that I wanted to start writing it up. But for life in the clinic with a cast of creative characters, each of whom was continuing to do things that were fascinating and important, postponing writing was a small price to pay. The clinic was such an active, alive, intellectually stimulating place that leaving it would produce a large gaping hole in my daily life. The second reason is a consequence of the first. None of the wondrous people who were my colleagues at the clinic were regarded as worthy of promotion by my department. That did not surprise me because the department never considered it *their* clinic but *mine*, my responsibility to do whatever was necessary to create and sustain it. As I have discussed in detail elsewhere (Sarason, 2001), American psychology has little or no interest in schools, viewing research in that arena as applied and, therefore, not as important or worthy as basic research; the goose that lays the golden eggs of basic psychological laws. Their disinterest in education extended to the clinic. The members of the department never said anything derogatory about me or the clinic. At worst they saw me as moving in new and strange directions far from the mainstream of American psychology. And that is how they viewed my younger colleagues at the clinic.

I do not take kindly to separations from close friends, and the people at the clinic were more like kin than friends. So during the years at the clinic I experienced one separation after another as younger colleagues left for positions elsewhere. The increasing strength of my reactions to these separations was, in terms of when I stepped down, the propelling factor in my decision. I no longer wanted to bring in new people, get to know and live with them, and then see them leave. So I stepped down, and that was the end of the clinic.

This chapter has primarily been concerned with two things. One was the phenomenology of the reformer, how the reform process changes the reformer, and how incomplete was my understanding of what I was getting to. Let me now turn to the phenomenology of those who are the objects of school change. Here again my understanding was grievously incomplete, and it showed up in what I *now* see as mistakes. What I understood was right, but it was incomplete. I did not take seriously what I knew from past personal experience.

Chapter 3

The Teacher's Phenomenology of Change

Clichés are verbal bromides that are rarely helpful in the arena of action. When we offer condolences to a sick friend or someone who has lost a loved one, we are trying to be sympathetic and reassuring at the same time we usually know that our words are not or cannot be therapeutic. That may be true even if we have experienced serious illness and loss of a loved one. More often than not we are no longer aware of or able to remember the sustained turmoil we experienced hour by hour, day by day, and month by month. We know we had a very rough time, but we no longer reexperience the depths and poignancies of the turmoil, the anxieties, the conflicts that had beset us. Repression has its virtues! That is what we mean when we hear ourselves say, "Time is a healer." But what if time does not heal, or minimally so? What are the conditions in which it does heal, which is another way of asking what are the conditions in which change does or does not occur in small or large degree? What conditions, internal or external, individual or social, play significant roles?

I never gave these questions the serious consideration they deserved in my different efforts, in action or writing, at educational reform. In my prereform days and in subsequent years I had to confront many occasions, some catastrophic, which required me, like it or not, to change in very significant ways. For example, as a child, I had contracted polio in both arms and throat which required an operation so that my right arm would not be a total dead weight; I was encased in a bulky, heavy plaster of paris cast, which for 6 months kept both arms raised, benediction style. Another example: I had read about the "empty nest" syndrome, but when our only child left home for college, I was a mess. (As I said earlier, I have never taken separations with anything like aplomb.)

More directly to the point of this chapter, from the time in college when I read Freud, I was no end impressed (an understatement) with how much he understood individual change and resistance to it: He was talking about me! That was the major reason I sought psychoanalysis after I finished graduate school, took my first professional job, and had the funds to pay for it. I had personal problems, period. And when I came to Yale almost immediately after World War II ended, I taught what probably was the first course in psychoanalytic theory in a psychology department. And a major theme in that seminar was change and resistance to it. What I had learned personally from extensive reading and from being a patient on the psychoanalytic couch was abundantly confirmed in my role as psychotherapist as well as supervisor of graduate students in their therapeutic endeavors. For me, change and resistance to it was the name of the game.

I and every other educational reformer have sought significant change. There are two conditions from which reform efforts arise. The first is external and takes two forms. An individual, almost always from the university, convinces the upper hierarchy in a school system that he or she has a program—accompanied by funding or the promise of it—that will improve the quality and outcomes of schooling. The hierarchy agrees that it is in its self-interest to, so to speak, buy into the program. The school system is not always perceived by the hierarchy as failing but goes along because it sees the program as adding quality to the existing program; in some cases it goes along primarily for reasons of status: a relationship with a prestigious university and/or with a member of its faculty who is respected and very well known. The system wants to be perceived as always seeking to take advantage of the newest good idea. Sometimes, of course, the system is ineffective or failing and will listen attentively to an external source whose program they have read or heard about in the mass media. Indeed, it is by no means infrequent that such schools will take the initiative to contact the external person in the hope that his or her program can be instituted in their school system.

The second condition from which a reform effort arises is internal in that there are individuals within the system who advocate for change and pressure the hierarchy and board of education to take actions for change. These advocates may or may not have a specific program: Using their political, community, and social networks they seek to exert pressure for change. If they are successful, it almost always means that external sources of help will be sought either because they can be helpful as individuals or they already have a program for change. In any event, what started internally almost always soon involves external agents, although leadership for what is done may remain internal.

The reform efforts from either of the two conditions can be somewhat different in their history and consequences. I shall be little concerned with such differences but rather with their similarities, among which are the following:

1. The assumption that before implementation begins those who will be the objects of change (e.g., the teachers) will have become willing par-

ticipants in the effort. Willing means they understand the rationale for the change and what the change means for them.

2. The identity and responsibilities of the leader are unambiguous. One of those responsibilities is to maintain open lines of communication with those who have ultimate and formal legal authority, e.g., the superintendent and board of education. Another responsibility is to know well what those to whom responsibility is delegated are thinking, experiencing, and confronting. Still another is to have some means that to some degree provide personal knowledge of how teachers and parents feel about the dynamics of the implementation process.

3. The assumption that when differences of opinion and conflicts arise, they will or can be resolved sensitively, fairly, and amicably.

4. The assumption that personnel turnover will be minimal, that key people of influence and/or power will remain in their positions, e.g., the superintendent, members of the board of education, opinion makers among teachers, principals.

The history of educational reform confirms that each of these four points can be of decisive importance in determining the course, ups and downs, and even the fate of the reform effort. For the purposes of this chapter I shall restrict the discussion to the first point because it is so early in the implementation process and it is one that on the levels of action and writing my thinking was incomplete and too superficial. That my omissions were also those of all other reformers with whom I have spoken or whose schools I observed in the role of consultant or advisor is no source of solace to me.

Why is it that so many people, young and old, continue to smoke even though they are bombarded with messages that it is dangerous to health? They may even experience some of its dangers: coughing, accelerated heart beat, temporary dizziness, irritations of the throat. But they continue to smoke. We say they are addicted, by which we ordinarily mean that the psychological and social benefits of smoking outweigh its negative consequences for the individuals, so much so that the individual enjoys smoking and will not give it up, change. Just as the person knows that the sun will rise tomorrow morning, that person knows that smoking is dangerous to health. But that is factual knowledge, just as knowing that there was an American civil war is factual knowledge. The smoker has another kind of knowledge: the intimate, personal knowledge that smoking serves a purpose (or purposes) that he or she needs and wants to satisfy and, therefore, will not seek to change. There are smokers who want to quit and when they do stop they find that quitting is a very psychologically destabilizing affair. How many times do we hear smokers say, "I have quit smoking hundreds of times"? They may intend humor when they say that, but they are also revealing how difficult it is to change, how the habit plays a role in diverse parts of daily existence. How many times have you heard individuals who have not smoked in years say, "When I have my morning coffee or after a particularly enjoyable dinner, I still yearn for a smoke." Smoking, whatever its origins, has personal and social contexts which are experienced, become evident, when the person seeks to quit, to change.

Whatever the precursor dynamics may have been, I started to smoke 58 years ago when my first professional job required a good deal of writing. The association between smoking and writing has continued to this day. I can go on trips for a month or more and not smoke or have a desire to do so. But as soon as I take pen to paper I start to smoke. Writing is central to my existence. When I am at home and a day has passed without writing, I feel I have shortchanged myself. The only time I think is when I write. I have tried to break the connection but writing—which I experience as a diluted form of Chinese torture—becomes near impossible; I become ill at ease, distracted, ashamed of my lack of will power, anxious about the future, miserable in the present. I ask myself: Do I write because I want to smoke, or do I smoke because I want to write? I have no answer, nor do I seriously seek one. What I know at a gut level is that for me writing is where I get my kicks, my highs, the feeling that I have learned something I want others to know. I do not want to change. In 1993, as a result of an auto accident in which my wife was killed, I spent almost 3 months in three hospitals. I never smoked or wanted to. Indeed, the smell of smoke was unpleasant. The overriding fear was that the nature of my physical injuries would prevent me from writing. Coping with the death of my wife was hard to contemplate. But if in addition I could not write, I entertained thoughts of ending it all. I shall not attempt to describe the physical difficulties I had, and the seating arrangements with which I experimented, when I forced myself to start writing when I returned home. I again started to smoke, of course. It was not an external crutch; it was, as it had been, as much a part of writing as pen, paper, and thinking.

In my writings on educational reform I have said that resistance to change is as predictable as death and taxes. Saying that was a form of cliché. Of course it was true, but the fact is that I vastly underemphasized the forms, depths, and subtle manifestations that the resistance of school personnel to change *had* to experience. That, I should hasten to add, is true even when school personnel willingly say that they will participate in the change effort. And they may mean it sincerely at the same time they, like me, cannot transfer and utilize experiences of change at other times in their lives to other arenas of living. They, like me, can envision with approval the substance and goals of the change, but between the beginning and end points of the change is psychological space empty of the turmoil of personal change. Wish and hope blot out what they have previously experienced about personal change.

Let us take the many frequent instances in which a superintendent, the board of education, and the larger community (or the state board of education) identify a failing school that has been unable to improve educational outcomes, to "get its act together." They seek and obtain the services of an external group whose leader is well known and acclaimed. The group presents its program to the personnel of the school, invites and answers questions, and seeks to obtain the willing acceptance of the personnel (mostly teachers, of course) to the described changes that will be instituted.

What are the likely psychological reactions of the teachers to what they have been told? One very likely reaction is in the form of a question: Do we have a choice? What other programs were considered? Why this one? Far more often than not they did not have a choice. They agree that their school needs to change, they are far from satisfied with conditions as they exist. Each of them has his or her diagnosis about why these conditions exist and why past efforts have failed. That point is very important because there are always instances where there have been past efforts on the part of the school system to improve conditions. However, I have never known an instance, or heard about one, where the new reformers *seriously and sincerely* sought to elicit the diagnoses of those who are now being asked to change their thinking and actions. Even if such actions were elicited, there are built-in factors that set limits to what teachers will reveal. After all, the reformers are strangers to the teachers, they are personal unknowns who may have credentials and a reputation but are they *really* interested in what I (we) think? How much of what I (we) know and experienced is it safe to say out loud? Why should I (we) embrace this knight in white armor? I (we) have been through this before. We have no alternative to rolling with the punch. And it is a punch that implies—it is very much on the internal psychological surface—that the teachers have been part of the problem, they played a role in "causing" or exacerbating it. It is not the first time they have heard such criticisms which sometimes have been not implicit but unambiguously explicit.

I have no doubt that there are teachers in such failing schools who are incompetent, temperamentally unsuited to be teachers, or whose conceptions of teaching, learning, and students are, to say the least, counterproductive, or whose capacity to direct blame to external factors (parents, poverty, neighborhood) is bottomless. But in such schools I came to know rather well there have always been some teachers, admittedly few, able to provide perceptive and helpful diagnoses of why the school was what it was. None of what they told me was revealed until they felt I could be trusted, that I was not intent on criticizing everyone and everything. I wished I had had an inkling much earlier in my relationship to the school, that I should have, could have, spent more time in different ways before the intervention formally started. My time perspective would have been more realistic and my tactics (not goals) somewhat different.

The point here is that resistance to change should be regarded as a given from day one even though it is not overt. And if you do not regard it as a given, it is likely that you are rendered insensitive to overt indicators: few questions are asked, everyone is very polite and respectful, and when the initial session is over they quickly depart the scene. To be satisfied and relieved by such reactions belies your lack of understanding of resistance to change, an understanding that makes for sympathy, not criticism. To expect that resistance is absent or minimal is to pave the road of reform with gaping potholes if not with caved-in craters. I use the word *sympathy* advisedly because reformers are like everyone else. By that I mean that when the reformer encounters overt resistance and/or criticism, the reformer is likely to take it personally, an attack on his or her competence and status. It is what has been called the "who are you to tell *me* that I do not know what I am doing" syndrome. This syndrome is exhibited in parent-child, teacher-student, boss-employee relationships, if not in all human relationships in which there are differences in perceived power or authority. So, when the reformer is the recipient of criticism, it is crucial to curb retaliation and to view the criticism as a direct or indirect manifestation of resistance. But what if the criticism is merited? Any reformer who cannot entertain such a possibility should, like the incompetent teacher, consider another line of work. Reformers and teachers have psychological tendencies in common by virtue of being members of the species we call human. "Know thyself" is a cliché. In light of what I have said I hope the reader does not regard as a cliché this assertion about school reformers and those who are the objects of his or her change efforts: "Know thyself in a way that allows you to know others." Let me elaborate this by analogy.

A very wealthy individual seeks psychotherapeutic help because of psychological problems causing interpersonal conflict, stress, and unhappiness. She is advised that an intensive, lengthy therapy is the treatment of choice. She approaches the therapy with the predictable and understandable fantasy that the therapist will tell her why she is unhappy and how she might change her thinking and actions. At the least, the therapist will express opinions, give advice, he will not be a passive listener. Although the patient knows in the abstract that there are no magical cures or quick fixes, she entertains visions of an altered, conflict-free personality at the end of therapy. If she knows there are no quick fixes, she nevertheless wants to, needs to, feel from day one that she is on the road to personal repair, and that she can judge progress not only by how she feels but by what the therapist says.

But the therapist is not very forthcoming; he listens attentively, asks questions, expresses puzzlement, but does not offer direct advice. This irritates, even angers, the patient who asks (sometimes demands) why the therapist is not being helpful. "After all," the patient may feel and say, "why am I paying you money if not for you to tell me how I can or should change my ways?" The therapist may remind her that she knew that the therapy would not be easy or quick. Besides, he would say, the very fact that the patient wants the therapist to be directive and offer "solutions" is a trap: a form of resistance to taking personal responsibility for personal change, a way of bypassing the turmoil and pain associated with actively seeking to understand one's self and history.

Resistance to change in therapy, any type of the many therapies, may be expressed in diverse ways: withholding information about feelings, habits, or rituals; missing appointments; frequently showing up late; lying; or just not showing up again. Therapies differ widely in their theoretical rationale, methods, breadth of focus, length, goals, and expectations. Each of them claims to be effective for certain patients and problems, and some, by no means all, present credible research evidence for their claims. Nevertheless, I have never known a practitioner of any of these therapies who denied that resistance to change is a ubiquitous variable. Because no therapy is anything like a magic bullet, we do not know (we are not told) to what degree the variable of resistance influenced the claims made for its effectiveness.

There is another feature about which all therapists and all patients are in total agreement: When the therapy is over, the problems which propelled the person to begin therapy are still present but with diluted strength and ramifying consequences. What has changed are new ways to handle and limit them: There are in the literal sense no final solutions. Change is a foe that never totally surrenders. Armistice, yes. Total surrender, no.

One-on-one psychotherapy is a cup of tea compared to the brew served up in educational reform efforts. It is not only because more people are being asked to change but rather because, unlike psychotherapy, those who are the objects of change (almost always teachers) did not seek "institutional psychotherapy" (if I may put it that way). Over the decades I have had teachers say to me (paraphrased), "We are the targets of change, but I don't see them targeting principals, administrators, the superintendent, or the board of education. It's as if we, and we alone, caused the problems we have. That is unfair and untrue." One teacher put it very succinctly: "It's the 'Papa knows best' attitude. We are the children who have to go along with Papa." Whether teachers' reactions are valid or invalid to any degree is not the point. The point is that a reform effort inevitably arouses resistance in varying degrees in different teachers. And it is not infrequent that one source of resistance in *some* teachers is that the reform effort requires them to establish and maintain new relationships with other teachers. Any noncosmetic school reform requires not only that individual teachers change what they have done in their classrooms but, in addition, how and why they will interact with other teachers. That is a glimpse of the obvious to the teachers, but it is not obvious to the reformers eager to begin implementation, as if the process of implementation will work its magic, will transform and overcome differences in personal style, age, length of experience, and perceived status and influence (among teachers). Just as in marriage there is a honeymoon period undergirded by the belief that love and good intentions will overcome whatever problems and conflicts arise, a similar honeymoon period is usually enjoyed by the reformers, less frequently by the teachers who inhibit expression of their reservations either because they do not want to be perceived as a stumbling block or wet blanket or because they know things should, must change and they allow themselves to hope that their doubts will be proved groundless. At some point the honeymoon period ends as problems and differences of opinion come to the fore. How they are expressed and handled is crucial for the fate of the reform; more correctly, how they are *interpreted* and handled. Too often the reformers interpret the problems as resistance to the letter and spirit of the reform, or lack of understanding, or even incompetence, or all of these in combination. Less frequently, the reformer begins to understand that some of these problems *antedated* the reformer's appearance on the scene; they have a history in the social relationships in the school. That is to say, the resistance may be to the reform, but it is also powered by social-interpersonal factors in the prereform era. Resistance has diverse sources in time.

How do teachers interpret the problems in the posthoneymoon period? The answer returns us to when the reformer first appears on the scene and teachers ask themselves two questions. Does the reformer *really* know what schools are like, what students are like in classrooms, and the complexities of the teacher's role? Does the reformer appear to be the kind of person who will try to understand *this* school as well as get to know me because I may have knowledge that may be helpful to him? In brief, teachers are asking questions about the reformer's credentials: personal and experiential. These are the identical questions they ask when a new principal takes over or when a new superintendent is chosen. They are the same questions we ask when we meet a stranger with whom we will have to interact and live. Those questions come up early, and they are answered with differing degrees of strength and security depending on how the reform effort unfolds, the problems that arise, and how they are handled. It is not infrequent that the reformer plays little or no role in implementation but rather has a staff to whom the responsibility for implementation is delegated; which means that teachers are asking themselves questions about more than one stranger. It is (or should be) understandable if teachers find this unnerving, a source of distraction or interference, and worrisome.

It can get quite complicated, psychologically speaking, and if the reformer is not sensitive to the complexity, his or her interpretation of the ups and downs of the reform effort will at best be incomplete and at worst counterproductive. When I first began to work in schools, it took me several months to get a vague idea of how teachers had been and were now regarding me. To myself, I described how they seemed to relate to me: ranging from an obvious wariness to a superficial friendliness to a very impersonal civility bordering on coldness. That bothered me because I saw myself as a nice guy who wanted to be helpful in whatever ways teachers thought I could be helpful. My intentions were honorable and on the table. Why were they so slow to call on me, so initially cool to me? Yes, I was a professor at a Yale unbeloved (an understatement) by the community and had few professional credentials in the field of education. That, I assumed, would be intimidating to teachers, but I believed I could overcome such attitudes. To a large extent I did, but only after months went by in that first year and teachers began to be revealing. I learned from them.

Over the decades I have had many opportunities to meet with small and large groups of educators. With few exceptions I had been invited to present my views of the results of educational reform movements, views which cannot be placed in the category of good news. I used to wonder why I was invited in light of the fact that in my writings I was critical of the educational community, including schools of education. Granted that my criticisms were not ad hominen, they were explicit that, generally speaking, the educational community was part of the problem. Early on I began to understand why I was being invited. The major reason was that what I had experienced and observed in reform efforts was strikingly similar to that of many in these audiences, especially teachers, more than a few of whom in the question and answer period confirmed what I have said in this chapter. In addition, after the meeting ended I could count on being surrounded by small groups of teachers who wanted to relate their "war stories" in which they were the objects of change. *The point here is not whether and to what degree these stories were valid, i.e., justified. Neither I nor the reader has a basis for passing judgment. The point is that these teachers felt put upon, misunderstood, disappointed, and angry.*

The rationale of any reform effort which is insensitive to or underestimates how difficult and agonizing it can be for teachers to change their accustomed ways of thinking, acting, and interrelating is like the boxer who begins the fight with chin out and his hands down. That does not mean that the reform effort is inevitably doomed; that depends on the resourcefulness and capacity for fast learning on the part of the reformers. In my experience there are two kinds of "mistakes." The first is when erupting problems are handled in a way that makes a bad situation worse. The second is when the eruption becomes an occasion for "clearing the air," for rethinking and even redirecting the course of the reform effort. If conflict and misunderstanding are predictable, and they certainly are, that is no warrant for viewing them as visitations from devilish sources. They can be exploited for learning and growth by all (or almost all!). That assertion is relevant to a similarity in the phenomenology of reformers and teachers, a similarity that goes unnoticed.

When people approach their first independent teaching positions, the one dominant fear they have is that they will encounter discipline problems and challenges to their ability to handle them well. Not infrequently they do have such problems, obvious and difficult ones. Such instances are responded to differently by different teachers but, generally speaking, they fall into two groups. The first group includes the anxious, insecure teacher who becomes more authoritarian, or punitive-critical, or controlling in seeking ways to be, or appear to be, the unquestioned authority who will brook no misbehavior. The situation may get worse, or if on the surface it has not, a wide interpersonal gulf between teacher and students endures. The teacher may be insensitive to what has happened because he is so absorbed with *his* feelings of fear, failure, and exposure that he is rendered incapable of taking distance from what happened and is happening. Self-absorption is a form of interpersonal blindness. The second group is comprised of those teachers who, seeing that their tactics are counterproductive, will change tactics because on reflection they decide that such a change is necessary. That type of change is possible only if a teacher has decided that his or her previous tactics with *this* student (or *these* students) did not or will not work. There are few teachers who do not view their early weeks as a first-time teacher as at best very trying or at worst a baptism of fire. In my book *Teaching as a Performing Art* (1999), I give a long account of a first-time teacher who was confronted with as difficult a class of students as one can imagine, a class in a school that was as disorganized as it was disorganizing for everyone in it. She deserves the equivalent of the Nobel Peace Prize for her flexibility, ingenuity, and creativity, as well as for what she accomplished with her students. From the moment she walked into the school and then into the classroom, she knew that what she had been taught about discipline was useless. I have no doubt that if I were in her place, I would have quit on the spot. Admittedly, what that teacher encountered is an extreme case, but nonetheless it illustrates how difficult it is to confront the necessity to change. To my knowledge, neither I nor anybody else has adequately recognized and emphasized the dynamics of that difficulty for teachers.

What I have said is no less the case for the person who for the first time is spearheading an effort at school reform. That person has high hopes but also anxieties about how smooth the process will be. The level and strength of those anxieties will to a significant degree be a function of how well the reformer knows the reform literature or has made it his business to talk to people who have initiated a reform but never wrote about it because the reform was for all practical purposes a failure or was aborted. The frequency of these instances is dramatically more frequent than one would conclude from the literature. Even if one restricts oneself to those relatively few published reports which seek to explain why the reforms failed, or fell far short of their mark, these reports often contain advice about how *not* to proceed. The reason I have written this book is my belief, based on my own experience and that of others with whom I have talked, that these reports ignore or vastly underemphasize the role of teachers' phenomenology toward change in the culture of schools.

That underemphasis should not be a surprise, at least it should not have been to me as I reviewed my own experience. Prior to my interest in school reform and on the basis of truly personal experience as well as in the professional role as clinical psychologist, I had learned that unlearning old habits of thinking and acting, and learning new ones is rough stuff. There is some wisdom to that roughness because it is a preventive to the too-easy acceptance of fads, fashions, nostrums, and panaceas which are never absent in the educational air. That, so to speak, is the good news. The bad news is that even when there is sincere agreement that a noncosmetic change should be attempted, that things cannot go on as before, that the future should and must not be a carbon copy of the present, the resistance to the change, far from being absent or minimal, will be daunting. In fact, I would say that when the change process appears to encounter no formidable issues and problems, the desired goals of the reform are not likely to be realized. The name of the game is not change but how to recognize, react to, and work through the turmoil of change which is always deeply personal and social in nature and context.

In any noncosmetic effort at change the stakes are high both for reformer and teachers. The reformer has invested a lot of time and energy in arriving at ideas and methods for changing and improving educational quality and outcomes. The reformer may be quite aware how much he has changed in getting to the point where he seeks to implement his ideas. What the reformer seeks to do is not a side show; it usually has become his total

professional life, an investment from which he clearly seeks a profit, a turning point in his life. He is so self-absorbed with his ideas, methods, and
goals that he cannot use his personal experience of change as a way of
understanding that he is asking teachers to go through a similar, difficult
experience, usually without the kinds of support (e.g., time, colleagues,
institutional support) he enjoyed. I am reminded here of how hard it was
for our daughter, Julie, to give up using a pacifier. My wife and I were both
psychologists quite knowledgeable and articulate (more correctly, perhaps,
voluble) about resistance to change. We knew it would not be easy for Julie,
and she did try, but at some point after we went to bed she would ask for
the pacifier. We were puzzled, even disappointed that despite her trying
she could not give it up. It took months before she could give it up. I have
often mused about why we thought it was taking so long. The answer, I
think, is obvious: For Julie, our asking her (we never demanded) to give
up the pacifier indicated that we did not understand what function the
pacifier had in going to sleep. We thought it was taking too long; Julie did
not. Imagine our surprise when one evening she said she would not need
the pacifier! (I have never tried to explain *that*.)

It is no different with teachers. They have experienced numerous tran-
sitions which required change: elementary, middle, and high school; college; entering a preparatory program; practice teaching; their first job;
moving to a new school. These milestones differed in the degree of difficulty they experienced. Many teachers have told me that it was practice
teaching when they had real doubts whether they were cut out to be a
teacher because it would require changes in personal style they doubted
they could make. Many more said that their first year of teaching was one
of fast and difficult change because it was so different from what they expected or were led to believe, or they were alone without support, or they
had not been prepared, as one teacher said, "for understanding and dealing
with individual differences in a class of 25 kids," or they could not or did
not want to be under the time pressures of a calendar-driven curriculum. I
have never known a teacher who did not say that he or she had changed a
good deal from the time he or she had entered a preparatory program to when
we talked. Some teachers tended to interpret my questions—they were not
standardized questions, I was not doing a formal study—as if I was interested in whether they had learned a lot. When I then would say that I was
especially interested in how smooth or difficult it was to change in the way
they did to allow them to remain in teaching, in one or another way they
said, as one teacher expressed with a loud laugh, "You must be kidding.
There were times I thought I should see a shrink or quit. Or both."

There is an irony here. Everything I have said about teachers is no less
true of teachers who become principals, or middle-level administrators, or

superintendents. The irony inherent in that fact is that one of the most frequent criticisms teachers make of their administrators is that they have forgotten or have become insensitive to what teachers experience in the culture of the school. I agree with the teachers just as I agree with some of their criticisms of reformers who have asked them to change, and I am not exempting myself.

From what I have said in this chapter, the reader might conclude that I have far more sympathy for teachers than I have for reformers. That is not at all the case. I have tried to describe and understand why and how teachers respond to reform efforts because it has been underemphasized, and wrongly or superficially interpreted. But there is another reason, a more important one: *I want to make the point that teachers, no less and no more than reformers, too often fail to mine previous experience as a source of insight and guidance for the change the reform effort requires.* There are reformers and there are reformers, just as there are teachers and there are teachers, which is to say that within each group there is variability in regard to personality, style, rigidity, sensitivities, temperament, prejudice, courage, openness, and more. Neither has cornered the market on human virtues. Each may blame the other, and they both may be correct, although they usually do not know that. It is usually the case that reformers have more perceived status and influence than teachers, a fact that very much complicates their relationship and that the reformers downplay at their peril. But teachers are not without power; when they experience the struggles associated with change, they can and they often do devise ways of resisting the change and impoverishing or distorting the outcomes of the reform effort.

The reader may conclude that I am describing battles in a war. The metaphor is an appropriate one although I hasten to add that there have been and will continue to be instances, their frequency unknown, when there have been at worst small skirmishes. If their number is unknown, the written reports provide little basis for understanding why there were not battles or wars.

We are used to saying that teachers, like parents, should be role models for their students. People differ of course in how they scale the characteristics which comprise their model. I doubt that very many people will have "openness" on their list. It is by no means an easy characteristic to determine, so let me draw upon my concrete experience. I have sat in scores of classrooms. It took me a while before I realized that *I had never heard a teacher say that he or she was wrong about anything or that he or she wondered whether the students thought that what and how he or she was teaching a particular segment of the curriculum was creating problems for them.* Also, in most (not all) instances students knew little or nothing about the teacher's out of school life: where he or she lived, the kind of house; the names, sex, and ages of his or her children (if any); the name and occupation of his or her spouse; what they like to do during breaks or vacations; and more. Why should teachers consider talking about themselves in these matters? I am clearly not suggesting that teachers reveal what I can only call "personal-personal" matters. What I am suggesting is that teachers reveal little or nothing to deal with questions about which students have an understandable curiosity. I am being descriptive when I say that the relationship between teachers and students is an impersonal one, as if a relatively superficial openness is off limits and pedagogically counterproductive.

Openness is also not the way you would characterize relationships among teachers and between teachers and principals or other supervisors. I am not referring to openness about "personal-personal" matters but to matters of pedagogical conceptions, beliefs, practice, and classroom problems. It is as if openness is dangerous because it may be perceived by others as a sign of self-inadequacy or a criticism of others. I did not understand this when I started to work in schools and unreflectively assumed that because teachers were working in the same school they had some degree of personal-professional relationship with each other, that they talked meaningfully with each other about professional matters—not gossip, but about teaching and learning. That was rarely the case. It took me longer than it should have to realize two things. First, preparatory programs and practice teaching do not take up issues and dilemmas of collegiality; they reinforce the situation I have described. Second, it clearly is no different on the college and university level where there is nothing resembling a teacher preparation program. When I started to teach at Yale, I felt alone, anxious, fearful, unprepared (to indulge in understatement), and envious of my colleagues who seemed so much more secure and mature than I was. No one offered advice or sympathy and, of course, it never occurred to me to seek any of them out for counsel. My students and teaching style were my business and mine alone. I wrongly assumed that it would not be the same in public schools. It was a case of assuming that the grass is greener elsewhere, for teachers at least. You could say I was naive. You would be right. Unless what I have learned from direct observations and discussions with other school reformers is grossly atypical, my naiveté was not atypical.

When you consider that a fair number of school reformers are academics who in their bailiwicks talk cynically but realistically about the lack of a professionally and interpersonally rewarding collegiality, it is not surprising that they are flustered by the realization that openness among school teachers, as well as between them (the reformers) and teachers is no small problem.

But how open is the reformer to those to whom a major role in implementation is given? For example, how open is the person about the *pre-*

dictable problems the educators will have dealing with change? What forums will she suggest where she and they can articulate their perceptions and advice? How sensitively and when is the reformer prepared to put her cards on the table? When the reform effort is described as one in which "we are all in this together," it is a "collaborative effort requiring mutuality," how prepared is the reformer to be as open as she hopes others will be? Under what conditions is the reformer prepared to change her accustomed style and time perspective? We have no answers to these questions. Reform efforts are written up in a way that is disappointingly and misleadingly largely impersonal, even though from beginning to end the process is deeply personal for everyone. As a result, one does not know what to conclude or what would constitute a replication. In addition, we do not know how to explain why an effort failed or had minimal consequences, or even why it was successful to the degree claimed. Frankly, when I read the educational reform literature, I end up not knowing what to conclude or believe. That is as true for the successes as well as the failures. I stress that point because the differences in their outcomes are in part, and only in part (I assume), because the issues I have discussed in these pages were differently perceived and dealt with.

The reader may feel that I am thinking and writing like a psychologist whose stock in trade is the complexity of human relationships. That is to say, I am transforming educational issues surrounding teaching and learning into the confines of the vicissitudes of human relationships. That is true but only in part. The reader acquainted with my previous books will know that I regard the inadequacies of school as incomprehensible apart from cultural, historical, political, and philosophical considerations. It is these considerations which are the parameters, the backdrop, which determine why and how human relationships in schools take the forms and directions they do. I knew that in an abstract way before I began to work in schools, just as I knew that to be the case in any complicated institution, public or private, religious or secular. The fact is that I started to realize that I had a lot to learn about these parameters if my psychological knowledge and experience were not to mislead me because they were not the whole picture; they were embedded in a larger picture in which there were no simple cause-and-effect relationships. Only in recent years did I wake up to the fact that I had shortchanged, so to speak, the complexity, the dynamics, of relationships among school personnel and between them and external agents for reform. It was that realization that led me to write this book, to examine my own thinking and experience in light of that realization. It is not undue modesty on my part to say that I long ago adapted to my belief that I could not put the whole picture together, or do justice to all the factors that make schools what they are, how similar they are to each other, and why they are resistant to efforts to change them. One of my all time favorite caveats is that by Mencken: For any major problem there is a simple explanation that is wrong. I have not in the past offered simple explanations. That is not to say that my explanations were valid. I believe they were largely valid but that I did not do justice to how psychological factors enter the reform process in ways that help in part to explain why educational reform efforts are a sometime thing, sources of disappointment that have the major consequence that those within or outside schools eagerly embrace the quick fix.

What I have said and will say in this book will not be a source of comfort to many people because in the past I have said that meaningful school reform is a very, very complicated affair. What the self-scrutiny process has taught me is that it is even more complicated than I realized. Why that has to be so I shall discuss in the next chapter when I take up time as a variable in efforts of educational change. Moreover, if what I have said is taken seriously, the variable of time will be seen as a major problem and obstacle to school reform. In saying that, I am reminded of a logo I saw on the rear fender of a car: Why be difficult when with a little bit of effort you can be utterly impossible?

Chapter 4

Time Perspective: The Disconnect Between Fantasy and Reality

An idea is, so to speak, born, it is developed, and it is implemented to a point where judgment is passed as to its quality and validity. How long should the entire process take? I assume that the reader, like me, would say that is a stupid question because there are myriad factors that predictably and unpredictably can determine the answer. Nevertheless, the fact remains that the answer always explicitly or implicitly involves a time perspective: The individual or group with the idea makes a judgment, however vague, about how long the process will take. There are usually two judgments about time. The first is what I call the "if God is on our side" judgment, and the other is one based on Murphy's and Sarason's law. Murphy's law states that if anything can go wrong, it will. Sarason's law asserts that Murphy's law is a gross understatement. I first heard about Murphy's when I came to Yale, and it came from graduate students who were working on their doctoral dissertations, and when I would ask them when their task would be completed, their answers provided personal experience confirming Murphy's law. I did not formulate Sarason's law until I entered the educational reform arena. You would think that having supervised many doctoral theses and having been on the committees of even more, it would be second nature for me to give a lot of importance to time as a variable. But it was not second nature. What was second nature, for me and most people, was the assumption that what I had experienced and learned in one arena would be quite different from the lessons I would draw in another arena. Fortunately, I learned fast, and it all came together in my mind as a result of a very upsetting experience in air travel. It was at a time when I was trying to understand why educational reform, which then was less a movement than occasional forays, clearly was, to say the least, ineffectual.

It was just before the era of jet travel. I was on a four-engine plane going from Idlewild (later Kennedy) airport in New York to Dallas. An hour or so out of New York the pilot told us, "Those of you on the right side of the airplane can see that one of our Evinrudes (He was, I can assure you, a frustrated disc jockey, but that would take too long to relate) is in trouble. We knew there was a problem 10 minutes ago. We will put down in Cincinnati." When I looked out the window, thick black smoke was coming out of one of the engines. It reminded me of the war movies I had seen as a child in the days of the silent movies. I was terrified. We put down in Cincinnati. We waited 3 hours for another plane to arrive. During the wait I saw the pilot and told him my imagery from childhood. He listened, smiled, and then said "There is only one thing you have to worry about: *You cannot put these monsters down quickly."* And it was then that it hit me that schools and school systems were kin to the monstrous 707 and that they could not be changed quickly or according to the time perspective that reformers had conveyed to the general public. I had other reasons at the time for predicting that the reform effort, generally speaking, would go nowhere, and the plane experience provided yet one more reason, one that should have been obvious to me but was not.

I trust that readers are not offended by my calling schools and school systems monstrous affairs. They are monstrous in the sense that a single school has anywhere from a couple of hundred students to several thousands; the complexity of relationships among students is hard to discern and fathom and that is also true for relationships among teachers and administrators; classrooms vary considerably in ambiance and educational outcomes; contacts between teachers and parents can vary from less than infrequent (e.g., in high schools) to frequent in terms of rationale, quality, and substance; relationships between unions and management vary considerably in terms of militancy, level of conflict, and frequency of resort to grievance procedures; and more. Is it surprising that reformers come to regard schools and school systems as tailor-made primarily for those with masochistic needs, or for those whose initial fantasy that schools can be changed, "turned around," quickly founders on the rocks of reality? Schools are not Piper Cub airplanes, just as the American Airlines pilot told me that his monster 707 was not a one-engine affair that could be put down in relatively short order on an interstate highway. Let me illustrate the point by a "modest" proposal I made decades ago (Sarason, 1976).

The proposal was intended as a way of altering the role of parents in their child's schooling, as a way of changing the quality and goals of teacher-parent relationships. Briefly, before the school year begins, the teacher meets with the child's parents and says, "You know your child better than I do, and therefore, there is much about your child you can tell me that would be very helpful to my understanding him as a learner and citizen in my class. You know what his interests are, what turns him on and off, what he does well or not so well, his assets and vulnerabilities. There is much that you know that would be very helpful to me. You and I have to feel comfortable to contact each other anytime we have a question and not wait until we are sure there is a problem. I will always make time to be available to you either during or after school, or in the evening if that is the only time we can meet." I emphasize in that article that this meeting should not take place unless teachers sincerely believe that parents know their child in ways and contexts that the teachers cannot; it is not an empty go-through-the-motions ritual. The teacher has to believe that parents are a resource to them and that their relationship is one of mutual rights and obligations.

What are the predictable obstacles to implementation of the proposal? There will be teachers who will feel that such an initial meeting will not be all that productive, that they have felt no need to involve parents in the way I described, that parents are notoriously reluctant to say anything "bad" about their child. There will be teachers who will look favorably on the proposal but who will look very unfavorably on cutting short their customary summer pursuits or employment. Teachers should not be expected to give such time out of the goodness of their hearts. Will the board of education budget for their time and persuade the community to increase the school budget? Will the proposal open up the sluice gates in that some parents will feel entitled to expect that the teacher will be available to them at any time for any reason and that they can pass judgment on the teacher's handling of that child?

Back in the 1960s I met once a week for 10 weeks with teachers in a nearby school system. In the fifth session I jocularly asked a question which says a good deal about the substance of previous meetings: "I get the feeling that if you had to decide between two options, I think I know which option you would choose. The first is that you never have to meet with parents. The second is that you get a thousand-dollar raise." The response was nervous laughter, then silence, and the direction of the conversation changed. Generally speaking, teachers do not look forward to meeting with parents; they do not find it a source of satisfaction especially if the parents are not shrinking violets. This particular school was in an affluent community where parents were articulate and from the standpoint of the teachers were "demanding" and quick to judge their competence and authority. For the teachers, parents were "complainers," not a source of information and advice; teachers know best! Over the years I have talked with about a dozen teachers who said what I have just said: They were teachers who had met with *their* child's teacher and were seething because the teacher responded to them as if what the parent had to say was too subjective, ill advised, and wrong. As one teacher put it to me, "She wanted to do all the talking. I was supposed to acquiesce and be more respectful than she obviously thought I was."

I am not playing the blame-assignment game for the simple reason that in their preparatory training future teachers are not exposed for as long as 5 seconds to how one should be with and relate to parents. Two assumptions seem to explain this: Talking to parents is a simple affair, or the future teacher has the requisite genes for mutually satisfactory relationships. I have discussed this in the many talks I have given in schools of education, always adding the suggestion that teaching films be made portraying both how and how not to engage with parents with this or that problem concerning the parents' child in the classroom. There have been no takers. Changing schools in some noncosmetic way is as difficult as changing preparatory programs. To change either one requires an effort based on a realistic time perspective, which is why the reform movement can point only to few successes.

With the above as prologue, I turn now to a community educational program based on a rationale that takes the variable of time very seriously, with a notable degree of success. This is in marked contrast to the unrealistic time perspective ordinarily undergirding the rationale for school reform efforts. Although originally the rationale and the actions derived from it could be characterized under the rubric "community organizing," it has in recent years expanded its activities to include school reform.

The story begins before World War II. It is the story of Saul Alinsky who, in my opinion, was one of the most remarkable thinkers and activists of the past century. His name will not be familiar to most readers. For those whose interest may be piqued by what I shall say, I suggest they read Horwitt's (1992) very readable and fascinating biography of Alinsky, *Let Them Call Me Rebel*. As for Alinsky's speaking for himself, and he spoke for himself extraordinarily well, I recommend his two books: *Reveille for Radicals* (1946) and *Rules for Radicals: A Practical Primer for Realistic Radicals* (1971). The reader will be surprised by the two books if only because of Alinsky's critique of and even disdain for well-intentioned, self-styled reformers and radicals who have a paternalistic, traditional conception of the nature, sources, and the uses of power. I will not attempt to discuss in detail Alinsky's thinking and actions but rather briefly distill what I consider to be a few of his basic conceptions most relevant to my present purposes. I had read Alinsky long before I got involved in educational reform, but it was long after my involvement that I began to see his relevance for such reform. That is another instance of how easy it is for two arenas of thinking and experience to remain unconnected despite their obvious relevance for each other. My early interest in Alinsky derived from my own experience in radical political movements. When I much later became part of the educational reform movement, it did not occur to me to ask, What was the relevance of Alinsky to what I saw happening in that movement? We are used to saying that we learn from our mistakes. In my experience what is equally or more consequential is why we have such difficulty making connections with different arenas of past experience.

What the reader needs to know for what follows is that Alinsky created the Industrial Areas Foundation (IAF) whose mission was to work exclusively with those segments of the community who were aggrieved, or oppressed, or rendered, for all practical purposes, powerless by the more powerful segments, the "establishment." The IAF consisted of highly selected "organizers" who would respond to invitations from one or more agencies in the aggrieved parts of the community in a manner consistent with the IAF rationale (to be described below). These agencies historically have been churches indigenous to that community. That was the case in Alinsky's work in the 1930s when the conditions, economic and moral, of most Chicago stockyards were more than deplorable. It was the Catholic bishop of Chicago who was Alinsky's most solid supporter. Today the IAF is most active in the Southwest where Ernesto Cortes is, to say the least, a presence in the Chicano and Black communities. Cortes is religiously devout, a formally and autodidacticly educated person for whom the label charismatic is appropriate. I first came to know him a decade ago in connection with Paul Heckman's school reform project in Tucson. Cortes is a thinker and activist par excellence. So was Alinsky, but his temperament and interpersonal skills tended to create as many problems as they resolved. Cortes' approach derives from that of Alinsky but differs in tone and pace. It is almost always the case that the invitation for an IAF organizer is extended by two or more parish congregations who will pay the organizers' salaries for 2 years, an agreement the justification for which is why I am writing this chapter. Let me now turn to the guts of Alinsky's rationale.

1. Reformers who seek institutional change—and more often than not they are external to the institution—proceed by trying to develop supportive constituencies within the institution. These reformers see themselves as leaders of the effort and wish to be perceived as such by the constituents. He or she is the directing force and the most influential person in planning, tactics, and decision making. This person is publicly recognized as the leader. The clearest example is when a national labor union appoints a person to organize factory workers, municipal workers, teachers, and so forth. What all these and similar efforts have in common is that a person is given or assumes the role of leader, the standard bearer. In all of these instances there is a challenge to power relations between the constituents and the institutional establishment.

2. Prior to the arrival of the external organizers, individuals in the targeted group vary, often considerably, in their willingness to take part in

militant action. Most are discouraged, passive, and feel impotent. Some are discouraged and respond favorably to the organizer's message and leadership. The task of the organizer is to increase the number of those who will join the reform effort. When a sufficient number sign up, the tactics and strategy of the reform become concretized, and so to speak, the battle begins. Throughout this process it is the organizer who is the major driving force. For all practical purposes he or she is the leader. This is not to say that the organizer is insensitive to the ideas and feelings of the constituents but rather that by tradition and previous experience he or she assumes and is accorded the role of leader.

3. A dependency relation between constituents and organizer develops, although no one would describe it in that way. The organizer is perceived as the fount of knowledge and direction, a needed and welcome one if the challenge to power relationships is to succeed. But, throughout, the organizer is the major initiator and director of action and goals. Indigenous individuals may demonstrate leadership qualities which is welcomed by and utilized by the organizer in ways he or she deems most appropriate.

4. When an aggrieved group is poor, disparaged, and discriminated against, who regard their fate with hopelessness and passivity, who do not or cannot envision that there is power in numbers or that they are capable of being initiators and of taking responsibility for their own actions to change their conditions—when these are the dominant attitudes and self-definition, the conventional conception of "organizing" (whether initiated from within or without) is counterproductive and inappropriate, if not doomed to result in failure. It reinforces rather than dilutes dependency, its needs, and manifestations.

5. In these instances, almost always in urban areas, the task of the Alinsky-Cortes organizer is fourfold. The first is to meet people *individually or in very small groups in their homes* with the limited purpose of getting from citizens what they see as grievances, inequities, injustices; why these have not been addressed by the establishment in the community. The organizer listens, rather than being an initiator of ideas, and he or she avoids conveying the impression of being a leader or savior who, so to speak, will run interference for them in any action whatsoever. Second, it is in these "house meetings" that the organizer begins to discern those individuals who seem to possess leadership attributes. They appear to be opinion makers and not fearful of action. Third, at some unpredictable point it is recognized that the nature of certain grievances about which there is consensus needs to be substantiated by concrete data, that opinion and feeling are not enough as a basis for public action. It is not the responsibility of the organizer to obtain those data, it is the responsibility of the people to figure out how to obtain the data, to use their social networks to get assis-

tance to obtain the data. It is also the responsibility of the group, which can become very large, to decide on and take complete responsibility for an initial public action to address grievances. It will not be an action they have been persuaded by the organizer to take but one for which they have willingly decided to assume responsibility, an action which if it fails in whole or in part cannot be blamed on the organizer.

I assume that this brief presentation of the rationale has raised certain questions in the minds of readers. One question has to do with what appears to be the passive, nondirective role of the organizer. Why should people talk with him or her and give vent to their frustrations? Why should a number of them agree to invite a small number of neighbors and friends to their homes for a "house meeting"? Let us remember that these people know (or have been told) by their parish leaders that money has been raised to secure the services of the organizer for the purpose of invigorating and stimulating the community to change and improve its conditions. These are segments of the community for whom their churches are safe and rewarding places. They are, so to speak, primed to welcome and be curious about such a person. It goes without saying that the organizer not only knows how to listen but also to convey sincere interest and understanding. He or she is not the expert on *their* problems in *this* community; they are the experts who can help the organizer become knowledgeable, and that is possible only in relationships of mutual trust. The reader, like me, can assume that organizers vary in personal style and efficacy. But organizers vary much less in the degree and clarity with which they convey the basic message: Citizens, not the organizer, take responsibility for whatever actions they take. That does not mean that the organizer, especially after some weeks or months, does not throw out ideas and suggestions, or glosses over the significance of the goal of people taking responsibility for whatever actions they agree on. There is a difference between being passive and laid back and being interested and probing, treating the person with respect because that person can be part of the solution.

As I said earlier, my first direct experience with the IAF was more than a decade ago in connection with my initial visit to Paul Heckman's project: an attempt to alter schools in the poorest (Hispanic) sections of Tucson, and to do so by drawing on agencies and parents with a stake in these schools. Here is what I wrote about that first meeting:

> At the first meeting I attended I was struck by the heterogeneity among the participants, ranging from individuals whose speech I had difficulty comprehending to those, mostly affiliated with local churches, who were obviously well educated in the conventional sense. I was also struck by their stance: they

were not coming hat-in-hand to ask for help from a university-based project. They had been invited to the meeting for what they thought was clarification of a basis that would be mutually enhancing both to community needs, which went far beyond school improvement, and the school project. There were no confrontations. It was a discussion centering around how the resources of each party could be interconnected, i.e., how the resources of each could be increased.

In previous years, I had been involved in scores of meetings among parents, community agencies, and school personnel. In all such meetings the stance of the educators was: "Here is how we think you can be helpful to us." The stance of the other participants was: "Tell us how we can be helpful, and we will see if and how we can be helpful." At that first Tucson meeting it was refreshingly clear that whatever agreements emerged it would not, could not, be of the one-way-street variety. That was not explicitly articulated, but it was what the conversation was all about.

The active, incisive, and creative participation of parents increased dramatically over the five-year period; they did not get bored and frustrated and drift away. The truly dramatic point of all this is that one of the participants—clearly a well-educated, very well-spoken Anglo—contributed only rarely to the discussions. It was obvious that he was totally attentive to what was being said but he was silent for the most part. He never, so to speak, carried the ball. Others from the community did so. The silent participant was Frank Pearson, the IAF organizer. He had done his job extraordinarily well. (Sarason & Lorentz, 1992, p. 132)

Another relevant excerpt is from a member of the San Antonio Communities Organized for Public Service (COPS):

I got out of the house when I joined COPS. It was like a whole new world. I never knew I had so many talents. In 1982, I was elected area vice president. One of my first actions was to go before the city council to demand [to know] where money allocated for our neighborhood had gone. Christine, the organizer, coached me. We did a lot of research. There was $300,000 allocated for Amistad, and the money was moved elsewhere. We formed a committee and met with our city council representative and then the head of Community Development Block Grants. We demanded to see the notes of a meeting when the money was discussed. We learned that it was moved to another part of the city as a loan and we could not demand it back. I always remember the day we went to city council. My throat was dry, my legs were shaking. I was petrified. Just before I started to speak, I turned around. There were 40 leaders from my parish behind me. I'll never forget that. That is the strength we have. (p. 133)

A member of Valley Interfaith in South Texas related the following:

People in the Valley had been taught to understand that the system was only supposed to work for a few. People were passive. In the men's class I attended at my church, I was watching the same problems go on and on. I didn't see why my people had to get help through cheese lines—waiting, sometimes two to three hours in the sun, to get five pounds of cheese and some canned goods. It was embarrassing, insulting, and I became angry—an anger that makes you want to struggle against those who don't understand. . . . It's been real growth for me. I couldn't stand in front of people and talk when I started. Now I have been on stage in front of 5,000 and 10,000 people. When I see these people, I am energized. I see through their eyes that I am growing. Seven years ago, I never would have thought that one day I would be in Washington talking to one of the Congressmen. It is a "university of the people"—that's what we call our organization in the Valley. At this point, I don't know where or when to stop. (p. 134)

Now I must tell the reader something that I deliberately omitted for two reasons. First, I wanted to sketch the rationale. Second, I wanted to contrast two very different conceptions of organizing. (Indeed, I hope the reader will agree with me that the Alinsky-Cortes use of the label "organizer" obscures more than it illuminates: It is an unfortunate label because it is so discrepant from conventional imagery of an organizer.) Third, and most important of all, the omission provides my justification for this chapter, and therefore, I felt it should not be part of a sketch, it deserves special emphasis.

I said that the organizer starts with a one-on-one house meeting, and when the interpersonal chemistry appears appropriate, an individual is asked if he or she could arrange a second meeting in his or her home with a few friends or neighbors. *House meetings may occupy the organizer's time for many months.* That time perspective is, of course, dictated by the goals of the IAF rationale. To help people change their self-perceptions, assume an unaccustomed role in decision making, commit themselves to assertive actions, take responsibility for those actions, and see those initial actions as beginning points for the broader purpose of community change—that has to take time, it cannot be achieved by a predetermined time schedule. The reader may be familiar with the classroom "October 7" syndrome: "By October 7 we must be on page x in the textbook." The IAF rationale mandates a time perspective which is the polar opposite. That kind of realistic time perspective has been almost totally absent in efforts at educational reform. It is an absence I never took as seriously as I should have, even though I had known about Alinsky and regarded his efforts with the highest respect. And, to add personally inflicted insult to injury, my experience as a clinical psychologist working with individuals—not with complicated, layered, traditional institutions—demonstrated the difference between a realistic and an unrealistic time perspective. In my books on educational reform I have railed, often polemically, against the quick-fix mentality but not in a sufficiently detailed and concrete way, which explains why I am writing this book.

An educational reform effort always reflects how certain questions are asked and answered. What are our ultimate goals? What are the *predictable* obstacles we will encounter? How will we prepare for and deal with these obstacles? What is required of us in the "tooling up" period? How will we determine when and to what degree those who are the objects of change are prepared to change? Is there a reasonable match between what we know we want and must do and the available time and money?

All of these questions enter into the time perspective that is adopted. Over the decades I have been asked to sit in on numerous meetings for planning an educational reform effort. All of my most recent experiences have been in meetings for the planning of charter schools. In all but one instance the discussion and development of a time perspective—a truly searching discussion—was glossed over as if hope, opinion, good intentions, and divine providence would be allies in whatever lay ahead. That is one of the several reasons I wrote *Charter Schools: Another Flawed Educational Reform?* (1998a).

Imagine the situation where a group of educators and child psychologists are meeting to discuss learning to read and reading problems. In comes a stranger who listens for a while to the discussion. After a few minutes he asks the group if they would answer a question that has long plagued him, a question containing an opinion, he says, that may anger them. "I have concluded that professionals like you have sold the public a bill of goods about how long it takes to teach a child to read. You make it sound so complicated that it requires as much patience as time. I do not know where and how this thinking originated, but it is my opinion that children can be taught to read in a matter of a few months at the most, not the 1–3 years you people proclaim."

Undoubtedly, the first reaction to the stranger would be, "How do we get this kook out of here?" How would we justify that reaction? Even if we were patient and polite and took an hour or more to tell him the major variables that play a role in learning to read—variables antedating the beginning of school, sensory factors, motivation, cognitive factors, personality-social characteristics—as well as highlights of the theoretical and research literature, would we not end up feeling that our quick and dirty course in child and social development was an exercise in the most extreme form of futility? And would we be at all surprised if when we were through the stranger left the room saying, "You have proved my point. You have a stake in making a simple problem appear to be horribly complicated." Would we not shamefacedly conclude that we had made the same error as the stranger did: We had attempted to change someone's mind and do it on the basis of an egregiously simple time perspective?

Today when I discuss with educators the disconnect between the time-perspective issue and educational reform, I come away with one of two feelings, or both: I am regarded as unduly complicating a complicated picture, or I am placing too much emphasis on the time issue. As one person put it to me, "If what you say is taken seriously, there would be far fewer reform efforts. Time is money." That person vastly underestimates the frequency and depth of the quick-fix mentality.

Let us return to the IAF because beginning a decade ago Ernesto Cortes turned his attention to the power relationships between parents and schools in poor urban areas in Texas. Just as no one had to tell Cortes that the plight of people in these areas reflected their passive stance toward the political-economic establishment in the larger community, no one had to tell him that the school system has its own power establishment which, ironically, contained more than a few members of the racial or ethnic minorities. Of course, this is not an autonomous establishment because it is the creation of the political-economic-social one. Cortes knew that and did not make the mistake of taking dead aim only at schools. He knew that at some point IAF would have to confront the truly powerful establishment, and by IAF I mean the parents and others who already had been part of IAF community actions.

I shall not attempt a description of the IAF–Alliance Schools reform effort. That has already been done by Dennis Shirley in his richly detailed book *Community Organizing for Urban School Reform* (1997), which I strongly recommend to the reader. It is one of the best and best-balanced books on urban school reform I have read. Persuasive as he is about the scope of IAF's accomplishments, he does not neglect to point out some of its problems.

The following are the last two paragraphs of Shirley's (not slim) book. I present them for two reasons. First, they are pithy and to the point. Second, they allow me to discuss some personal IAF observations relevant to the purposes of this chapter.

> Whatever fruits such strategies may produce must remain a matter of speculation for the immediate future. Even with the different setbacks that the Alliance Schools have experienced, one may posit that Texas IAF's work has accrued sufficient momentum and staying power to initiate a reconceptualization of American public education. Instead of pursuing marketplace models of school reform, the Alliance Schools indicate that we need to support neighborhood schools by strengthening their ties to their immediate communities. Instead of focusing on fixing the school in isolation from its environment, the Alliance Schools suggest that one can develop integrated strategies of neighborhood improvement and school revitalization. Instead of asking parents

to become involved in strengthening the existing culture of the school, we can challenge parents to become engaged in agitating and transforming the school's culture. Instead of relegating parents and students to the roles of clients, consumers, and recipients of information, we can challenge them to become citizens with the skills and commitment to strengthen our struggling urban schools and neighborhoods. The future is open and there are no guarantees. Nonetheless, the development and popularity of the Alliance Schools in Texas provides a powerful counter-example to the dominant rhetoric of privatization and marketplace models of reform.

The diffusion of the Alliance Schools concept beyond Texas is currently under way. As of this writing, the spread of Alliance Schools has taken its most advanced form in Arizona, where IAF organizations in Tucson and Phoenix have organized twenty Alliance Schools in collaboration with local districts and the state department of education. Unlike the Texas Alliance Schools, however, they have not acquired funds from the commissioner of education or waivers for school development programs. "Our superintendent of schools doesn't have the same power that the commissioner in Texas does," said Frank Pierson of Pima County Interfaith. "And the development of our Alliance Schools will inevitably look different than the Texas network. Still, the central thread which emphasizes a culture of conversations and teaching people about power and their self-interests will be the same." Arizona's Alliance Schools have already won important victories by gaining funding for after-school programs and youth employment projects; they have also gone further than Texas' Alliance Schools by formalizing relationships with local chapters of the American Federation of Teachers. Arizona will provide an intriguing laboratory for the further dissemination and development of the kind of school improvement and neighborhood organizing promoted by the IAF. (Shirley, 1997, p. 294)

Texas IAF leaders and organizers now have over a decade of intense organizing in education behind them. They have fought for parental engagement, increased school funding, better student-teacher ratios, and a new kind of community-based political power mobilized for public school reform. Although the Alliance Schools are still at an early stage of development, they represent one source for educational and civic renewal that should attract widespread attention in the national quest for prosperous cities with safe, diverse, and thriving schools and neighborhoods.

The schools in the Alliance initially did not roll out the welcome mat for IAF. Initially, there were a principal or a few teachers who were favorable to being part of an IAF-Alliance partnership. But, as Shirley described it, at times it seemed to have some of the features of a forced marriage. To have expected otherwise was, Cortes knew well, not in the cards. Changing traditional power relationships is never easy for those who are the objects of change. It appears, however, that to an undetermined but significant degree resistance was overcome. The fact is that we do not know how much resistance remains below the surface or how or when its subtle or not-so-subtle manifestations will appear. On two occasions I was invited to address the annual meeting of the IAF–School Alliance. Each meeting had about one thousand or more attendees. As best I could determine there were clearly more parents than educators, which is what one would expect given the fact that for any one school there are fewer educators than IAF members. I called them meetings, but it would not be an exaggeration to say that at times they had a revivalist flavor, and in no way do I imply anything pejorative. On the contrary, I found the meetings inspiring. I have never observed a parent-teacher affair anytime, anywhere, that came near in the enthusiasm I saw and heard on these two occasions. But it was my impression that the revivalist ambience was created by the IAF members plus Cortes who is a master orator who knows how to galvanize an audience and whose ability to use biblical stories appropriately to concretize his messages is equally masterful. Not so incidentally, at each of these meetings there were several people from around the country who had heard about Cortes and wanted to get some direct sense of what was going on in Texas. In addition, there were also several well known speakers from academia whose writings were in substance and conceptualization right up Cortes' moral, conceptual, and action alley. The second annual meeting was held as the Democratic and Republican presidential nominating campaigns were picking up steam. Cortes made a point of caustically criticizing George W. Bush for his superficial conception of the differences between contexts of productive and unproductive learning as well as his narrow conception of the goals of education and who should play a role in achieving those goals. Cortes would not claim to have cornered the market on "educational" truths in the narrow sense of that word. I would claim that he has cornered the market on some moral-social truths in the absence of which a graduation diploma testifies that a student has conformed to attendance requirements and has passed tests which reveal little or nothing about the quality of the student's thinking or sense of responsibility to his or her community and responsibility.

I have learned—not as well as I should have—not to be taken in by appearances. Therefore, at those two annual meetings I made it my business to converse one-on-one with as many participants as time would allow. I was able to talk with a few organizers, parents, and teachers. I asked them this question, What problems have there been and may still remain to some degree at least in forging alliances between IAF and schools? The organizers said there were always some principals and some teachers who were enthusiastic about IAF goals, and the same was the case with some in higher echelons of the school system and in the political establishment;

there was a greater number of principals and teachers who were puzzled about and/or silently resistant to what would clearly be a change in power relationships. They recognized, however, that IAF parents were an organized, activist group that was not going away and would therefore have to be recognized and dealt with. Things have gone as well as or better than could have been expected (although schools vary in this respect), and it is probably the case that more than a few school people have a puzzled, unclear understanding of the IAF rationale; this is not to say that they seek to undercut the alliance but rather that the IAF rationale is so new and strange to them, there is nothing in their experience and training to make for quick assimilation.

The parents were far more than favorable about the IAF–School Alliance and despite probing on my part said nothing about problems or even anything negative about teachers. Of the four teachers with whom I talked, none was critical of the Alliance, they said nothing to suggest that the Alliance was a misguided effort in some ways. However, three of them in guarded fashion indicated that the IAF was not as knowledgeable about schools and classroom learning as they should be; in response to one of my questions, the four teachers said that in their schools there were teachers who had reservations about the Alliance.

Obviously, I spoke with a piddling number of individuals. I do not know how the four teachers were selected or self-selected to come to the meeting. Nor do I know how their schools were different from or similar to other schools. In short, I have no basis for making generalizations. But I do have a basis for raising a question I had when I first heard that IAF was going to form alliances with schools; more correctly, two interrelated questions. The first question is this: How well do Cortes and his organizers understand the traditions and culture of schools? I knew that Cortes did not, to put it mildly, consider schools as contexts of productive learning. When he talks about the modal classroom, he waxes derisive, angry, and passionate. He sees IAF as educationally revolutionary. Here is how Shirley dispassionately puts it:

> The social crisis of American education, according to the Texas IAF vision paper, requires a threefold change in the culture of public schools. First, schools must abandon the model of the "mass-production assembly line" approach to education which has dominated urban public schools for most of the twentieth century: "In our vision, the model of a school shifts from efficiency to effectiveness: from that of students as passive learners to that of a community whose members are committed to learning the skills of problem solving, teaching themselves and others, and collaboration." Second, schools must free themselves from the top-down directives of the 1980s which mandated a pernicious uniformity in instruction, curriculum, and assessment

in public schools. Instead, "Schools should have the authority to design and implement their own program of instruction, including planning curriculum, determining the use of time and space, and choosing instructional materials and classroom management techniques." Third, schools must cease to ignore the crisis confronting American families and design innovative strategies which make the school a resource for families and a cultural center of the community.

The Texas IAF's vision paper proposes a triple revolution for public schools. First, it calls for a transformation of the kind of learning that transpires in schools from an emphasis upon memorization and standardization to critical thinking, collaboration, and alternative forms of assessment. Second, the paper promotes a development of school organization away from centralization and bureaucracy and toward decentralization and democracy. Third, it advocates a transformation of community relations from marginalization and exclusion to participation and empowerment.

The Texas IAF's threefold strategy for change was not designed in a vacuum. Generations of critics of American public education in the twentieth century have attacked the anti-intellectual propensities of urban "factory schools" that emphasize obedience over autonomy, memorization over creativity, and uniform over personalized instruction. Although the democratic localist spirit of public schools has been undermined by the rise of powerful state departments of education, teachers and parents have challenged that hegemony and sought to revitalize community control. In spite of numerous attacks, however, urban school districts have proven to be extraordinarily successful in deflecting criticism and perpetuating centralized control and bureaucratic power.

The originality of the Texas IAF contribution does not stem from the critique of the factory school or its proposals regarding instruction, curriculum, and assessment. Virtually ever major school reformer in the country now advocates similar proposals in the same areas as the Texas IAF. Schools collaborate with the Texas IAF experiment with portfolio assessment, interdisciplinary curriculum development, and child-centered pedagogies in a manner entirely congruent with a host of grass-roots reforms which have enlivened and improved American education in the last decade. The unique feature of the Texas IAF approach, which gives its collaboratives a different feel and nuance, lies in its unusually bold interpretation of what it means to engage a community in school improvement. (1997, p. 71)

I completely agree with both Cortes and Shirley. If Cortes has a very sophisticated conception of productive learning, it is my impression that organizers do not. No educator can talk down to Cortes who is very well read in the educational reform literature in terms of theory and research. That does not appear to be the case with organizers; they are not the voracious reader and absorber that Cortes is. In his meetings with organizers he always asks, What have you been reading?

The second question I raise is this: Given what Cortes knows about schools, will he and his colleagues devote that amount of time in the preaction phase that would allow educators to grasp why a relationship with IAF would be mutually beneficial, to set the stage for a collaboration that avoids the perception that educators collaborate because they have been backed unwillingly into a corner? I am talking of a preaction phase that respects the fact that teachers are being asked to change. It will not be easy, it cannot be easy, there will be problems, they are not intractable problems, but with mutual effort can be surmounted. That is not a phase the purposes of which can be achieved by several meetings. The kind of change that the IAF school vision will require cannot be short-circuited, as the failed efforts of many other noncosmetic reform efforts have amply demonstrated. What I am in effect raising here is a question about the IAF–School Alliance for which I have no direct experience to answer now: In terms of the time variable, has IAF thought through how it approaches schools as thoughtfully and realistically as it did its approach to the communities it organized?

When you review the history of IAF beginning with Saul Alinsky—Shirley's book contains that history's highlights—schooling is virtually absent. It has taken someone like Cortes to put it on the agenda. It is very likely that in the future, IAF–School Alliances will be forged nationally wherever IAF puts down roots. That raises a question I raised in my talk at the year 2000 meeting of the alliances in the Southwest. It is a question I have discussed in almost all of my writings beginning years ago (Sarason, Davidson, & Blatt, 1962/1986). Very briefly, here is what I said:

1. Any noncosmetic reform effort encounters all kinds of resistance, subtle and otherwise, from educators. Shirley's book (he was at the meeting) contains relevant examples.

2. Those resistances are time consuming and frustrating for IAF; they are sources of conflict which imperil the goals and outcomes of the IAF educational vision.

3. It would be a mistake to judge educators in ad hominem terms, such as rigid, self-serving, oppositional, insensitive, and tradition-bound people. That they are "problems" for IAF goes without saying. But educators are also victims, and IAF should not fall into the trap of blaming the victim.

4. There is nothing in the formal preparation of teachers that exposes them or stimulates them to think about the values, goals, and methods of the IAF rationale or even one similar to it in some ways. Preparatory programs are very narrow in scope, especially in regard to how schools could or should relate to the community in which they are embedded. Teachers emerge from these programs with the view that professional educators, and

only they, determine matters of pedagogy, goals, curriculum, and assessment. At best, teachers absorb the noblesse oblige stance: The role of parents and other community individuals and groups is to support what the educators deem best and appropriate for students *and the community*. At worst, in our urban areas with economically poor ethnic and racial groups, parents are viewed in terms of their educational deficits, as if they have no assets, real or potential.

5. *Just as IAF came to see that it had to turn its attention to schools, at some point it will have to focus on preparatory programs. If that is not done, or put off into the indefinite future, IAF will continue to have to confront the obstacles, frustrations, uphill battles that it has experienced. That not only imperils the quality and outcomes of the current efforts but guarantees the same problems in the future.*

My talk had little impact. Indeed, there seemed to be a disturbing absence of self-scrutiny at the meeting, which, as I said earlier, had a self-congratulating atmosphere. Although I can understand that—IAF has reason to take pride in how far it has come—the fact remains that IAF is caught up in a mode of repair and giving little or no thought to preventing or at least diluting problems long overlooked by the educational community even though there have been individuals in the past century who have said that preparatory programs, like the apocryphal emperor, are not only naked but have a terminal disease. I have been writing about this for more than 40 years, which was one of the reasons I had decided, as I said in the early pages of this book, that I had no more to say about educational reform and I should devote my remaining energies elsewhere. Some people have a midlife crisis. I had a postcareer crisis.

I was invited to come again to an IAF–School Alliance meeting. I was reluctant to accept the invitation. Even if the audience would probably be respectful and even interested, I did not want to hear myself sound like a broken record. But then I realized that IAF potentially posed the most substantive, concrete, practical challenge inherent in the features of the basic IAF rationale: its emphasis on people's assets and not on their deficits, its concern with the moral issues reflected in relationships between groups of unequal power, its development of methods of action to change those relationships, and the bedrock importance of knowing how the psychology of poor, oppressed, and discriminated-against minorities contributes to a passivity and hopelessness that masks hopes, personal resources, capabilities, and a willingness to take responsibility for action. The IAF rationale is psychological-educational in nature, substance, and goals. It does not rivet on subject matter (although subject matter is important). It goes far beyond the encapsulated classroom in the encapsulated school. It is as applicable to and necessary for classroom teachers as it is for IAF parents and their children in school. Of all the critiques of and challenges to preparatory programs I have read, none is as encompassing, concrete, or specific, or has the internal moral and psychological logic or its accomplishments as the IAF rationale. And by "none" I include what I have written. Yes, I have touched on most of the features of the IAF rationale, but I did not go beyond touching.

I am not Cortes, just as he is not I. Cortes has been a social activist, a religiously inspired one, all of his adult life; he has experienced all that is involved in an activism challenging social-economic injustice, establishment power, defeats and victories in a geographical area of the country where discrimination against his ethnic minority was the order of the day, every day, over more than a century. He had the good fortune to be educated about the IAF rationale by Ed Chambers, a colleague of Alinsky, who changed aspects of the IAF rationale and who, Shirley notes, has not been given the recognition he deserves. Except for the decade I spent planning and directing the Yale Psycho-Educational Clinic, I was an Ivy League academic in the protective cloisters of Yale where there was no department of education and where educators and the field of education were scorned and derided, unfit to be part of Yale. I learned what I did through my role as advisor or consultant to educational programs around the country. I learned a great deal, and I wrote about what I had learned. But in matters of community organization and educational reform I never experienced confrontations of the political, economic, social, and educational establishments. I knew, of course, about those establishments and was explicitly critical of them. But as John Dewey pointed out eons ago, there are two kinds of knowing: Knowledge we have gained on a conceptual level, and knowledge based on concrete experience which becomes part of your psychological bloodstream. So, for example, I knew that hospitals were not places where sick people receive sensitive and compassionate care, where what was happening in your head was, to hospital personnel, of little interest, which is par for the course in large, bureaucratic organizations containing a layered assortment of status-enamored professionals. I had nothing to do with hospitals in my adult years until 1993 when I spent 3 months in three different hospitals. Only then did I really come to "know" about care in hospitals. What Cortes knew I did not know, just as there were things I learned about schools Cortes did not know but which he is now learning.

I am not claiming that Cortes and the IAF are paragons of virtues, and I have been at pains in this book to indicate that neither am I taking undiluted satisfaction and pride in what I have done and written. I am not unduly modest, but I have never kidded myself that I knew all I needed to know and that anything I wrote was as complete as it could or should have been.

Let me conclude by returning to something I learned from supervising doctoral dissertations of graduate students. The student would prepare a short paper containing the theory (assumptions, hypotheses, predictions) he or she would test and validate. After reading the paper I would, far more often than not, find myself saying, "There is a difference between a career and a thesis. What you want to accomplish in this dissertation requires a career, not the one or two years you say you can devote to the thesis. If you had more time and financial resources, you could approximate your goal." It usually took at least two more meetings for the student to understand the time implications of what he had proposed to do and then to begin to restate the problem, or an aspect of it, that he could do without becoming a student emeritus. It was not, I would emphasize, that the initial statement of the thesis was faulty, far from it, but rather that he could not do justice to it within the time he was able to devote to it. If some of the students benefited from my advice, the fact is that when I entered the educational reform arena, I tended to make the same mistake my students had made. I had no supervisor, the literature on school reform contained no warnings to heed, indeed it was totally silent on the issue, and for all practical purposes it still is. There is something in the phenomenology of the reformer, in any arena of human affairs, that makes it too easy to develop a disconnect between what you want to accomplish and the time perspective you adopt. I learned a lot about this disconnect, but I continue to be puzzled why reports of reform efforts continue to be silent about it.

Chapter 5

Educational Reform and Foreign Aid: Similar Problems, Different Labels

This chapter continues discussion of the theme that I robbed myself of opportunities to bring together experiences and bodies of knowledge that would have broadened, deepened, and made more persuasive major points central to my writings. I have railed against the steady rise of professional specialization which makes it difficult (often impossible) for people in a particular discipline (e.g., education, psychology, anthropology, and so forth) to be aware of, let alone talk meaningfully with most other people in that discipline. By the luck of the draw, and it was luck, I came to know a handful of people who prevented me from remaining a conventional, too-parochial psychologist. None of them was a psychologist (Sarason, 1988, chap. 16). I have always been a voracious, even indiscriminate reader who even near the end of his life cannot enter a library without feeling sad that I will not be able to read all the books in it. And I also experience guilt because I know in the way that I know the sun will rise tomorrow that in regard to what I may be thinking and writing, there have been others who *must* have written things with which I should be familiar. In my opinion, among the many books I have written, there are only two about which I had no feelings of scholarly guilt. One was *The Creation of Settings and Future Societies* (1972); the other was *Teaching as a Performing Art* (1999). In both instances I tried hard to locate writings relevant to the way I was formulating a problem, but I found amazingly little. If I did not feel guilt, I certainly felt anxiety.

In previous books I emphasized that schools are not unique institutions, they are different. That point should have but did not remind me that there was a strand of economic thinking tailor-made for relating the substance of that strand to issues in educational reform. That is why much of this chapter will be about foreign aid and development, what we mean by freedom, and assumptions about what should be basic in the political-social arena. And, I shall try to show, there is a point-by-point correspondence between what on the surface are two very different sets of problems. The human capacity to categorize and label is not without drawbacks; labels serve the purposes of differentiation and mask similarities.

In my 1971 book, *The Culture of the School and the Problem of Change*, I ask the reader to imagine the situation where Congress in its infinite wisdom passes a law mandating that in all schools everywhere class size will be drastically reduced. I point out that we possess the knowledge and means to build the very large numbers of schools that would be required. But I go on to say that we have neither the knowledge nor means to obtain the number of new teachers the law would require. I was saying that at a time when there was a sizeable teacher shortage, just as in year 2000 there is what appears to be an even larger shortage. But in passing the law Congress made clear that its intent was to improve the quality of teaching; its intent was not merely to insure that each classroom would have a teacher, a live, newly minted one; the several million new teachers would be expected to be (at least on average) better than the average teacher of the past. So the question becomes not only where are large number of teachers going to come from, but also how will the quality of their teaching be improved? How will quality be defined and by whom? Do they, or do we, have the knowledge and means to achieve the intent of the law? My answer was no, and for several reasons. My previous experience with and observation of preparatory programs had already convinced me that those programs were not part of a solution but part of the problem. Our 1962 book (Sarason, Davidson, & Blatt, 1986) had already explained why, even though as I came later to see, the case we marshaled was at best incomplete. Then I wrote *The Case for Change: Rethinking the Preparation of Educators* (1993a) in which I fleshed out a more comprehensive case. For me at least, rethinking is far more difficult than what is ordinarily called thinking. Hence the resistance I had starting the present book. Rethinking opens the door to self-criticism and who embraces *that*? The arguments in that book have clear and comprehensive implications for the economic aspects of institutional change, but I did not pursue them in any detail; my purpose was to indicate why educational reforms would go nowhere if preparatory programs did not change. And then when in 1999 I wrote *Teaching as a Performing Art*, it was (in my opinion) the final nail in the coffin of the congressional law to reduce class size and improve the quality of teaching.

So what do the above prefatory remarks have to do with economics and foreign aid, both of which seem truly "foreign" to educational reform? I can assure the reader that I am quite aware that schools are not underdeveloped countries and that the field of economics has had at best a slight passing interest in education even though in narrow economic terms education is a very big business, far bigger than foreign aid in which economists have a serious interest. I could argue, but shall not here, that when economists have written about education, they have muddied the waters by applying concepts, methods, and language that have the appearance of a preciseness and rigor that betrays an almost total ignorance of fundamental, substantive problems in education that are at their roots not at all economic in nature: They are social, political, philosophical, moral, and historical. Indeed they are problems that, beginning with the ancient Greeks, have been posed and discussed over subsequent millennia. Why and how should a society educate its youth? Not how *does* a society educate its youth, but how *should* it do so consistent with ideals and purposes of the society. Those who over the millennia thought and wrote about those questions were never in doubt about two things. First, ideals are ideals, they are challenges, spurs to actions consistent with those ideals. Second, to have no ideals, or to give lip service to them, is to insure actions having the characteristics of travesty and societal tragedy. To fall short of the mark is not a secular sin; not to have a mark is such a sin.

Small Is Beautiful: Economics as if People Mattered is the title of a book by E. F. Schumacher published in 1973. It had and still has a surprisingly large sale, especially among young adults many of whom regard it as a classic. If by classic is meant a book that by virtue of its new ideas or theory or data transforms the way the world is understood and redirects the actions of individuals, groups, and societies, the book is not a classic and it would not be so regarded by Schumacher. The impact of the book had two major sources. The first was a writing style that few people possess. He avoids mind-numbing academic jargon and lofty abstractions; the reader is never in doubt about where Schumacher stands and why; he uses concrete examples any literate person will understand (whether they agree with his conclusion or not); he is passionate but not a dogmatist; he talks to and not down at the reader; and he respects his readers in that it is as if he is saying to them, "Our world has many crazy, self-defeating features which you undoubtedly have thought about but for one or another reason you felt incompetent to fathom"—he was wont to say, "We are not blind! We are men and women with eyes and brains . . . and we don't have to be drawn hither and thither by the blind workings of the Market, or of History, or of any other abstraction." You literally enjoy the way he writes. Even when you disagree with him, you do not stop reading, "something tells you" that you are very likely to be rewarded. Just looking at the table of contents of the book arouses your curiosity! What a strange, intellectual menu this writer has prepared for us to digest! Clearly, he is not the conventional economist of today who writes "as if people do not matter." Schumacher is a loose cannon in the dismal science of economics.

The second source of the book's impact is that it came out after the turbulent 1960s and early 1970s. The substance and character of those years of rebellion were worldwide phenomena; they were not just a feature of American society. Every major societal institution, secular and religious, was militantly challenged. Generational conflict, war, pollution, civil rights, the women's liberation revolution, racial discrimination, sexual life styles, ever enlarging corporate organizations—all of these and more preoccupied everyone. There is no simple explanation for what happened and why, but one thing is sure: Together they added up to a condemnation of the society as it was, a society in which people did not matter, the individual a cipher expected to conform to an anonymous role in giant, bureaucratic, impersonal, insensitive, mind-destroying organizations. The slogan "You can't trust anybody over 30" gives something of the flavor of the times. So when this book comes out with the title *Small Is Beautiful*, millions of people (not only the young) had been primed to embrace it.

So what is the relevance of Schumacher's book to educational reform? Why did I not see the connection? I could say that I allowed myself to be misled by the obvious: Schumacher was writing about economics, and I was steeping myself in matters of educational reform. To say that is a form of cop-out because it has always been bedrock to my thinking that a major purpose of education is to see connections, to counter the tendency to pigeonhole ideas and experience in labeled categories, to go beyond surface differences and appearances in the quest for their commonalities. Parochialism is the enemy of the personal sense of growth, the sense that you are not what you have been and that you willingly look forward to the future. Although they cannot verbalize it, that is the way children approach their introduction to schooling but, unfortunately, by the time they have been graduated from high school (if they have), that sense of growth has withered. In a more broad way and on a much more general world stage, it is the withering of that sense of growth about which Schumacher is talking. Although he does not talk directly or in detail about what we conventionally mean by schooling, his devastating critique of economics is no less applicable to the field of education.

In his introduction to the American paperback edition, Roszak pithily states Schumacher's basic point.

> "The great majority of economists," Schumacher laments, "are still pursuing the absurd idea of making their 'science' as scientific and precise as physics, as if there were no qualitative difference between mindless atoms and men made in the image of God." He reminds us that economics has only become scientific by becoming statistical. But at the bottom of its statistics, sunk well out of sight, are so many sweeping assumptions about people like you and me—about our needs and motivations and the purpose we have given to our lives. Again and again Schumacher insists that economics as it is practiced today—whether it is socialist or capitalist economics—is a "derived body of thought." It is derived from dubious, "meta-economic" preconceptions regarding man and nature that are never questioned if economic science is to

be the science it purports to be rather than (as it should be) a humanistic social wisdom that trusts to experienced intuition, plays by ear, and risks a moral
exhortation or two. (In Schumacher, 1973, p. 9)

Anyone familiar with my writings will know that much of it is about
our enamorment of measurement as reflected in the statistical problems
of test development; issues of test reliability and validity; comparisons
between schools, school systems, states, and other countries; program
evaluation; comparisons of test performance between males and females,
this racial or ethnic group with that one; the relative contribution of nature and nurture to mental ability and performance; and, of course, the
controversies that have surrounded and still surround the use of this or
that statistic in analyzing data. The importance of the field's emphasis on
measurement has not escaped public attention and acceptance. So, for example, in the year 2000 presidential-nominating campaign the candidates
loudly and proudly proclaimed that the outcomes of the educational reforms they would initiate would, of course, be rigorously and objectively
measured and evaluated; they were not about to be gulled by subjective
opinion. There were to be clear statements of educational standards and a
scientifically derived basis for determining how well those standards were
being met. Public acceptance of educational-psychological measurement
goes back a long way to when measurement by psychological tests determined the fate of many immigrants; test scores were in numbers, and numbers conveyed a precision "ordinary" people accepted. My first professional
job was in 1942 in a state residential institution for retarded individuals. It
was the state policy that only individuals with an IQ below 70 could be
admitted. If they had an IQ of 71 or 72 you had to prepare something akin
to a lawyer's brief to receive permission to admit them. And it is not a secret that today there are colleges and universities who have cutoff points
for admission to undergraduate and graduate programs. And that is also
the case in the personnel offices of many large corporations.

Writing about issues of measurements in research, educational policy,
and educational practice has always been a problem to me. On one hand,
I did not want to appear antimeasurement or antiscientific, because in principle I am not. On the other hand, I was never in doubt that *in practice* educational measurement was at best a distraction from, and at worst a moral
insensitivity to, as Roszak put it "people like you and me—about our needs
and motivations and the purpose we have given to our lives" (p. 9). Before going on let us listen to Schumacher:

> When people ask for education they normally mean something more than
> mere training, something more than mere knowledge of facts, and something
> more than a mere diversion. Maybe they cannot themselves formulate pre-

cisely what they are looking for; but I think what they are really looking for is ideas that would make the world, and their own lives, intelligible to them. When a thing is not intelligible you have a sense of estrangement. "Well, I don't know," you hear people say, as an impotent protest against the unintelligibility of the world as they meet it. If the mind cannot bring to the world a set or, shall we say, a tool-box of powerful ideas, the world must appear to it as a chaos, a mass of unrelated phenomena, of meaningless events. Such a man is like a person in a strange land without any signs of civilization, without maps or signposts or indicators of any kind. Nothing has any meaning to him; nothing can hold his vital interest; he has no means of making anything intelligible to himself: Estrangement breeds loneliness and despair, the "encounter with nothingness," cynicism, empty gestures of defiance, as we can see in the greater part of existentialist philosophies and general literature today. Or it suddenly turns—as I have mentioned before—into the ardent adoption of a fanatical teaching which, by a monstrous simplification of reality, pretends to answer all questions. So what is the cause of estrangement? Never has science been more triumphant; never has man's power over his environment been more complete nor his progress faster. It cannot be a lack of know-how that causes the despair not only of religious thinkers like Kierkegaard but also of leading mathematicians and scientists like Russell and Hoyle. We know how to do many things, but we do not know *what* to do? Ortega y Gasset put it succinctly: "We cannot live on the human level without ideas. Upon them depends what we do. Living is more or less than doing one thing instead of another." What, then, is education? It is the transmission of ideas which enable man to choose between one thing and another, or to quote Ortega again, "to live a life which is something above meaningless tragedy or inward disgrace." (1973, pp. 89–90)

Schumacher was not antiscience or technology. He was not a professional educator, and there is no evidence that in his adult years he had any direct knowledge of and experience with schooling. But what he says is where any discussion of schooling should begin: What is the purpose of education? I use the word *purpose* in the singular because it is obvious in his book that he has a conception of what people are, what they want, what they need, what causes in them a feeling of bewilderment in a world they do not but want to understand, why an impoverished sense of personal agency leads to a mind-impoverishing conformity.

The last time I read Schumacher's book I had the fantasy that he asked me what is it about schools that bothers me the most. "Give me two examples," he asks, "that will explain to me why you regard schools as antieducational places. You say that my book persuaded you that your intuitions about a superficial, misdirected, iatrogenic economics were right on target, a case of the emperor not only being naked but also having a terminal disease. Apparently, that is the way you regard education. So I need a couple of examples, like some of the concrete ones I have in my book. Take a few minutes to order your thoughts." I did not need a few minutes because I had asked for the meeting in order to give him examples for which his critique of economics seemed incisively appropriate, if I had understood what he wrote in the way he intended. " My first example is the evidence that in the modal classroom period of 45–55 minutes, students ask on an average about two substantive questions, and those two questions may have been asked by only one student. During that same period teachers ask dramatically more questions. My second example is based on the evidence that as students go from elementary to middle to high school their interest in learning goes steadily downhill." To which Schumacher replies, "What you are indicating is that classrooms are places where the educational experts, like my economic experts, are amazingly insensitive to what developing youngsters need, want, expected, and hoped for. Are you saying that educators, like economists, have no first principles, no vision, no values that inform what they do and why they do it, that they view human development and growth as the assimilation of and accommodation to a world of brute, unconnected facts which have little or no personal meaning and give no direction to choice and living? Are you trying to persuade me that educators have made the same mistake that economists have made in regard to foreign aid? That is to say, with the best of intentions, albeit very misguided, they look upon students as underdeveloped countries who are required to drastically alter their accustomed ways of thinking, working, and relating even though those requirements do violence to their motivations, aspirations, and capabilities. Students, like undeveloped countries, are deficit ridden, they have few if any assets, they have to learn to be other than what they are if they are ever to grow up. And you are telling me that a lot of students do not buy that message? Outwardly they conform, inwardly they feel estranged? They really do not want the equivalent of foreign aid. They play the game because it is the only game in town."

Since it is my fantasy, I allow myself the final words. "Frankly, when I read your book, I did not appreciate how relevant it was to education and educational reform, even though you were critiquing economics in much the same way I was critiquing education. But as time went on, I became increasingly discouraged because stakeholders in education—educators, colleges and universities with preparatory programs, parents, politicians/policy makers—went merrily on their self-defeating ways. I don't know why but I went back and read your book and then the connections emerged. However, in certain respects, the situation in education is a wee bit less gloomy than in economics. But only a wee bit. For example, I got into the habit of asking parents and educators this question: When your child graduates from high school what is the one overarching characteristic you want your child to possess? I know you want him or her to possess more than one major characteristic, but is there one of such importance that if it is not possessed will subvert possessing the others? They have a great difficulty with the question because they are so aware that education serves more than one purpose they consider important. So I give them my answer: When my child graduates, I want her to *want* to learn more about herself, others, and the world, not a small piece of it but a good deal of it in its complexity. That stops them for a couple of minutes and then I get unanimous agreement. More than a few parents have said that they wish they had that characteristic when they were graduated because if they had, their lives would have been more enriched. I relate this to you, Dr. Schumacher, because it is a source of encouragement that people can be brought to see that not all important characteristics are of equal value over the course of a lifetime. Not so incidentally, teachers initially have more difficulty with my assertion than parents because, I think, they know full well, especially if they are high school teachers, that only a few students possess the overarching characteristic. One final thing. It is both a source of encouragement and despair. The fact is that child developmentalists have over the course of the twentieth century learned a great deal about what I call contexts of productive and unproductive learning. That is the good news. The bad news is (1) the bulk of this research has been carried out on preschool children, and (2) child psychologists have little interest in school contexts and school learning. Institutionally speaking, psychologists don't talk to educators whom they regard, as does the university generally, as 'underdeveloped' people in an intellectually 'underdeveloped' arena of human activity."

Thus far I have only discussed that part of Schumacher's book concerned with issues others have discussed over past centuries: Human institutions should be judged by the degree to which their outcomes are consistent with their implicit or explicit conceptions of what people are, should be, can be. They are primarily philosophical, psychological, moral issues. They are, so to speak, first principles which come with the obligation to act in accord with them. Science at its root is a moral enterprise because it is based on the assumption, really a fact, that scientists, like all people, are imperfect organisms who cannot be trusted to be perfectly rational, logical, meticulous in reporting what they think, do, and find. Therefore—and here come the shoulds and oughts—they are obliged to submit their methods and findings in a form that allows for replication by peers; personal opinion is a frail reed on which to claim validity. To assume the human capacity to delude self and others is small is a folly that could never have given rise to science as we know it. Science rests on conceptions of what people are and should be that are fundamentally moral. Schumacher criticizes economics either for ignoring its metaphysical preconceptions or not taking them seriously. And that is precisely why I have been so critical of education and educational reform. If I had made the connection between what Schumacher wrote and what I had been thinking and writing, it would have provided a more solid base for my assertion that schools are not unique institutions, they are different, and they have more in common with other institutions than I had indicated. We are used to hearing from architects that form should follow function, by which is meant that the form of a building has to be hospitable to the characteristics, purposes, and functions of those who live and work in it. In that sense, analogously, the purposes and functions of schooling are not obtainable given the preconceptions on which they are based and the organizational forms to which they have given rise.

Now let me turn to the concrete issue which caused Schumacher to write the book about aid to developing countries. I shall not attempt to summarize what he says in any detail but rather focus on those aspects which are of direct relevance to what the central problem is in education, be it in a classroom or in a Third World country targeted for foreign aid. On what conceptions of learning should foreign aid be based? Put in another way, why has foreign aid had such disappointing outcomes? Here are the barebones of an outline of his argument.

1. Developing countries are characterized by a "dual economy." Two worlds in which there is a gulf between rich and poor are hard for westerners to comprehend. Schumacher wonders how many economists have ever seen the manifestations of that gulf in those countries.

2. When we visit one of our modern industrial establishments, we are awed by its vastness and complexity. How did such an establishment come about? What we see is the tip of an iceberg. What we cannot see is far greater than what we can see: how the raw materials come to the site and from where, how a host of products is properly prepared and labeled, and then reaches innumerable customers via a fantastically complicated distribution system.

3. When we think about how this modern establishment came to exist, we explain it in terms of an evolutionary process, not as one of instant creation. Development experts have made the grievous mistake of confusing development with creation. They start with the philosophy that "what is best for rich countries must be best for the poor, and they go on to implant—create—in these countries the types of establishments which depend on *special* education, *special* organization, and *special* discipline such are not inherent in the recipient society—requirements that will not promote healthy development but will more likely hinder it" (Schumacher, 1973, p. 175).

4. What is required is an "intermediate technology," the seeds of which already exist among the very poor in the hinterlands or are within the capabilities of the people and relatively easy to acquire. In addition, there is a communication infrastructure within small geographical regions or districts that allows both for the dissemination and exchange of the know-how and needs of others, as well as facilitating possibilities for cooperation among people in the region. (An American example would be when in the nineteenth century the county agricultural agent was created to help farmers—largely uneducated, technologically unsophisticated—help themselves, learn from the experience of other farmers, and be a source of technical and scientific information unknown and unavailable to farmers in the middle of nowhere but of potential significance to the problems and goals of farming. What we rightly consider the glories of American agriculture derived from a developmental process over scores of decades. Farmers did not unwillingly leave their farms until after World War II with the rise of giant agribusiness, making farming uneconomical for the small farmer for whom big was not beautiful and people did matter.)

I have presented in barebones fashion—and without any of his examples or moral passion—Schumacher's argument in order to indicate its relevance for how we conceive of education and educational reform. I regret that I only belatedly saw its relevance because if I had seen it earlier, it would have prevented me from being as conceptually parochial as I have been. It is not that I was wrong in what I thought and wrote, but rather that the issues I was concerned with and the conclusions I drew were far more general than I knew. If the purpose of education and living is to broaden and deepen knowledge of yourself and the world you live in, you should have the obligation (and so should your teachers), it seems to me, to beware of a parochialism that not only gives you a very restricted view of the world but also prevents you from going beyond appearances of differences to the commonalities with which the human endeavor confronts us, whether it is about schooling in America or foreign aid to underdeveloped countries. Apples and oranges are obviously different, but we call them both fruit. Men and women are obviously different in numerous ways, but when we call them people, we do so because we know that both are also similar in numerous ways; in this instance, let us not forget, it is only recently in human history that the similarities in what men and women can be has begun to be generally acknowledged.

The first way in which Schumacher's book is relevant to my purposes, past and present, can be put this way: Just as foreign aid is only secondarily an economic problem, the educational enterprise is not initially the province of the professional educator. Indeed, it is not the province of any one discipline. Its foundations are moral, philosophical, social, and psychological. And by psychological I do not mean it in a narrow sense. What are the abilities, motivations, hopes, and dreams of people? How do these features combine to allow people to experience the sense of freedom, growth, choice, and the obligations of social responsibility? How should we, ought we, must we create the conditions in which developing youth are provided a basis for assimilating the knowledge, skills, and values consistent with our conceptions of what our society deems to be autonomous, responsible adults who are concerned with their obligations to their society as well as to their own personal and intellectual welfare? In my experience, relatively few people are in the habit of clearly articulating, or even thinking about, these questions even though in rearing our children these questions arise in different ways at different times in our relationship to our children and their future. These are, some would say, the "big" questions that only special or elevated minds can contemplate and extrapolate from. They are not only big questions but also very messy ones and divisive in dangerous ways because as soon as you ask, "What do I want out of life that I expect others to want out of life?" it becomes apparent that what you want is not possible for many other people given the history and nature of the society; better not to pursue the questions very far. The fact is that we know in an inchoate way that by not pursuing or answering the questions we become part of the problem and not part of the answer.

How individuals answer these questions and the degree to which there is consensus about how to answer them is of an enormous, practical significance because those answers are the criteria by which derived actions should be judged. If, as was once the case, it was thought that women had neither the intellectual and rational qualities to have the right to vote, action consistent with that view was the norm. If, as was long the case in human history, it was believed that only a select few could benefit from education, depriving the bulk of people of any education was deemed right, natural, and proper. If you believed that the waves of immigrants coming here in the nineteenth and early twentieth centuries were a threat to the social fabric, you were in favor of a compulsory education that would tame and socialize their young, an education in which the concept of individuality was truly an alien idea. The examples are legion. And that is why Schumacher's subtitle to his book is so important and revealing. Whether or how people matter depends on (1) your picture or vision of what people are, can be, and should be, (2) the degree to which the actions taken are consistent or inconsistent with that picture, and (3) the *courage* (a nonscientific, nonquantifiable, but identifiable term of bedrock importance) to indict inconsistencies that make a mockery of the picture or vision. Schumacher does not stop there. He goes on to present guidelines for action, practical actions, that take seriously the phrase, "as if people matter." He knows that he has given us guidelines, that he has not cornered the market on truth, that the more we act and learn, the more we will have to act and learn.

The 1776 Declaration of Independence was a brief document about what people are and can be and their obligation to take that vision seriously. That became the task of the Continental Congress which came up with the Articles of Confederation, which, it soon became clear, were inadequate in action. To repair their inadequacies, omissions, and dangers (real and potential) was the task of the 1787 Constitutional Convention. That task took 3 months and what is fascinating about the substance of the proceedings were disagreements about what people are and can be. Can you trust people who are largely uneducated—the members of the congress were highly educated—to act responsibly and rationally consistent with the obligations of a free people, of a democratic ethos? Can the elected officials in the federal government resist the lures to misuse and seek more power, to resist the sources of corruption? Since the states differ widely in size, population, and economic base, will the larger states be capable of refraining from dominating the smaller ones? Are the people and their elected representatives capable of distinguishing between self-interest and the larger good of the country? Are people capable of resisting the vices of narrow, political partisanship? The founding fathers were not sentimentalists or misty-eyed utopians. Far from it, they were too aware of human imperfections, they knew the history of man's inhumanity to man extraordinarily well. From beginning to end the "should and oughts" of social living, the potentials and inalienable rights of people were either on the table or certainly not far from it at the Constitutional Convention.

What organization of government can we agree on that stands a chance of being in action consistent with the nature, rights, and hopes of people? That was the question that ultimately was answered by the constitution they developed. That document was not ratified by the states until 2 years later and only because the Bill of Rights was added to it, an addition reflective of the general mistrust of "rulers" to be consistent with first principles. Good intentions and verbal agreement on first principles were one thing; explicit criteria by which to judge consistency in action was quite another thing.

The fact is, I confess, that my critique of schooling and educational reform lacked two things. The first is passion, a watering down of the resentment, even anger, that I felt at the scandalously superficial view that educators had about what children are, can be, need, and deserve. Why? I think it was because I wanted to appear to be a friendly, constructive, sympathetic critic, not a carping one who delights in taking dead aim at well-intentioned educators. In all of my books I have said, "Educators are not villains who deliberately set out to create and sustain a deplorable state of affairs. Just as teachers are victims by virtue of their preparation and the culture of schools, so students are victims of teachers whose understanding of children and learning is, to indulge understatement, inadequate." I still believe that, even though at the same time I would write those words I felt I was talking to a wall. In talking to economists, Schumacher knew he was talking to a wall, that given the training-education of economists and their almost total ignorance or eschewing of matters psychological, there was no point to expecting them to change. It is as if he had decided that the time had come to call a spade a spade, to judge ignorance and insensitivity as immoral.

In 1993 I wrote *Letters to a Serious Education President*, an effort to tell that fictional president how he should think about schooling and learning. It was a chatty, semihumorous (I think!) book, yet very serious. The book was sent to the President at the time (Clinton) and his major advisors. While writing the book, I would entertain the fantasy that the President would read it, and invite me to come and talk. Hope springs eternal. Fantasies are wonderful because they have little to do with the real world. And yet in my saner moments I realized that the world would go on in its unmerry ways. So, when in 1998 I wrote *Political Leadership and Educational Failure*, I sort of vented my spleen at politicians whose ignorance is bottomless, matched only by their juvenile arrogance. I would like to believe that if Schumacher were alive he would say that I finally got the point, which is that stakeholders in the educational system grounded their thinking and actions on presuppositions that guarantee that little or nothing will change.

Another way in which Schumacher's book is relevant to education was for me a true eye-opener because it involves what I consider to be the most important theoretical and practical problem in education, a problem central to all I have written. It is a problem which if it is ignored or glossed over, as it has been, will undercut even the most laudable, unassailable statement of first principles about what people are, can be, and should be. In its simplest form the problem is in the form of this question, What do we mean by productive learning?

I shall not go over old ground, but one of its features was second nature to Schumacher. You start the learning process by taking seriously what the learners are and where they are coming from: their assets of interests, curiosity, and knowledge, what they can and do do. They may be living in miserable poverty, expecting the future to be like the present, passively resigning themselves to a barebones existence. But they have a repertoire of actions and skills that allow them to persist and exist. We in the Western world are so impressed with what we observe from our vantage point that we can only see deficits in Third World peoples. The concept and presence of assets cannot occur to us. So, as Schumacher says, with the best of intentions we seek to "aid" them to think, learn, and do as we do. We start where *we* are coming from, not what they are and where they are coming from. Our "aid" is truly foreign to them. Schumacher's concept of "intermediate technology" rests on a polar opposite way of thinking about learning. *You do not start where the learner is in order to keep him there but rather as a starting point on the road to broader horizons, to new possibilities, knowledge, and skills.* That feature of a context of productive learning is, the usual few exceptions aside, absent in American classrooms. Which is why I have said that American schools should be viewed as the equivalent of underdeveloped countries. Schumacher's *psychological* rationale for an intermediate technology is identical to mine for contexts of productive learning. I could not see the connection when I first read his book. My experience had not prepared me to see the connection, and I did not yet have clarity about the values or first principles by which to judge the process of learning and its consequences. In my autobiography (1988) I described my career as one which began in a fog, the fog dissipated, and the sun came out, then another fog-dissipation-sun, and on and on and on. I am tempted to say that I am not now in a fog, but the still, small voice within me warns, "Famous last words."

Let us now turn to another book *Development as Freedom* by the economist Amartya Sen, who was awarded the Nobel Prize in economic science in 1998. That award was greeted with surprise by many economists. That was predictable from the words of the Nobel Prize committee which said that Sen "had *restored* an ethical dimension to the study of economic problems and opened up new fields of study for subsequent generations of researchers." I italicized "restored" for two reasons. First, Sen (like Schumacher) makes it perfectly clear that, beginning with Aristotle, ethics and economics were indissolubly related. More correctly, ethical considerations were the only basis on which one could justify economic practice and organization. Second, the committee was undoubtedly aware that previous winners reflected well the pride that the field of economics takes in its effort to be a scientific enterprise: the rigors of logic, the abstractness and the impersonal nature of mathematics, theory building to explain this or that aspect of economic activity by the use of indices of aggregated data. "Economic man," the individual, was rarely if ever in the picture. What could be dignified as psychological behavior was absent or so oversimplified as to cause one to be undecided about whether to laugh or cry. If you peruse, as you should, the most used and respected introductory textbooks in economics, you will see what I mean and what the Nobel Prize committee was alluding to. And if those texts leave you with any doubt, try reading any level of textbook above the introductory one.

Sen's is not a small book, but his basic argument against the conventional wisdom in regard to foreign aid is very clear.

> Let me start off with a distinction between two general attitudes to the process of development that can be found both in professional economic analysis and in public discussions and debates. One view sees development as a "fierce" process, with much "blood, sweat and tears"—a world in which wisdom demands toughness. In particular, it demands calculated neglect of various concerns that are seen as "soft-headed" (even if the critics are often too polite to call them that). Depending on what the author's favorite poison is, the temptations to be resisted can include having social safety nets that protect the very poor, providing social services for the population at large, departing from rugged institutional guidelines in response to identified hardship, and favoring—"much too early"—political and civil rights and the "luxury" of democracy. These things, it is argued in this austere attitudinal mode, could be supported later on, when the development process has borne enough fruit: what is needed here and now is "toughness and discipline." The different theories that share this general outlook diverge from one another in pointing to distinct areas of softness that are particularly to be avoided, varying from financial softness to political relaxation, from plentiful social expenditures to complaisant poverty relief.
>
> This hard-knocks attitude contrasts with an alternative outlook that sees development as essentially a "friendly" process. Depending on the particular version of this attitude, the congeniality of the process is seen as exemplified by such things as mutually beneficial exchanges (of which Adam Smith spoke eloquently), or by the working of social safety nets, or of political liberties, or of social development—or some combination or other of these supportive activities. (1998, pp. 35–36)

His book is not small because he devotes his attention to the philosophical, logical, moral basis in contrast to the conventional wisdom approach to foreign aid. And in doing so he very creatively employs easily comprehensible economic indices to indicate where his argument applies to highly developed countries. Nor does he put all underdeveloped countries in one category but rather compares and illuminates why their economic development varies because of historical and cultural differences in regard to certain freedom variables, specifically the attitude to education in China and India.

Here are those aspects of his position most relevant to my purposes.

1. Regardless of the society, its primary objective is to develop, protect, and sustain basic political freedom, economic facilities, and social security. Those are *primary* ends, bedrock *constituents* of freedom. They are also the *instrumental means* of development. Concentrating only on eco-

nomic development is tantamount to defeating both the constituents of freedom and economic development.

> This approach goes against—and to a great extent undermines—the belief that has been so dominant in many policy circles that "human development" (as the process of expanding education, health care and other conditions of human life is often called) is really a kind of luxury that only richer countries can afford. Perhaps the most important impact of the type of success that the East Asian economies, beginning with Japan, have had is the total undermining of that implicit prejudice. These economies went comparatively early for massive expansion of education, and later also of health care, and this they did, in many cases, before they broke the restraints of general poverty. And they have reaped as they have sown. (Sen, 1998, p. 41)

2. As instrumental means in development, the freedoms are interactive with each other, the denial or support of one affects the others.

3. The lack of freedom means the absence of justice as well as deprivation of the individual's capabilities for growth.

4. Economic-statistical indices of development are inadequate and misleading to the extent that they are neither interpreted or related to or judged by the constituent freedoms or their employment as instrumental means for development.

When you finish reading Sen, you are very unlikely to continue to think about development in narrow economic terms. On the contrary, you will see development as a very, very complicated conceptual, moral, strategic-tactical problem. It is as if everything is related to everything else. And because you cannot deal with everything at the same time, and because each country is distinctively different in important ways from other underdeveloped countries, your approach to aid has to take those differences into account. The one universal feature to all approaches is that they are informed, directed, and powered by the freedoms as ends and as instrumental means.

What does all this have to do with educational reform? There is a prior question: Why did I buy and read the book? The answer is that in the course of reading two reviews of the book I got the feeling that Sen's critique of economic aid was similar, if not identical, to my critique of educational reform. I was right. Let me explain.

In all that I have written I have always said that when it comes to schooling there are two interrelated questions that must be answered. The first question has two parts. The first is what we ordinarily mean by philosophical: What kind of thinking-feeling-social person do we want our developing youth to become? The second part is more empirical-scientific:

What are the capabilities they do or can display in the course of their development?

Once the two-part first question is answered, then comes the second one: What does that mean for life and learning in the classroom? When we observe classrooms, what do we expect to see that allows us to conclude that how we answered the first two-part question is being taken seriously? Unfortunately, the usual exceptions aside, the philosophical question is couched in words that are so general and vague as to give us no guidelines whatever telling us what we should look for when we observe classrooms. In science, for example, a most damning criticism of a study is one that says that the experimental data are irrelevant to the hypothesis from which the study derived. Hypotheses are not formulated for the hell of it. They are guidelines obligating you to choose methods that provide data and outcomes consistent with the hypotheses. Consistency is the name of the game. When the study is published, it is "observed" by a relevant community of scientists who individually feel obligated to read the study for, among other things, its consistency with the hypotheses.

What we observe in a classroom is not science. It is not intended to be (nor should it be) seen as such. But it is intended to be consistent with first principles articulated in how the two major questions were answered.

In schooling, however, the obligation of consistency runs smack up against a very practical problem, against a brute fact: In the real world we have neither the resources nor knowledge allowing us to be consistent with all the purposes stated in the first question as well as with all the capabilities and talents we say young people potentially or actually possess. We *have to make choices.* You may believe (or assume) that all children can at some level learn and enjoy to play a musical instrument, or that they have the capability to acquire at some level or another a personally satisfying artistic skill. But those are not capabilities we can help all children develop. It is possible, of course, if you extend the school day, find the thousands of teachers and money required, and be able to buy the thousands of instruments that would be necessary. *We have to make choices.* But on what basis? Money? An already too-crowded curriculum? My answer is that you make choices on the basis of your conception of what children are, can be, and should be, and their need to experience growth and competence, features that can inform a lifetime. Therefore, I could argue, as I have, that I would choose music and art over physical education. I know I am in a minuscule minority! The crucial point is that choices are or should be determined by what you think people are, can be, should be.

What I have said about education is in almost all respects identical to how Sen approached the problems and failures of foreign aid. In fact, when I finished his book, I realized that I had long regarded schooling as if it were an underdeveloped country which many people were trying to put on the road to effective reform, with little success. Initially, increased funding for schools was the major way to improve schools. Then came a second answer: Teachers needed to have a firm grasp of subject matter. Soon after came the era of curriculum reform. In light of disappointing results came the rise of the parent and community involvement movement. Beginning in the 1980s came the clamor for high standards: We should expect more from students, anathema was pronounced on the "dumbing down" of standards, and the implicit message was that it was the educators—the rulers of these underdeveloped sites—who should be accountable (blamed) for past failures and lowering of standards. Finally, in recent years when it became crystal clear that presidential expectations that by year 2000 American schoolchildren would be at the top of all countries in terms of achievement test scores would not happen, the school voucher and charter school movement gained a great deal of momentum. If success has been in short supply, that is certainly not true for hope and answers.

Let me give several concrete examples of why I regard the applicability of Sen's book for education so highly. I assume that no reader will deny that test scores loom large in matters of educational policy and practice. For students and parents it looms frighteningly large and that has also become the case for teachers whose competencies and rewards (and sometimes their jobs) depend on the test scores of their students. In principle and practice it is different in economics where they have indices (= scores) by the bushel. They are indices that seek to explain this or that aspect of the economic systems as well as the relation of one index to others. Sen, like me, is not opposed to indices. He emphasizes, however, that the interpretation and uses of them has to be in terms of the freedoms he considers of basic importance. If you ignore that judgment, you are in effect giving a value to the indices that is contradictory to the basic freedoms which, at least in Western society, are given verbal support. Sen makes this point clearly and succinctly in the following quote:

> Take for example the well-known argument in economics that a competitive market mechanism can achieve a type of efficiency that a centralized system cannot plausibly achieve both because of the economy of information (each person acting in the market does not have to know very much) and the compatibility of incentives (each person's canny actions can merge nicely with those of others). *Consider now, contrary to what is generally assumed, a case in which the same economic result is brought about by a fully centralized system with all the decisions of everyone regarding production and allocation being made by a dictator. Would that have been just as good an achievement?* (1998, p. 27; emphasis added)

Imagine the following: Each school system is a truly autonomous unit in a market of comparable units. Each unit is free to "wheel and deal" as it sees fit, to scan, know, and use the market for the purposes and ends it has proclaimed. The overarching aim of all units is to demonstrate that the preponderance of students will meet or exceed academic standards of achievement. All units have the same standards and utilize the same tests by which those standards are to be judged. In one half of the units, each teacher is free to use knowledge of the external market as well as the system's internal one (other teachers, parents) in whatever ways maximize the chances that his or her students will meet the standards.

In the other half of the units all educational decisions and programs are developed and made in a centralized office: What the tests and curriculum will be, how much time will be devoted to this or that aspect of the curriculum, the pedagogy to be employed, the organization of the school day, how this or that infraction of disciplinary rules is to be handled and punishment meted out, and so forth.

When the results of all units are tabulated, it turns out that there are no differences whatever between the two types of units. Is the achievement of the top-down "dictatorial" units as good an achievement as the other? *Indices in economics and test scores in education have different uses for different purposes. But when they are used as a basis of action and policy, they always reflect and must be judged by axioms of value, the "givens" for what the society wants its people to become. To assume that such axioms do not exist, that they are not moral imperatives by which concrete actions are to be judged, is tantamount to a denial that choice is a basic, pervasive feature of individual and social life. Numbers are numbers. Their precision in no way means that the meanings we attribute to them are consistent with our axioms.*

Sen devotes his book to what I have just said. In each of my books I have discussed aspects of the problem, only aspects. I never dealt with the problem head-on. I did not realize that the problem was not peculiar to education just as Sen seems unaware that it is not peculiar to economics. He talks about the importance of education for economic development as if what underdeveloped countries need is what we call education. As a highly trained economist it is understandable he has no experience in schools, our schools, and as a consequence it cannot occur to him that the types of freedom he rightly espouses are applicable to life in classrooms. The fact is that in obvious and subtle ways his freedoms are applicable to life and learning in the classroom and, as I have tried to show in my writings, that when you do apply them you begin to see why I regard the modal classroom as a context of unproductive learning. Sen's emphasis on freedoms (*plural*) is very important. If early on I had looked at schools from the standpoint of Sen's freedoms, they would have given force to several points I have made time and again. First, schools are not unique institutions with unique purposes. Second, if (as Yeats wrote) the substance and process of education "is not to fill empty buckets, but to light fires," schools do not get a passing grade. Third, the interests, curiosity, and capabilities of developing youth are either unrecognized or underestimated, or blunted. *Fourth, as John Dewey said eons ago, school is not a preparation for life, it is life itself and therefore contains all the problems and challenges of social living and purposes, just as Sen opposes the notion that freedoms in underdeveloped countries can only come about after economic development, a notion notable for its failed consequences.*

In one respect Sen's book was therapeutic for me. Comforting would be a better word. I read his book shortly before I started the self-scrutinizing ordeal in an effort to understand why I had the feeling that educational reform was a near hopeless affair and why and how that feeling stemmed from the realization that educational reform was both conceptually and practically a horribly complicated affair. I use the word *horribly* advisedly because I was overwhelmed by how many different factors *and their interrelationships* you had to take into account when we describe what we too blithely call our educational system. A system contains interacting parts, and the more parts, the more complicated the system. In a system it is as if everything is related or dependent upon everything else. So, when a human system is malfunctioning, and that system is complicated, traditional, and rooted in a complicated larger society and its history, you (I) should be pardoned if you (I) feel overwhelmed. In the case of human systems in which no one part stands alone, how do you identify a single source of malfunction? Conceptually, realistically, that makes no sense. But you have to start somewhere, the malfunction must be identified even though you know you are not dealing with single causes and effects and you assume (rightly or wrongly) that not all parts are equally fateful for the system's functioning. In several of my books (1993a, b, c, 1999; Sarason et al., 1962/1986), I have said that I would start with radical changes in preparatory programs. What I did not say, but should have, is that if you start there, you will run into some knotty problems and issues (to indulge understatement) that will sorely try you to the point where you look for other starting points. I shall have more to say about this later in this book. My present point is that educational reform is far more complicated than intervention theory and the existing literature suggests. And if I did not discuss it in any detail, it is because I am overwhelmed by its complexity. I still believe that my starting point is the most fruitful one, that it is not tinkering at the edges, but it is one that will expose (1) that dealing with a part inevitably will fall short of the mark because parts interact with each other, (2) that we are never dealing with problems that will be solved in the sense that

4 ÷ 2 is a solution, and (3) that educational reform—on the level of conception or theory or practice—should only be undertaken by those who know what their mark is and also know and accept the fact that they will fall short of the mark; unless, of course, their conception of the system qua system is so superficial that they do not know what Adelaide knew and lamented in her song in *Guys and Dolls*—"That's not where the problem is"—or what the king sang in *The King and I*—"It's a puzzlement."

What Sen gives us in his book is how horribly complicated the problem of foreign aid is, far more complicated than past experts and their policies have imagined. In fact, although Sen knows that his conceptualization of the problem is the polar opposite of conventional economic wisdom and, therefore, the number of choices with which one is confronted is large and thorny, he never examines what any aspect, alone or in combination, will encounter in *action*. Sen knows what he is against and what he is for on the conceptual-moral level, but he tells us nothing about starting points and action. Although Schumacher is not the formal, systematic conceptualizer that Sen is, they are essentially in agreement about values and goals. Schumacher, however, comes up with the concept of "intermediate technology" as a focus of action which strikes me as very practical on the level of action and implementation.

Sen is a scholar in a university, a very creative scholar who does what scholars are supposed to do: to examine, interpret, dissect, and organize ideas about a problem (in the present or past) that exists or existed in the real world, for the purpose of adding to and clarifying our knowledge of the problem. The scholar is rarely a person of action, a social activist whose ideas derived from social action and who seeks to implement them. Schumacher, in contrast, spent his years as a civil servant, which required him to initiate, oversee, and then evaluate the consequences of ideas and policy. He had vast experience adapting policies to needs. He was a very practical thinker, which is not to say that he lacked the scholarly bent. He did not lack it. Schumacher knew how complicated the problem of foreign aid is. What he sought was a starting point which would have relatively quick and percolating effects for individuals and society. And he understood individual needs and capabilities in a way that Sen does not. I am grateful to Sen for providing me, in an area in which I have had no experience, an example of a social problem in which everything is and should be seen as interrelated. It confirmed for me conclusions I had arrived at in matters of educational reform. And I am grateful to Schumacher for illuminating how absolutely essential it is to think through choices about starting points. And I am indebted to both for confirming me in my belief that starting points not derived from clarity about values and first principles will add to that mountain-sized collection of failures, all of them demonstrating the adage that the more things change the more they remain the same.

As I was writing this chapter (April, 2000), the World Bank and the International Monetary Fund were meeting in Washington, under siege by thousands of protesters critical of the past policies of these agencies. Some of their criticisms are precisely those made by Schumacher and Sen, especially in regard to the increasing gulf in underdeveloped countries between rich and poor. How the two international agencies will react is unknowable at this time. But on the basis of what educated protesters from these countries have said in numerous TV interviews, they do not have anything resembling concrete implementation plans that will have the effects they desire. On one thing they agree: The debts these countries have incurred to these agencies should be canceled and used to begin to lift these countries from their disastrous economic and social morass. I agree. But if you take Sen seriously, these are countries where the freedoms he espouses and considers indispensable accompaniments to development hardly exist and in some cases even the word *freedom* is inappropriate. It is interesting and important to note that Sen's book is an elaboration of lectures he gave at the World Bank, lectures critical of that agency's past policies. One has to assume that inviting him to give these lectures indicates a recognition by the World Bank that its past policies and programs have been either ineffective or counterproductive. As I said earlier, Sen's conceptualizations are not tied to specific scenarios for implementation. Schumacher's approach is tied to suggested scenarios, but there is no reason to believe that either of the two agencies have ever taken him seriously, if they have read him at all. I say that for two reasons. First, Schumacher was not a conventional economist; indeed, he was and is regarded by mainstream economists as a fuzzy, bleeding-heart, sloganeering do-gooder, one of those philosophical types who does not understand how economies develop and work. And that judgment was reinforced by the appeal his book had from an "unknowledgeable" public in the late 1970s and the subsequent decades. Why does Sen—a mainstream but controversial economist—never mention or refer to Schumacher? I find that omission astounding and, I must say, inexcusable. People matter for Sen, but it is a cerebral kind of mattering. People matter for Schumacher, but his is a passionate mattering that requires him to come up with ideas and programs for action he believes speaks directly to where people are coming from and therefore dictates what are appropriate actions by which capabilities and growth can be part of their experience. Action in itself may be neither virtuous nor productive. But action is the crucible in which conceptualizations which give rise to them have to be judged.

What is most discouraging is when the conceptualizations from which actions are derived have rarely if ever born edible fruit. And that brings me in the next chapter to an article on educational reform that appeared on the front page of the *New York Times* at the same time that the protesters were gearing up to protest the policies of the World Bank and the International Monetary Fund. The two events are conceptually kissing cousins. The front page article on educational reform is about an "agency" under siege, and if the international agencies respond in the same fashion as the educational one, only fruitless consequences should be expected. That article forced on me the realization that I was derelict in failing to say what I will now say in the next chapter. I learned a lot from the self-scrutiny process, but the article reminded me that self-scrutiny, however seriously taken, never overcomes all obstacles to truth telling.

Chapter 6

Teacher Unions: Part of the Problem, Not of the Solution

The Great Depression forever changed me. I experienced what it was to know that eating tomorrow would be a sometime thing. It further exacerbated an incompatible relationship between my parents. My sister—who had contracted polio 15 years before—dropped out of school to seek work, any work her infirmities would permit. In 1934 I contracted polio, making me, as a neighbor told me, a "cripple." All this predisposed me to be drawn to a left-wing political outlook. And that meant that I supported labor unions seeking economic change and justice. Cross a picket line? How more sinful can you be? It justified consigning such a person to a secular equivalent of the religious hell. I became a follower of Leon Trotsky in his denunciation of Stalin's dictatorship and terror. I accepted Trotsky's position that even though Stalin's Soviet Union was a "degraded" workers' state, it was still a workers' state and therefore had to be defended against the capitalist world. By the time I started graduate school in 1939, which coincided with the beginning of World War II in Europe and Stalin's "nonaggression" pact with Hitler, my disenchantment with Trotsky and any communist ideology was total. But one thing did not change: my unwavering support of labor unions and the use of the strike to achieve their goals. That blind support slowly weakened over the years but never anywhere near the point where I could be described as antiunion. I remained and still am pro–labor unions.

When under the leadership of Albert Shanker the American Federation of Teachers began in the 1950s to be militant, strong, and successful, I was no end pleased and supportive. My research on test anxiety had made me knowledgeable about schools, teachers, school administrators, and boards of education. As individuals, teachers had no power, they had no voice in decision making about salary or matters educational. Their salaries were scandalously low; they had no choice but to accept whatever financial crumbs were thrown their way. They were the voiceless, unrespected, large bottom of an organizational pyramid on the top of which was a largely faceless few who made all of the decisions and who, when unions sought to involve them in collective bargaining negotiations, viewed the teachers as unprofessional, at best, and un-American, at worst. And when a district local here and there would call a strike, it was national news, as if the army was rebelling against the government. It was a classic case of what happens when the powerless come to see there is power in numbers and courage. More to the point of this chapter, it is also a case where achieving influence and power entrenches parochialism, vested interests, and the tendency, understandable but ultimately self-defeating, to direct criticism only to those perceived as opponents. Self-scrutiny is both dangerous and humbling; it is not pleasant, let alone easy, to admit imperfections and mistakes. When this characterizes an entire professional organization, however, both the profession and the society pay a high price.

A front page article appeared in the *New York Times* on April 14, 2000. The large headline read: "Union is Urging a National Test for New Teachers." There were two smaller headlines. The first was: "High Standards Sought." The second was: "Reform Advocates Hope Better Preparation Will Improve Esteem of Profession." The union was the American Federation of Teachers. Here are the guts of the report.

1. Prospective teachers should have to pass two tests, one after their sophomore year in college and one before entering the classroom. The purpose of the tests would be for teachers to demonstrate college-level knowledge in math, science, English, history, and geography. The proposal addresses the common complaint that "teachers learn too much pedagogy and not enough subject matter, that is, they learn how to teach but not what to teach."

2. A national core curriculum should be created for schools.

3. Entrance requirements for teacher education programs should be raised. Initially, students would need a grade point average of 2.75, with a requirement for a 3.0 average phased in over time.

4. Teachers should have a major in the subject they want to teach.

5. Teacher preparatory programs should be expanded to 5 years, with the fifth year devoted to observing and working in schools under the aegis of more experienced mentors.

The report was commented on and applauded by the national media in the form of news reports or editorials. There was one paragraph in the *New York Times* article which aroused in me a mixture of guilt and shame.

"People from the outside need permission to talk about teacher quality without it seeming like bashing teachers," said Kati Haycock, executive director of the Education Trust, a nonprofit group in Washington that has studied teacher preparation and advocates for poor and minority students. "When the second-largest national teachers union talks about teacher quality, it gives other people permission to talk about it, and to do something."

Let me explain the historical background of my feelings of guilt-shame.

I have already said that early on I was totally supportive of the union's goal of increasing the immorally, scandalously low salaries of teachers. In fact, in the first book to come out of the Yale Psycho-Educational Clinic in 1966 (Sarason, Levine, Goldenberg, Cherlin, & Bennett), I made it a point to say that I agreed with John Dewey that a school teacher should be paid the same as a university professor. Dewey said that because he knew and appreciated what teachers needed to know and do if they were to do justice to the complexities and importance of their task. Dewey spoke with disdain about how teachers of his day were prepared for those tasks. But everything that he thought, learned, and did at his lab school at the University of Chicago left him in no doubt that if and when preparatory programs took his ideas seriously, the knowledge they would require, and the pedagogical artistry they would employ ranked in importance, difficulty, and complexity with what we expect of professors. Dewey moved to Chicago only after the university agreed to combine psychology and pedagogy in one department. Theory without practice, practice not derived from theory, theory uninfluenced and/or unchanged by practice, teaching that becomes mindless routine for teacher and student—for Dewey you did not "become" a teacher, period. Teaching, learning, and changing should be never-ending affairs, and to nurture that stance in teachers is precisely the stance it is the obligation of the teacher to help students acquire. That obligation holds as much for the teacher as for professors. At the point of a gun I would confess that discharging that obligation is more complex and difficult for teachers than it is for professors.

Although I was supportive of the union goal, I had reservations I should have but did not express; in diluted form I expressed those reservations decades later and even then I steered clear of clearly, unequivocally, expressing those reservations. I was a union man—one did not give ammunition to the enemy! Chronologically, my first reaction was not a reservation. What the unions were implying in their messages to the public was that if salaries were increased, teachers would respond with increased motivation that would make for improvement in the quality and outcomes of schooling. I, for one, got the impression that unions were implying that teachers were discouraged and resentful, not respected as professionals, treated as if they were expendable, and that it was unreasonable to expect that they would or could give their best. With one exception, all of this was true. The exception was the assumption that higher salaries would make for better educational outcomes. Instead of saying that teachers deserved higher incomes on the basis of morality and comparative equity—in those days garbage collectors were paid discernibly better than teachers—the unions were emphasizing an improvement in educational outcomes. This both mystified and bothered me. I had already been in many schools, observed and talked to scores of teachers, enough to have come to two conclusions. First, and generally speaking, teachers were dedicated people. Second, teachers' conceptions of teaching and learning violated almost every feature of what constitutes productive learning. Concomitant with my in-school experience was what I had been learning about preparatory programs. Those were the years of the "great debate" in which proponents and opponents of change in preparatory programs locked horns, the former taking dead aim at teachers' superficial knowledge of subject matter, and the latter describing these proponents as ignorant, at best, and elitist, at worst, or both. The proponents described schools of education as anti-intellectual and diploma mills; the opponents said that they were also in favor of change but that what the proponents were advocating was an example of throwing the baby out with the bath water. All of this took place at a time of a growing teacher shortage, evidence of impoverished educational outcomes, and the recognition that local, state, and national funding for schools would have to increase.

Over a period of 2 years, and spurred by the growth and success of the unions, I read the official contracts between unions and schools of at least 20 Connecticut school districts. Serendipitously, I also read summaries of school grievance and arbitration cases published by the American Arbitration Association. The cases were from around the country. These readings made clear to me a question I heard administrators and board of education members asking in their meetings when they were discussing a change, small or large, directly or indirectly educational in substance: "How will the union react? Will they consider it a breach of contract?" The question was a legitimate one in that there was a contract which had to be honored; the day was past when teachers could be expected to submit passively to unilaterally made decisions. But two things bothered me. First, the administrators saw the union as "the enemy," not a force to work with but one to be circumvented, if possible. I sometimes got the impression that they used this stance as an excuse for not pushing a program or idea, or as a ploy to make it appear that the union was an obstacle to progress. Second, the union seemed primed to say no to any idea which in its opinion would alter in some way the duties and obligations of any individual or class of individuals in the union. The substance of a proposed change seemed not to be an issue but rather whether it meant that some teachers would be treated selectively. For the years I am talking about (1960–1970)

I cannot come up with an instance when a union conceived and presented an idea or program which would alter and improve educational outcomes. Granted, the union was a labor union, and therefore it was off limits to intrude in any way on the prerogatives of management. I considered that an excuse, however, and not an explanation of why the union was totally passive about educational policy issues and so zealously protective about "bread-and-butter" issues. The union seemed either unaware of or uninterested in the fact that the public was coming to see the union as concerned only with increases in salary. Reluctantly, I had to agree, by which I mean that for all practical purposes the union was clear about what it was against; it said nothing about what it was for in matters of educational reform. Let me give a personal example.

In the early 1970s I had several long meetings with Albert Shanker. I always read his Sunday columns in the *New York Times*. I had a great deal of admiration and respect for what he had accomplished as president of the New York Federation of Teachers and then as national president. Meeting with him deepened my positive feelings for him as a leader and thinker. Shanker knew the educational game and score better than 99½% of all those in the educational community. I was surprised how candid he was with me and how undefensive he was to some of my criticisms. At one point I said to him, "You know how I feel about preparatory programs. They are disaster areas. And from some of the things you have said to me you seem to agree. Why is it that you have *never* voiced your feelings in *any* [I emphasized the italicized words] of your columns?" His almost instant reply was, "Because many of the college faculty in those programs are members of my union." I had two instant reactions which I did not voice. First, if Shanker took on preparatory programs—which would imply that he was critical of the quality of many teachers in the union—he would not remain president very long. Second, in the several hundred columns he wrote in the Sunday *New York Times*, only once did he raise this question: Could or should the union continue to restrict itself, in the tradition of labor unions, only to bread-and-butter issues and continue to leave educational policy issues to "management"? It was obvious to me that Shanker, whose desire to improve the quality of education was bottomless, was constrained by the traditions of the labor movement and the self-interests of union members. He was a superb leader who would not remain long in office if he stood for actions that were critical of the members of his union. The disparity between what he knew and what he could do was striking. It had elements of the tragic.

As the years rolled on, I said next to nothing along these lines. Whatever lingering hope I had that the unions could be a force for educational reform was extinguished. Indeed, I, like much of the general public, came to see them as part of the problem and not of even a part of the solution. That is why, when the charter school movement rose above the educational horizon, I was not surprised that the unions fought vigorously to kill it or contain it, thus providing additional fodder to the public's view that the unions were bulwarks of a failing status quo. In principle I was in favor of charter schools because they rested on an unarticulated assumption I had come to regard as a fact: If you want to initiate and sustain a noncosmetic educational reform, your chances for success in the existing system are slightly above zero; you have to go outside the system, and if you do, you can expect hostile opposition from the unions. And that is what has happened in almost all instances I know or have heard about. In my book *Charter Schools: Another Flawed Educational Reform?* (1998) I alluded to the opposition of the union, but I should have said more, much more, because I no longer had any doubt that the union was an instance of the maxim, "With friends like that, educational reform would not lack enemies." I confess that I was aware when I wrote that book that I was avoiding writing the critique the union stance deserved. Old loyalties are hard to overcome! I say that as explanation and not as justifiable excuse.

So what happens when the union finally comes up with proposals—as it did on April 14, 2000—to take concrete actions to improve education? Early in this chapter I described the proposals. My first reaction was to the fact that there was no indication (or hint of one) that the union was acknowledging that, in general, teachers' grounding in subject matter was inadequate, a long standing criticism to which the union had remained silent or opposed. I could say that it is asking too much to expect that the union would say out loud that it had been wrong. But I could also say that if it was seeking to elevate the public's esteem of teachers (and the union), it should have admitted its past mistake if only as a way of signaling that it was capable of learning from its mistakes. I am reminded here of the convening of the historic Vatican Council by Pope John XXIII, who had the courage and foresight to say that there was much the church had to rethink and seek to change. Esteem for the church skyrocketed on the part of the Catholic and non-Catholic world. I am also reminded here of the legacy of the Vietnam War because that war caused a distrust of government that withheld its mistakes from the citizenry, as well as the knowledge that the war was basically unwinnable. Truth and esteem are highly correlated. Truth may reveal mistakes and imperfections, but it holds the promise that lessons have been learned. The teacher unions seem unable to recognize that their loss of public esteem stems from their past stance and policies and that the public needs to be assured that the unions have learned the appropriate lessons. I am not suggesting that the unions should have come up with a list of mea culpas and plead for forgiveness. The unions could and should have reminded people that "historically our first and sole task was to emancipate teachers from powerlessness and financial peonage. It was akin to a war in which those opposed to the unions used their considerable powers to try to maintain the status quo; the battles are far from over. During those years we riveted on bread-and-butter issues and avoided substantive educational policies that were and are ineffectual. We essentially left the war to the generals and that was unfortunate and wrong. Although we are solidly in the tradition of the labor movement, we can no longer remain silent on major issues of educational reform." The thrust of that kind of a message is what Albert Shanker believed and wrote about in only one of his columns. Why he said no more along those lines I cannot truly explain. And neither can I explain why that message in the recent report is absent. I consider that both unfortunate and wrong because most readers of the report are too young to remember the strength, unreasonableness, and insensitivity the union encountered from school administrators and the political system, far more than what it encountered from the general public. What the union implies is that it won the battles and lost the war in regard to public acceptance, respect, and esteem. Memory is a sometime thing that in the case of the individual has little or no untoward social consequences; the consequences for organizations are profound, especially when the memory of its public audience is faulty or grossly incomplete.

My initial personal reaction to the newspaper article was mild compared to those that followed. Take, for example, the proposal that prospective teachers pass subject matter tests after the sophomore year and also prior to entering the classroom; in addition the individual must have a college grade point average of 2.75 although over time the cutoff point would be raised to 3.0. In all of my writings I have emphasized (too weak a word) that I regarded as necessary and crucial that teachers have a very firm grasp of subject matter, far firmer than has been the case. If what has been reported about grade inflation is even partly true, a grade point average of 2.75 or even 3.0 are standards that would admit candidates whose grounding in subject matter would appear to be weak, of mediocre quality. It could be argued that those are minimal standards, but that is precisely the criticism that has been made of the academic requirements for selecting and certifying teachers: The minimum becomes the norm. And let us not gloss over the fact that subject matter courses are taught by faculty in the college of arts and sciences. I know of no evidence whatsoever that the quality of their teaching does not vary from the incompetent to poor, to average, to above average, to excellent. And I am assuming for the sake of argument that all such faculty have a firm grasp of the subject matter they teach: They are experts. Having been in the university for 45 years, plus 7 years in college and graduate school, I regard the assumption as nonsense. But suspend your experience and assume the assumption is valid. What you cannot assume as valid is the assumption that college faculty who teach the subject have an interest in how it might be applied by teachers in an age-graded public school. Such an interest is alien to them. They acquired their expertise in order to be a member of an arts and science faculty, not in a department or college of education. Their stance is: "Here is what I know, and it is my obligation to transmit that knowledge to you. How to adapt and transmit that knowledge to school children at different stages of development, is not my obligation. How to do that you will learn in a teacher preparatory program." That is a reasonable stance. We do not expect an undergraduate biology professor to take up how the subject matter in a course can and should be applied by the pre-med student to examining and treating a sick person, or a psychology professor to demonstrate how the contents of a child development course should be applied by a teacher in a classroom. This division of labor did not come about on the basis of educational theory or experience but rather because early on colleges of arts and sciences wanted nothing to do with teachers whom they regarded as operating far below what they considered professional in nature. Teaching school students was judged as a relatively simple affair for which a 2-year course of study in a "normal school" was sufficient after completing high school, an experience sufficient and appropriate for the tender, nonintellectual minds of women! That, in brief, explains why over time and accompanying the creation of schools of education, those schools were and still remain the least respected part of the university, an object of sarcasm, criticism, and ill-concealed disparagement. I discuss this in some detail in my 2001 book *American Psychology and Schools: A Critique.*

The colleges of arts and sciences and education are each based on assumptions that are irreconcilable. That is to say, one explicitly contradicts the other. In the college of arts and sciences the assumption is that a firm grasp of subject matter is sufficient to justify allowing someone to teach it. It is no secret that in many universities someone is asked to join the faculty who is not regarded at all highly as a teacher but whose research credentials and accomplishments are highly prized. They are delighted, of course, if the person is both a good teacher and a researcher or scholar, but when push comes to shove, the quality of his or her teaching takes a very back seat.

The department or college of education rests on the assumption that a firm grasp of subject matter is insufficient to justify allowing a person to teach it to students in schools. The task of the school teacher is to adapt and convey subject matter in ways appropriate to the cognitive capacity of this or that age student. The ideal teacher is one who understands and strives to meet the criterion put succinctly, as I have said before, by the poet Yeats: "Education is not about filling empty buckets, it is about lighting fires." *How* do you light and sustain such fires? That is by no means a burning question in the college of arts and sciences; it is somewhere between a secondary and tertiary question, if and when it is a question at all. But in the college of education it is the most important question. More correctly, it should be the most important, but it is not, rhetoric to the contrary notwithstanding. The most persistent criticism of teachers and colleges of education is that they do not light fires, that over the course of the school years they extinguish the fires children have in them when they start school.

Two things appalled me about the union proposals. The first was that the proposals would reinforce the view that by beefing up a teacher's grasp of subject matter the quality of teaching—the number, size, and duration of fires—would of course improve. The only explanation I could come up with for such proposals is that those who conceived them are totally ignorant of the subject matter on human learning. That they are not so ignorant is belied by the second thing that appalled me: the absence of a searching critique of preparatory programs, of a literature that demonstrates that teachers regard preparatory programs with disdain, chiefly on the basis that they were ill prepared for the realities of classrooms, schools, school systems, and students who vary considerably on a host of factors. The union leadership knows this. Albert Shanker certainly knew it and conveyed it to those who are now the leaders of the American Federation of Teachers. So, when the union *finally* comes up with proposals for educational reform that essentially require only cosmetic changes in preparatory programs, I trust the reader will understand why I feel guilt for not voicing in earlier years my reservations about the role of the union as a potentially positive force in reform.

By capitulating as they have to the well-intentioned but misguided proponents of more and more subject matter courses for teachers, the union has made a bad situation worse because its proposals are being read and interpreted as a kind of breakthrough which will be fruitful. That hoped-for goal will, as in the past, bear little or no fruit. Let us remember that after World War II two things happened. The first was converting free-standing teacher-preparatory schools into 4-year liberal arts colleges, a development that in part at least was intended to increase the variety and quality of subject matter courses available to prospective teachers. It was in response to the growing awareness that American schools were generally grossly inadequate in regard to educational outcomes. Many readers may be too young to remember the cascade of criticisms of teachers and colleges of education that started in the late 1950s and obviously has continued to this day. The major result was a slow but steady decrease in what the college of education could require, and increase in the subject matter courses teachers were required to take in the liberal arts and science departments. Second, and with great fanfare, many universities created MAT programs, the Master of Arts in Teaching, which admitted only those students who had completed a 4-year liberal arts and science program with, of course, a major in one subject matter area. And let us not forget that during those years many school systems allowed individuals to begin teaching without having had a single education course, provided that when they started teaching they would begin to take such courses. I know of no credible evidence that these "improvements" improved anyone or anything. And yet, the criticism of inadequate subject-matter preparation goes unabatedly on, a Johnny-one-note refrain sung today by the federal department of education, foundations, schools and academics, and now the American Federation of Teachers.

I am reminded here of the "Horse Story" which was placed in the mail box of Emory Cowen at the University of Rochester.

Horse Story

Common advice from knowledgeable horse trainers includes the adage, "If the horse you're riding dies, get off." Seems simple enough, yet, in the education business we don't always follow that advice. Instead, we often choose from an array of alternatives which include:

1. Buying a stronger whip.
2. Trying a new bit or bridle.
3. Switching riders.
4. Moving the horse to a new location.
5. Riding the horse for longer periods of time.
6. Saying things like, "This is the way we've always ridden this horse."
7. Appointing a committee to study the horse.
8. Arranging to visit other sites where they ride dead horses more efficiently.
9. Increasing the standards for riding dead horses.
10. Creating a test for measuring our riding ability.
11. Comparing how we're riding now with how we did ten or twenty years ago.
12. Complaining about the state of horses these days.
13. Coming up with new styles of riding.
14. Blaming the horse's parents. The problem is often in the breeding.
15. Tightening the cinch.

I am also reminded of a joke: It was in the dead of winter and this man did not feel at all well. He went to his physician who conducted an extraordinarily thorough examination. After studying all findings, the doctor said, "I want you to go home, take off all of your clothes, open all windows, stand in front of one of them, and inhale deeply." The patient was dumbfounded. "But doctor," he said, "if I do that I'll get pneumonia. It's freezing outside." To which the doctor replied, *"That* I know how to handle."

You can characterize the educational reform movement as doing what is familiar even though what is then done confirms the maxim that the more things change, the more they remain the same. Increasing budgets, requiring teachers to take more subject matter courses, changing curricula, more parental involvement, more of a role for teachers in decision making, open classrooms, raising standards, greater accountability—the list goes on and if, like me, you have lived through most of the twentieth century you have to put up with repeats. It ain't easy, there is no remote to turn off the repeats.

I know there are people who see me as akin to Henny-Penny forecasting doom and gloom. What keeps me going I am asked frequently? The process of self-scrutiny gave rise to several answers. The first is that the only time I think is when I take pen to paper. The rest of the time I am living, fantasizing, talking to friends on the phone, or what is most satisfying, being with them when their travels bring them east or mine bring me their way. But thinking, real thinking, only starts when I write. And that, believe me, is not easy. Because of my physical handicap from polio, there are many activities in which I would love to engage but cannot. Writing for me is a form of action, and, like all actions, its course can change as the road you are on takes you to byways you have ignored or overlooked. What seemed to be a well-paved road with a clear end point turns out to be a segment of interconnecting roads, some of which are unmarked and need to be explored. If making sense out of where the road is taking you can be frustrating—it always is—there is the sense of learning and changing. Although it did not seem so at the time, I was fortunate that in my professional career I have always been in a role that required me both to act and react to people in complicated organizations, and those actions and reactions almost always centered around efforts to improve an existing state of affairs. I made mistakes of diverse kinds, but in the course of my actions I was far more clear about the mistakes others were making. It was not until I would reflect and start to write about those experiences that I would see that what happened was more complicated than I had thought at the time and that I had imperfections that I wished I did not have, that the cauldron of action forces on you the recognition that you are not the hot shot you thought you were, and that we do not live in a predictable world. It always is more complicated. It is memory and arrogance that play the simplifying role, another example of unintended consequences.

Undoubtedly, a major factor which has kept me going is both reward-ing and discouraging. It has been rewarding because on all of the scores of occasions I have talked to groups of educators, no one has ever disagreed with the major thrusts of my criticisms of American schools and educational reform. On the contrary, they agreed with what I had said. They did not view me as a dyspeptic academic venting his spleen at beleaguered practitioners. More rewarding, because the letter writers were unknown to me, were the people who had read something I had written and wrote to tell me that their experience and conclusions were similar to mine. What was discouraging was the sense of impotence and hopelessness these practitioners conveyed about the possibility of change. It was via these face-to-face and impersonal (letter writing) occasions that I was confirmed in the conclusion that schools and school systems are nonlearning organizations. I trust the reader will understand why the satisfactions I have experienced are swamped by the opposite feeling that nothing will change. More about this later in this book.

That brings me to a mistake I made from the time the Yale Psycho-Educational Clinic was created in the early 1960s. In the opening chapter of this book I said that the self-scrutiny process in which I had engaged did not cause me to alter in any basic way the major aspects of what I have written. That is to say, what I had described and interpreted suffered from an insensitivity to the nitty-gritty tactics of action which caused me to over-emphasize this and de-emphasize that source of resistance to reform. They were mistakes of misplaced emphasis. The mistake I will now discuss is about a type of action I came to regard as of bedrock importance for edu-cational reform.

I can identify the occasion in which I first became aware of the mis-take. It was 10 years after I stepped down as director of the clinic. I was conducting a graduate seminar on Public Policy and Human Services In-stitutions (including education). I invited the local representative to the Connecticut legislature, a young, bright, articulate individual with a doc-torate in economics, to talk with us. I told him we hoped he would give us a realistic picture of how and on what basis legislators decided specific policies which, when enacted, would clearly impact on diverse people and organizations. I asked him to be as forthright as possible. And he was. Here is what he emphasized:

1. Being a legislator is not a full-time job. Until recently the Connecti-cut legislature met every 2 years.

2. The federal legislature provides each of its members with several staff people and in addition the considerable backup services of the Con-

gressional Library, the Congressional Budget Office, and more. The state legislator has, for all practical purposes, no staff or backup services.

3. Far more often than not, a legislator casts his or her vote on the basis of little or no knowledge or experience of the substance of the policy issues. For any one issue there are usually one or two legislators who have a special interest in and knowledge of the ins and outs of the issue, and they influence how the others will vote. That is the case in the caucus meetings of the two parties.

4. Generally speaking, legislators want to do the "best" and the "right" thing at the same time they know they are voting on the basis of ignorance or on the most superficial knowledge. Generally speaking, and despite public stereotypes about them, legislators agonize about the role in which they find themselves. Many feel guilty that they vote on important issues about which they know little.

5. Lobbyists play an influential role: They are often conveyors of relevant information, but they are also equally as often conveyors of a very narrow, black-white opinion of the issue for which they lobby. It is the rare instance when a legislator can say that he or she has a real feel for judging contrasting viewpoints and the data that purports to substantiate them.

A year later in another Yale venue Professor Wendell Garner and I conducted a seminar on Public Policy and the Social Sciences. We invited Senator Green of Rhode Island to come and talk with us. Senator Green had been in the Senate for years and had been chairman of committees particularly relevant to the social sciences. We plied him with questions. Between Garner and me and the graduate students, we covered what we thought was the social science waterfront. About 15 minutes before the 2-hour seminar ended, the Senator—a senior citizen with a quiet, reflective, quizzical manner—looked at us and said, "I would like now to share an experience with you that you might want to ponder." I do not remember his exact words, and I take the liberty of paraphrasing what he said, in my own words. "I have been in the Senate for many years. Countless times I have been visited by social scientists either as individuals or as representatives of their fields. They all had one message in common: There was something I could do for them or their field, usually in regard to funding for one or another research or training purpose. They were always clear and articulate about why such funding was important. I found them persuasive more often than not. My question to you is why in all those years no social scientist, as an individual or representing a professional organization, has ever come to me and asked, Is there any way I (we) can provide you with information about issues you feel you should know more about? My visitors are crystal clear about what they want me to do for them. It apparently is alien to their interests even to conceive that maybe, just maybe, they can be of help to me with problems peculiar to my senatorial responsibilities. You will pardon me if I regard that as narrow, even irresponsible."

Those two experiences forced on me the very humbling realization that in my zealousness to bring about educational reform I had totally neglected to make contact with legislators and other politicians (to me a nonpejorative term) who play such a crucial role in educational matters. I could and should have made such an effort. I should have not been content to criticize legislation that would probably be counterproductive and a source of future disillusionment. It would not have been difficult to make such contacts. I could have arranged to meet with legislators individually and in small groups, on the state and federal level. I had credentials that suggested that I was not a crackpot, a fool, an ideologue, or personally contentious and self-serving. How can you write off the political system when you must have been dumb, blind, and in a terminal coma to ignore the politicians whose responsibility is to act, to formulate legislation that affects education?

Action in and commerce with the real world has been my best teacher, especially if the actions hold out the promise of changing schools to become places of productive learning. But what the self-scrutiny revealed was that I had done what a lot of academics had done: engage in action, analyze your experience and data, and publish it in the hope that your readers will consider it a contribution. But who were my readers? I certainly hoped that those interested in reform would be one audience, although if I depended on the sale of my books to live as I do (semigraciously) I could be in real trouble. Given the size of the educational community the sale of my books is not small, it is minuscule. Any hope I ever had to reach a wide audience was dashed years ago. But the intellectual and personal kicks I get from writing keep me going. But the nagging question remains: If I was (and am) intent on improving the educational experience of students, and if I was aware that what I had to say was reaching few people in the educational community, why did I totally ignore the possibility that if I tried to establish meaningful contacts with people in key political positions, I might get to first base in that world of policy and action?

Was it because I did not take the obvious seriously, namely, that what the political system (local, state, federal) does is a difference that makes a difference for schooling? Was it because I was victim of holding the stereotype that politicians were intellectually narrow, superficial, self-serving types who had neither the time nor desire to listen and react to the likes of academic me? Was it that I valued thinking and writing so highly that I did not want to take the time to deal with these policy makers even though what I was writing recognized and criticized the failures of their policies? Was I oversocialized in the traditions and culture of the university cloister

where the outside world is seen as a source of contamination that negatively affects dispassionate thinking?

All but the last question has an affirmative answer. The last question
is the most personally aggravating one because during all the years I was
in the university, and during the decade or more since I retired, I have always been engaged with the "impure" outside world. For example, for 30
years after receiving my doctorate in 1942 I spent a significant part of my
time in and around the arena of mental retardation, first as a full-time
employee in a residential institution for the mentally retarded, then as a
participant in the creation of nonresidential regional centers, and then as a
colleague with Burton Blatt in changing preparatory programs for special
education teachers, all this overlapping with my developing interest in
education generally. I thrived on those involvements in the world of action, just as I would have if I had decided to come to grips in one or
another way with the political system.

There are ironies in what I have just said. For one thing, three of my
books (Sarason et al., 1977; Sarason & Lorentz, 1989, 1992)—not directly
on education—have dealt with the creation, enlarging, and sustaining of
resource exchange networks. I have always been a networker type who
early on learned how productive and enlivening it was to exploit the stance:
"I think I can be of some help to you and in return you can be of help to
me." It is what I call the barter approach to personal and professional relationships. It has opened many closed doors to me just as it has opened my
doors to people I did not know. The network I helped create was a vehicle
to facilitate such exchanges. The point is that I could have used my networks to get to almost anyone important to my purposes. However, in all
the years that network existed, getting to people in the political system was
not central to my purposes. As a result, I failed to exploit one golden opportunity: my relationship with Albert Shanker. He sought me out to discuss my book *Schooling in America: Scapegoat and Salvation* (1983), which he
liked very much. (Shanker was a reader, which is more than I can say about
current leaders in either of the two teacher unions.) In that and several
subsequent meetings we discussed his interest in bringing together in a
book columns of his writings in the Sunday *New York Times*. I offered to be
of help in selecting the columns, of which there were several hundred. He
sent me *all* the columns from which I selected perhaps a hundred. I offered
to write an introduction to such a book. Shanker was, to say the least, a
very busy man who in any one week spent a lot of time in an airplane. He
never followed through on his plans for the book. *If at that point in my life
I wanted to get to policy makers in the political system, Shanker could and would
have opened doors for me, receptive doors.* The irony does not stop there. *I could
have used our relationship to discuss a question he had raised but once in all of his*

columns: Had the time come when the union had to concern itself with more than bread-and-butter issues? I have little doubt that if I had a series of meetings with him, his staff, and key state union officers, ideas might have gained currency that would have prevented the leadership after Shanker's death from issuing the kind of infertile proposals their recent report contained.

Like everyone else I am capable of unrealistic optimism, even grandiose expectations. I can assure the reader that such a capability is nowhere in the picture when I say that any excursions on my part to be an influence with the union or with politicians might have paid off. Realistically, the payoff would have varied from nothing to the very small. Not to act is to engage in the self-fulfilling prophecy: You think it a waste of time to try to influence this or that individual or group, so you do nothing, and then judge their subsequent misguided actions as a confirmation of your wisdom in doing nothing. I was guilty of that, but I truly did not confront the implications of inaction until the self-scrutiny process began not long after my book *Political Leadership and Educational Failure* (1998b) was published. The central theme of that book was that improvement cannot be expected until political leaders begin to glimpse the major reasons why the educational reform movement has gone essentially nowhere in the post–World War II era. That is why I devoted a chapter in that book to the only president who deserves to be called the education president: Thomas Jefferson. He had clarity about the purposes of education, and he *acted* in accord with those purposes.

The teacher unions have always advocated smaller class size. So did I until 10 years ago, along with everyone else. The usual class size of 20–30 students (or more) was obviously the single, most important barrier preventing teachers from discharging their obligation to promote the cognitive and personal growth of their students, especially in urban schools. It was presented by the unions as a glimpse of the obvious. The public agreed. The problem, of course, was money. Where would the considerable increase in funding come from, especially (again) in urban areas where revenues from their tax base were inadequate for the way they were supporting education, let alone for what they should be doing?

It was in the course of writing *The Case for Change: Rethinking the Preparation of Educators* (1993a) that I began to question what I and everyone else regarded as a glimpse of the obvious. I remember well how, when I was writing the final chapter, this question popped into my mind: Why do I expect a teacher I regard as a poor or even a so-so one with a class of 25 students to become a more effective one with a class of, say, 15 students? That an effective teacher would accomplish more with a smaller class size, I had no doubt, but in my experience the number of such teachers was far smaller than the ineffective or so-so teacher. And by so-so I meant teachers who were motivated, dedicated, hardworking, but lacked the spark that lights fires in students. They were filling empty buckets, their students learned what they were told to learn, dutifully but without enthusiasm, rarely if ever asking a question suggesting that they were mulling over or thinking about what they were learning and why. However you define creativity, these teachers did not meet the definition.

I agonized over whether I should go back over the manuscript of the book and somewhere deal with the question which had popped into my mind. The book was already highly critical of preparatory programs. By raising and dealing with the question would everything else I said in the book be taken as coming from someone whose nihilism and dyspepsia knew no bounds? Besides, I had no evidence for my prediction that markedly reducing class size would make only a small difference in outcomes. I would have to say what was an indisputable truth: I was in favor of smaller class sizes for the same reason decades before I was in favor of the Head Start legislation. But just as in a public lecture I gave at Boston University in 1966 I said I was in favor of Head Start but predicted that its educational impact on the children would not, could not, be robust, that was what I was predicting for the effect of smaller class size.

So I agonized. What decided me not to deal with the question was the realization that a major aspect of the problem, perhaps the basic one, was the utterly inadequate criteria employed for the selection of individuals for admission to preparatory programs. And that aspect required more thought. So I did not deal with the question until my 1999 book *Teaching as a Performing Art*. That book came out many months before the American Federation of Teachers made public their proposals for "improving" the preparation of teachers. I have no reason to believe that anyone in the union leadership read the book or the earlier one I discussed above. If any one of them did read either of the books, they decided that what I said was inimical to their purposes.

On the evening of the day (May 12, 2000) I finished this chapter, the News Hour on PBS devoted a segment to an interview with Marilyn Whirry, national Teacher of the Year. She has a very lively manner and is refreshingly forthright in expressing her opinions. She left no viewer in doubt that she regarded the major obligation of the teacher was not to fill empty buckets but to light fires in students. She never expected to go into teaching because in her own schooling she had, with one exception, boring teachers. She uses the Socratic method because it gives students the opportunity to express their interests, ideas, and questions. At one point she said loud and clear that what schools needed were "wonderful, new teachers," a remark I interpreted as criticism of many who are now teaching. The interview segment lasted for approximately 10 minutes. At the end of 2 minutes I was hooked: This middle-aged woman was a force of nature. To the extent that one can pass judgment based on watching a 10-minute video segment, I concluded that Ms. Whirry meets my criteria of how a good teacher should think and act. Over the years PBS has had similar segments with Teacher of the Year honorees. I have seen, perhaps, 10 such segments. Ms. Whirry is in a class by herself. Even if I am only half right in my assessment, her students are fortunate to have her. They are warmed by the intellectual fires she lights in them.

In the 2000 presidential campaign the two major teacher unions spent millions of dollars and probably as many hours in support of the nominee of the Democratic party. At the nominating convention the single largest group was educators. The educational platform of the party was a collection of platitudes. Needless to say, undergirding all of the platitudes was the importance of increasing funding for school improvement, especially for smaller class size; increasing pay for teachers as recognition "for the professionals they are"; and for increasing the supply of "qualified" teachers. During the convention and the campaign no one, but no one, said "better qualified" teachers, and for two reasons: They had no idea what "better" would or should mean and, crucially, it would be a criticism of those who are now teachers. You do not bite the hand that feeds you! It was all empty rhetoric, instances of knowing what you are against and devoid of any substance about what you are for. The Replication platform was no less rhetorical albeit more specific. Where it was specific, it was mindlessly ahistorical or stupidly simplistic psychologically, or based on a conception of evidence that belies total ignorance of why educational reform *has to be* mind-bogglingly difficult and requires us to adopt, at the least, a stance of humbleness and self-criticism that makes it somewhat more easy for us to recognize that *maybe* we have met the enemy and it is us. That is something the teacher unions have not learned and, therefore, contribute nothing to clarifying anything. That is why I regard Al Shanker as a tragic figure: He knew as few others have that teacher unions potentially could play a significant role in educational reform but only if they were prepared to go beyond bread-and-butter issues. He was light years ahead of his membership.

Chapter 7

Again, Are Teachers Professionals?

We hear much today about the importance of staff developments for teachers. That belated recognition of its importance is not only a response to the criticisms of the inadequacies of schools as judged by conventional criteria of educational outcomes. No less a stimulus has been the recognition that it is at best folly and at worst self-defeatingly unrealistic and unfair to expect that those who finish their preparatory education and training are equipped to discharge their professional obligations at a high level. Sheer personal experience is, God knows, of bedrock importance; it is the crucible in which one's concepts and style of practice inevitably change and develop for good or for bad. The classroom and school are psychologically confining places which have omnipresent and demanding routines that leave little or no time for probing reflection, for examining and reexamining one's initial concepts and style of practice. And let us never forget that the beginning educational professional has been catapulted into a school and school system which seek to socialize and professionalize the individual according to its conceptions of what is right and wrong, permissible and unpermissible, what is innovative and what is off limits. This socialization consists of messages, implicit and explicit, which can be put this way: "Here is how we think about and do things in this school and school system." To the beginning teacher who is anxious, feels incompetent, and fears exposure, those messages are not ignored; that teacher's professional development has begun whether or not those messages conflict with his or her concepts, attitudes, and style of practice. How and to what degree those conflicts begin to be resolved is very much determined by the fact that the teacher will be *alone* in the classroom. I italicize alone to emphasize that the teacher is expected to be responsible for his or her professional development. That is why Murray Levine said, "Teaching is a lonely profession." For all practical purposes, schools do not have the tradition of forums for the discussion of concepts and practice. The teacher's professional development is largely determined by experience in the classroom which is his or her world of concepts and practice. If a *professional* is one who has something to "profess," something based on, justified by, more than personal opinion and experience, the teacher is not a professional.

A mother may claim to know a great deal about child development based on her experience with her children. She may indeed have learned a lot, but we would not say she is a child development professional, and for several reasons. Her experience is with a very limited sample of children; her assessment of what she has learned is very personal and subjective; she has no conceptual framework by which she can claim that what she did and how she did it was as good as, superior or inferior to other ways she might have proceeded; she has no credible evidence that allows others to accept what she says at its face value; her self-assessment may tell us what she says she has learned, but we know nothing about what she did or did not unlearn; one person's story is one person's story unless that story fits in with the stories of other parents as that has been determined by independent investigators; parents, like everybody else, can be self-deluding. To put it more succinctly, we expect a professional to make decisions and give advice on the basis of broad knowledge not only of the range of practices in his or her field but of their consequences as well. If the obligation of the professional is "do no harm," that obligation implies that your knowledge and experience are broad enough to help you avoid doing harm.

When you go to your physician, you assume that he or she has benefited from discussions with colleagues in a variety of venues. We expect him or her to know that how he or she prescribes and treats cannot ignore how other practitioners prescribe and treat, that as a solo practitioner the physician must not assume that he or she has cornered the market on truth about how to think and practice, that he or she has no need to learn more, change, develop. From colleagues near and far, from reading the clinical and research literature, from the pamphlets and articles the physician receives from pharmaceutical companies, we assume he or she has far more than a superficial grasp of what is going on in his or her specialty. Lay people are unaware that the hospital to which the physician sends patients has procedures and forums explicitly intended to review all instances in which the physician may have been negligent or unknowledgeable about what is considered appropriate handling of such cases. The physician may be a solo practitioner, but he or she is one who is, so to speak, swimming in a well-populated fish bowl, a fact ignored at peril and at the expense of the well-being of his or her patients.

Practicing physicians are clinicians trained in an atmosphere of the morality of science by which I mean that their training will be suffused by the importance of continuous learning: The more you know the more you have to know; changing how you think and practice is in the nature of the professional endeavor; resisting changing is sinful when it justifies a lack of curiosity and courage or a surfeit of mental laziness and passivity; the routinization of thinking and practice is a prescription for "standing still," an antidevelopment virus. Absent this kind of morality an individual has little basis to be included in the category professional.

What I have just said I could and should have said a long time ago: Many teachers are not professionals. The judgment was implied in all that I have written, but I could not bring myself to state it explicitly. We have long been in an era where regarding oneself as a professional is a badge of honor and status. Auto mechanics, policemen, hair stylists, builders, plumbers, electricians regard themselves as professionals and want others to so regard them. It is beyond my present purposes to discuss the defining features of a profession and its members. It is wholly understandable if people want to, have to, regard themselves as possessing special knowledge and craft and label such possessions by a term that in our culture commands respect. But when that label does not extend beyond special knowledge and craft, the moral obligations traditionally and explicitly associated with the label get lost and unexamined even though those obligations are of bedrock importance and have fateful consequences. To use the label "professional" indiscriminately totally obscures differences which make a difference in the real world. When so used, the label confuses meaning with significance, communication with shared meaning.

All this was clear to me decades ago when I began to be in, live in, schools. But I gingerly and silently avoided putting my judgment into my writings. You could say that I was not discharging my moral obligation to put what I truly thought into words. There is justice to that criticism. My excuse was that I did not want to alienate the educational community. More correctly, I did not want to create an unbridgeable gulf between me and the educational community by saying that they were wrong in regarding themselves as professionals or that they were in an occupation masquerading as a profession. If I said that unambiguously, I would lose whatever credibility I had and would be regarded as one of those self-important academics who from his elevated perch regards those "below" him as mindless drones. I could say, as I truly believed, that far from regarding educators as mindless drones I regarded them as victims. They would not have believed me because they literally could not listen to, let alone assimilate, a message so contrary to their self-regard. So I wrote about this or that aspect of the moral issue, which I never stated as clearly as I should have.

There are physicians who are not professionals and that judgment is usually harbored by other physicians who are reluctant to articulate the judgment and take action. But the nature of medical practice—which today is largely group practice and takes place for the most part in a hospital fish bowl—makes it likely that the unprofessional physician will not go unnoticed. Although there are forums for discussing such individuals, the truly professional physician is very reluctant to resort to action involving, as it would, reputations, livelihoods, public exposure, institutional practices, and self-esteem. But, at least, these forums exist even though resorted to less frequently than one would expect or hope. These forums and moral-professional traditions undergirding them hardly exist in public education. And up until the early decades of the twentieth century they hardly existed in medicine, a situation largely remedied by the consequences of the publication of the 1910 Flexner report. Returning to Murray Levine's comment that "teaching is a lonely profession," I believe that loneliness, reinforced by the school culture, allows the professional teacher to remain silent about an unprofessional teacher. Self-policing is not a notable feature of any profession. The point of this chapter is that it is worse in education.

Let me list and briefly discuss why and how my judgment that too many teachers are not professionals evolved.

1. My formal graduate training was in clinical psychology. A good part of one year was spent in a clinical service center where I attended conferences at which a staff member would present for discussion a case that he thought important, or instructive, or puzzling. The discussion was serious and (for the most part) friendly. If in the beginning of the internship I had any doubt that there was more than one way to diagnose, understand, and treat troubled people, those doubts almost instantly dissolved. The staff members came from different universities, they were different kinds of personalities, their theoretical orientation and clinical style were by no means identical, and they were not in doubt that it was their obligation to indicate why they disagreed (or agreed) with this or that point the presenter had made. I said earlier that these discussions were "for the most part" friendly because to a novice like me there were times when the discussion seemed so passionate that I wondered whether those in disagreement with each other would willingly discuss anything with each other after the case conference. I did not look forward to my postnovice years as a presenter. But by the end of that year it seemed obvious to me that the benefits of those case conferences far outweighed whatever downsides they had. And I learned that every staff member looked forward with eagerness and enthusiasm to the give-and-take of the meetings: They were interesting, challenging, instructive, and influential. I had no way of determining how influential they were in changing people's minds, but they influenced me forever in two ways. First, I should seek ways and forums where what I was thinking and doing could be challenged by knowledgeable colleagues, however much I might not like what they said. The second was that if, God forbid, I became a solo practitioner, I would professionally die on the vine if what I thought and did was based only on my experience in my isolated office devoid of little or no stimulation from beyond my isolated office confines.

2. The above explains why, when I started to work in schools, I was both surprised and appalled that there was no tradition for scheduled case conferences or, for that matter, any kind of meeting to discuss professional issues. I knew that at best there was a monthly faculty meeting where housekeeping, administrative, and central office directives constituted the agenda. I have never met a teacher who spoke positively about these meetings which were usually relatively short, humanely so. Central office directives came from people whom teachers regarded as semifaceless bureaucrats who made work for themselves by coming up with ideas that complicated the lives of teachers. It was the rare teacher, I learned, who felt obliged to heed directives once he or she entered the classroom and closed its door. Teachers were solo practitioners who did not look with favor on others, from in and out of the school, who entered their domain for the purpose of evaluation. For teachers, one of the defining characteristics of a "good" principal was that he or she rarely entered the classroom. And principals admitted that they knew that teachers did not want them to take seriously that they were instructional leaders. If a school was an interpersonally peaceful place, it was because everyone observed this rule: "You take care of your problems and classroom, I will take care of mine, we each have our own ways of doing things." I floated the idea of a case conference, but it sank. For one thing, the structure of the school day provided no time for such meetings which, therefore, would have to be after school. Some teachers said, and I had no reason to doubt them, that they had responsibilities at home that meant that as soon as the school day ended they had to depart. But the idea sank because most teachers made it politely clear that my proposal was misguided, however well intentioned. In a private conversation one teacher chided me by saying, "You obviously do not realize that your proposal is tantamount to opening a can of worms. Your intentions are good, but I for one am against it because it is a dangerous one that can upset the applecart." She was right, of course. I naively had assumed that the opportunity to learn from each other would be welcomed because it would dilute the sense of the unwanted privacy of the solo practitioner. Not only was it not welcomed, but it starkly revealed to me how teachers treasured and protected their solo practice. The traditions and the culture of schools support such a stance.

There is more to it than that, but that comes later in this chapter. Let me say that I should have written at greater length and with more concrete detail about the intellectual, professional, and institutional significance of the case conference, that is to say, its *potential* significance. Wrapped up in the rationale of the case conference is its potential to surface and discuss issues of student *and* teacher learning, teaching style and practice, a productive collegiality, and the moral obligation of teachers to develop, change, and grow. Can such a conference be upsetting? Of course. Can it engender or surface strong differences of opinion? Of course. Can such conferences be conducted in ways that make a mockery of the moral obligation of the do-no-harm maxim? Of course. Will such a conference increase (initially at least) in some teachers the fear of exposing themselves to the scrutiny of others, and increase the strength of their protective armor which shields them from feeling unsafe? Of course. To these questions I can only reply by asking this: By what conception of learning can you assume that learning, developing, and changing can be smooth, conflict-free, pleasurable, with no ups and downs or highs and lows? And by what conception of institutional change can one expect that an innovation takes hold quickly without ruffling feathers and that there is no need of time for an innovation to become a tradition consistent, to a discernible degree, with the spirit of it?

3. If the absence of the case conference and any other forum for discussion of issues of educational import surprised and appalled me, there was another observation that was more unsettling: School personnel hardly read or even had interest in the literature of their field. That was and even today is incomprehensible to me. How can you arrogate to yourself the label "professional" and read next to nothing about what is going on in your field, what the controversial issues are—the competing conceptions, the innovations, and the evidence they claim to provide? This hit me with truly full force when I learned that no teacher in the schools in which I worked had ever heard of a major governmental publication—which had received play in the national media—which had surveyed many scores of studies of reform efforts in order to determine which types of approach seemed to achieve their intended reform purposes. The major conclusion of the survey had been that the approach based on serious involvement of teachers and parents in the planning and implementation of the reform could claim to have been successful in varying degrees. All other approaches (the vast majority) could make no such claim. How could it be that no teacher had even heard of the report? How could you discuss a report you have never heard about? How can you continue thinking and acting as you do and have no curiosity about what others have thought and done? In my work with individual teachers there were occasions when I thought it would be helpful to the teacher to read a particular book or article. No teacher ever followed through on my suggestion. In the course of the many times I have been invited to talk at meetings and conferences, I have met teachers and administrators who clearly read the literature, but they were the usual exceptions. I confess that in my writings over the decades I never dealt with this "reading problem" precisely because I could not bring myself to say out loud what I believed, "You are ignorant and do not know that there

is a world of ideas and practices that you do not feel obligated at least to scan and mull over. I do not expect you to be scholars or sophisticated readers of the literature most relevant to you. But I do expect that you should feel obliged to read enough so as to prevent you from thinking that you have nothing left to learn, that what you think, believe, and do is not in need of challenge and change, that you have settled into a comfortable routine you do not want to disturb, that in the culture of schools learning and knowing do not pay off." How could I say that and not be perceived by the educational community as a very hostile, demeaning, ignorant, utopian academic foisting his values on others? I should have said it at the same time I could have sincerely said that teachers are as much agents as they are victims. (I will elaborate on that shortly.) I should have articulated *my* truths to discharge my moral obligation to my profession as well as to those in an arena I was seeking to influence. It would be predictable that those I would seek to influence would, to indulge understatement, not take kindly to what I would say. No one wants to be told that they are, unbeknownst to themselves, ignorant. So what if I alienated the very people I sought, by my lights, to influence in positive ways? My livelihood would not be in any way affected, nor would my status in my profession as a psychologist. If I were a professor in a school of education, it would be another story in terms of interpersonal relationships. There was another reason why I was silent: I did not want to give aid and comfort to those, in or out of the academy, who (1) would like nothing better than to see the withering and demise of public schools, (2) regard educators as inferior people who deliberately subvert the educational process and, so to speak, willed the present situation, and (3) possess a bottomless ignorance of the nature of teaching and the history of education. I will never forget when I said to one of these academics that at the beginning of the twentieth century the quality of medical education and practice was far worse than the situation in education today. She looked at me with staring disbelief and said, "I don't believe you. You do not know what you are talking about. I am no youngster [she was not], but I have lived long enough to know that in the twentieth century American medicine was the envy of the world." I told her she should read Flexner's 1910 report *Medical Education in the United States and Canada*. Who was Flexner, she asked. I replied, "He was not a physician, but he was one of the two most eminent educators of his times, the other one being John Dewey." It was instantly obvious that pairing Flexner with Dewey was to her proof positive that the conversation should be terminated. It was, but not before I told her that Flexner's report had been supported by the Carnegie Endowment for the Improvement of Teaching. There are many people like her. I do not know how to deal with such people, just as I did not know how to tell teachers they are ignorant and not professionals; for the former I have no sympathy (or patience), for the latter I do have sympathy because they are unwitting victims of a scandalously poor preparation in which the moral obligations of professionalism are shortchanged.

I have written critically about preparatory programs, but it never reflected the passion associated with my conclusions. I consciously tried to be balanced and reasonable, but I was not calling a spade a spade. It probably is obvious to the reader that the self-scrutinizing process which stimulated this book has resurfaced conflicts about what I did and did not do, what I could have but chose not to do for reasons I am still unable to say were right or wrong, advisable or inadvisable. You do not live as long as I have (ca. 83), look back over roads taken or bypassed, and not have regrets even though you know that there is no way you can resolve or assess those regrets, that today is the first day of the rest of your life, and you have to grow up.

The issues I have raised in this chapter I touched on in my book *You Are Thinking of Teaching?* (1993c). Although the title suggests that the book is for those who are making a career choice, it was really meant for those who prepare teachers. The last chapter in the book has the oxymoronic title "The Non-Reading Professional." In it I say that if I were appointed Czar of Education I would require that in every school there be a biweekly or monthly meeting to discuss an article or book bearing on practical issues of learning and teaching. I said it tongue-in-cheek because I make plain that the problem is not one which will be ameliorated by fiat but by engendering, reinforcing, and supporting *wanting* to read. That is as true for teachers as it is for their students. Directives have limited value, if they have any value at all. Having the power and authority to require a practice or an attitude or a value to be verbally proclaimed fuels resistance and unexpressed resentment. As a colleague said to me, "We need more directives and policies the way we need a hole in our heads." She was one of those rare principals who knew the difference between influence and power, between wanting "your way" and dictating it. Educational reform has a surfeit of czars.

So where does one start? With school personnel? With preparatory programs for teachers and administrators? Both? I regret that I never dealt as clearly as I should have with these kinds of questions even though early on I knew that the failures of educational reform had their source, far more often than not, in the simplistic way these questions were posed and, therefore, in the course of action taken. The reason I did not write more clearly and in greater detail about these issues was my belief that I would not clarify them unless I developed—by myself and the writings of others—a theory of institutional change which would begin to answer the questions above. The strategy and tactics of interventions geared to achieve institutional change have to derive from what we have learned about institutions in general and schools in particular. If you were a psychotherapist, you would have learned in a one-on-one relationship by training and experience a variety of strategies and tactics you could employ to help troubled clients. You would know that each client is different in many ways and that your strategy and tactics must be guided by that obvious fact. But you would also know that how you think and act rests on a conception or theory of personality which purports to explain how people become what they are, interpret and react to the challenges and opportunities that come their way, the psychological mechanisms or defenses they might employ, and more, much more. It is a general theory that prepares you, warns you, that the next client you see is not a clone of previous ones and that in some ways, large or small, that uniqueness must inform how you think or act. Your theory of personality and its development is not a cookbook for action. (The difference between a good and a bad cookbook is that a good one leaves you in no doubt that you have to exercise judgment about quality of ingredients, the characteristics of your oven or cookware, personal taste in regard to herbs and spices, and so forth. Reading a recipe is easy; following the recipe requires using sight, feel, smell, and taste.) This is what William James meant a century ago when he said that teachers should not expect that scientific psychology can tell them how to teach, that however valuable such a psychology is for teachers, it is the *artistry* with which teachers use that psychology that is crucial. A psychological theory is a *general* statement about all people, it does not tell you how you should act with your next client or classroom.

I consider it axiomatic that all institutions share characteristics at the same time each is in some way unique. From one standpoint schools are monotonously similar, but no two are by any means identical. That is a glimpse of the obvious which, however, has enormous significance if your goal is to change either of them. And that, of course, is true if your goal is to change the school system in which both are embedded. What do we need to know about institutions that will alert us *for the purposes of action* to commonality and uniqueness? Is changing IBM and a school system unrelated both in theory and action? Is changing middle and high schools, in theory and action, uniquely different from changing elementary schools? Is changing the ways our military is organized totally unrelated in theory or action to changing schools? Is what we have learned about how to help individuals change in a one-on-one situation of no relevance to how we think and act in helping an institution change? Is it likely that one source of the failure of most educational reform efforts is precisely what apparently accounts for the relatively nonrobust outcomes in psychotherapy, namely, that different therapists have very different theories which have very different implications for action?

Differences in theory and therefore actions are differences that make a difference. If that is true, as I have long believed, it was for me a daunting task, one that would require years for me to clarify (at least to my satisfaction). That would be a full time job! To have taken on such a task would have made it virtually impossible to think through the implications of what I was learning about a variety of other issues: what makes for a context of productive learning, why students in middle and high school "turn off," the role of parents, how governance structure resists innovation, the feckless role of preparatory programs, the artistry inherent in teaching as a performing art, and other related issues. The reality was and is that in regard to these problems I was learning that the more you learn the more you need to learn, the more you want to learn. Besides, I was having an intellectual ball, the feeling that I was growing up, that what I thought I understood needed reexamination. And yet there was always that gnawing conclusion that educational reform was doomed, or its effects mightily diluted, by the absence of a comprehensive theory of institutional change. I did not and do not need to defend what I experienced and have written about. But I should have said and emphasized that when it comes to actions for change, intervention, and innovation, we are flying blind and we have no instruments. Each reformer has his or her conception of how institutions change and should be approached, and it may be literally true that none of them in their writings has spelled out those conceptions, leaving us where we have long been: unable to determine the relationship between outcomes and the conception of institutional change powering action strategies and tactics.

Outcomes never have one cause. When I have observed or read the write-up of a reform effort, the explanation of outcomes, however positive or negative, is given in terms of a variety of causes almost all of which, and sometimes all of which, occurred *after* implementation began. In terms of causes, let us assume that each cause and its consequences did play the role attributed to it. But causes have causes which may—I would say always do—reflect the reformer's implicit and explicit theory of institutional change, which antedated and informed the implementation or intervention process. When the reformer's conceptions about institutional change are hardly made explicit in the write-up, we have no way of judging why and how the causes which are reported derive from that preimplementation conception of institutional change. (That is the case both for positive and negative outcomes.) *As a result, not only do I conclude that the explanation of causes is incomplete or misleading, but I have nothing like a secure basis for how to proceed if I decided to replicate the reform effort.* How can you replicate what has not been described in fair detail? Let me give an example.

In *Charter Schools: Another Flawed Educational Reform?* (1998a) I spell out why I predict that, generally speaking, charter schools will fall short of their mark. What permitted me to make such a dour prediction even though in principle I am a partisan of the concept of a charter school? There were two reasons. The first was my direct experience with some charter schools and what I read or was told about charter schools from others who were creating or consulting to charter schools. The second and more galvanizing reason was that in 1972 I had written *The Creation of Settings and the Future Societies.* It was a book about how new settings are created. It was a very personal book deriving from, among other things, my creation of the Yale Psycho-Educational Clinic. In that book I describe the *predictable* problems confronting anyone who is creating a new setting. And basic to my argument was the importance of what I called the before-the-beginning phase, a phase in which the seeds of crucial problems find hospitable soil. There is very little about schools in the book. Charter schools were, in 1972, far below the horizon of the educational scene. So when in the early 1990s charter schools—a singularly excellent example of a new setting—appeared on the educational horizon, I asked and answered this question: Do these well-intentioned people know what they *predictably* will confront? My answer based on what I was observing and learning was *no.* The hearts of these people were in the right place, but their heads were devoid of any warnings about what predictably lay ahead when a proposed "new" institution departs from a traditional, large, powerful, antagonistic institution, a departure requiring those in the new setting to change their highly overlearned ways of thinking and acting. Before the first day the charter schools opened, they were already under stress and experiencing conflict within and beyond the confines of the creators. They did not have a working conception of institutional, interpersonal, and personal change.

I conclude this chapter with a series of questions that an educational reformer should ask before the implementation phase begins. They are questions, certainly not all the questions, a theory of institutional change will have to pose, interrelate, and answer. I ask the reader to consider the answers to these questions as relevant for a question which rarely occurs to reformers: What are the *minimal* criteria by which you will decide whether to proceed with a reform effort or, so to speak, forget it? Enthusiasm, a high level of motivation, a laudable desire to rectify or improve an unsatisfactory state of affairs, a vision of what can and should be—these, like love, are not enough, hence the astronomical divorce rate and dispiriting reform failures.

1. What is distinctively different about the setting in which you seek to effect a change? Are you prepared and do you have the time to determine, to some degree at least, who has formal power and those who have informal influence or power? What is the previous history of efforts to change that setting and with what consequences? For example, will you find out how much turnover in personnel there has been in recent years?

2. Do you have criteria and ways to determine the degree to which those who are the objects of change see a need for change? And by "see" is meant a willingness to participate after they have been explicitly informed about why the proposed change effort has the goals and characteristics it does and after providing them safety to ask questions and express reservations, puzzlements, and suggestions?

3. Have you built into the change process meetings or forums in which you and the participants review and assess what has happened or has been accomplished or not? If a participant (or participants) advocates a midcourse correction in the plan of action, will you be temperamentally able to consider and discuss such suggestions? How will you judge whether the suggested changes in effect subvert the purposes of the changes you seek? What are the criteria for deciding the difference between acceptable and unacceptable compromise? Have you considered what you will do in the event you decide you should cut bait rather than continue to fish in muddied waters?

4. Because you know, you certainly should know, that one source of failure of a reform effort is that a person in a key role—such as the principal or superintendent—has decided to leave, what agreement should you seek that gives you a role in selecting a replacement?

5. Given the above questions, and assuming that you have dealt with them conceptually and realistically, do you have the funding, personnel, and time to do justice to the implications of these questions?

As I said, these are *some* of the questions which the reformer has to pose and answer before the process of change begins. More correctly, these questions represent the initial stage of the change process, and I would say the most fateful one because it illuminates the degree to which the reformer understands how complex the process is and will be. Although in my writings I have emphasized how complex the process is (conceptually and interpersonally), I did not discuss it in the comprehensive detail it requires, even though all along I knew it was one of the two most basic issues, the other being a framework for comprehending the culture of the school. Schools are not unique institutions, they are different types of settings. You can have a most comprehensive theory of institutional change, but how you use or adapt it depends on the institution of your interest and how well its culture, organization, and history are understood.

The questions above have at least one thing in common: *At every step of the change process, time is a crucial variable.* As I have experienced, observed, and read about change efforts, time and time perspective may well be the variables most unrealistically judged and planned for. As one reformer put it to me, "At the beginning of the change process I knew that time was a problem, but it was not until the change process began did this relatively nonobtrusive problem become an unrelenting one that subverted what I was after. Time became an implacable enemy whereas at the beginning I regarded it, say, as a friend I could count on. Was I ever wrong."

Engaging in this self-scrutinizing memoir revealed to me how right he was and how incompletely I had written about it. I could console myself with the thought that given the time and resources I had to devote to matters of educational reform, I could not expect to be able to identify and do justice to all or even most of the important aspects of reform. I do not need that kind of consolation. I always knew that I was playing to what I considered my strengths and, all things considered, I think I made the right choice for me. What I did not understand is that when you are playing to your strengths, you are, implicitly or explicitly, acknowledging your weaknesses.

What should not go unnoticed is that the current emphasis on staff development did not come from teachers. Indeed, the words "come from" are misleading because it obscures the fact that it was *mandated* by state departments of education, which were pressured by legislatures and/or governors frustrated by poor educational outcomes. So, it was not that teachers desired more professional development, but they were required to obtain more. There is, of course, a world of difference between wanting to learn more and being required to do so. And that difference has to manifest itself in better outcomes, and those outcomes have not been studied, let alone demonstrated. Unless my experience is very atypical, most teachers look upon staff development seminars, workshops, and courses the way they look upon preparatory programs: uninteresting rituals that have the virtues of continuing their license to teach or to receive an increase in salary. The law of staff development is honored but not its spirit. That should not be surprising because one of the egregious shortcomings of preparatory programs is their failure to instill in their candidates the moral obligation to view teaching as a growth process in which one willingly seeks new knowledge and skills that not only will benefit students but also the self-regard of the teacher who otherwise will wither on the vine of routine. And when one considers that the culture of the school supports such withering—it certainly does not counteract it—the charade of staff development continues. It is only in those exceptional instances where teachers have themselves collegially taken the initiative to learn more to expand their skills and horizons that I have seen the opposite of an empty ritual. I know I run the risk of sounding like a broken record when I say that if we do not radically transform how preparatory programs select and train teachers, educational reform will be an endless, self-defeating affair, and prevention an alien concept.

Chapter 8

Failure of Nerve: Or, Why Bang Your Head Against the Wall?

To explain the meaning of this chapter's title I start with an article by James Traub which appeared in the *New York Times Magazine* on January 16, 2000. The title of the article is "What No School Can Do." The cover of the magazine shows a child entering a school and in the middle of the cover is emblazoned the words "Schools Are Not the Answer." On the first page of the article, above its title and in crimson type is the following: "A child is in an inner city school for only so many hours. It's the rest of the day—as well as the rest of the neighborhood—that's the big influence and the problem."

Traub is explicit that the inner-city milieu he describes is representative of virtually every big city in this country. Though for 35 years we have poured billions of dollars into inner-city schools, and though we have fiddled with practically everything we could have fiddled with, we have done almost nothing to raise the trajectory of ghetto children. Why say anything that could encourage children and parents who desperately need encouragement? After all, Traub notes, we know that some reforms work better than others.

Traub then comes to the point of his article. How much better, he asks, can "a better educational mousetrap" counteract the disadvantages ghetto children bring with them to the school door and return to at home? Traub acknowledges that others before him have raised similar questions. But he is "amazed" how much of political discourse is "implicitly predicated on the notion" that schools can counteract the effects of the conditions in which inner-city school children live. He castigates political leaders whose policies rivet on school reform as if the context of social and family living outside of the school will thereby be ameliorated, or improved, or counteracted. Traub discusses some of the major efforts at educational improvement and concludes:

> Head Start, Title I and a host of other programs have gone a long way toward proving one of Coleman's central claims, which is that money does not buy educational equality. Although the premise of many a crusading volume,

including Jonathan Kozol's "Savage Inequalities," is that ghetto schools have been allowed to rot, many of the most catastrophically failing school districts, like Newark's, spend far more money per student than do middle-class communities nearby. Labor economists have had a field day proving that school spending is not correlated with school achievement. And that desegregation never had nearly the academic effect its advocates hoped for shows that equality of educational opportunity is much more elusive than it once seemed to be. (pp. 55–56)

In the last section of his article Traub advocates for preschool and after-school programs that are staffed by well-trained teachers, which is not the case in Head Start, and in settings which are well equipped and visually stimulating, again not like so many Head Start settings. They would be modeled after some programs he has visited. He knows that even to do that would require expenditures political leaders would shrink from contemplating, let alone advocating. It is important to emphasize that what Traub advocates derives from his aim to have inner-city children of preschool age spend essentially a whole day in educational contexts which will be physically and socially stimulating, will put flesh on the bones of educational "readiness," and will provide the children reasons to embrace a future that can be dramatically different than the present in which their families are mired. And it will also inculcate and engender personal values without which intellectual and social development cannot withstand the baleful influences of their neighborhood.

Traub deserves credit for saying out loud that money is not an answer. He also deserves credit for saying that preschool programs for the inner city are qualitatively poor and ineffective. And I understand why his assessment of the educational reform movement compels him to come up with an encompassing all-day school program that he hopes will reduce the influence of what these children see, experience, and absorb in their families and neighborhoods.

I have several criticisms of Traub's article, but since this is a book of my own mistakes, I shall restrict myself only to those criticisms of Traub which are relevant to the purposes of this book. For example, it took me more than a decade (1960–1975) to see the obvious: Educational reform would go nowhere even if more money, much more money, would be spent. But unlike Traub's, the reason for my conclusion was not that the educational mousetraps employed were faulty and we needed a better one. Nor was my conclusion relevant only to inner-city schools in which I had spent a lot of time. Granted that inner-city schools were especially ineffective, my conclusions applied to and were based on experience in suburban schools where reform efforts were notable for their lack of success. Test scores in suburban schools are dramatically higher on average than in inner-city schools, a fact which, together with "personal safety," lull people to conclude that all is well in suburbia. (In recent years extreme or murderous violence has been more frequent in suburban schools.) Just as inner-city children lose interest in and motivation for learning as they go through the grades, the same is true in suburbia. If you believe that it is the purpose of education to stimulate and sustain motivation for learning, you have cause to worry about suburban schools, unless the only thing that is important to you is test scores. But people who think that way think very differently when it comes to inner-city schools where test scores are abysmal, motivation is low, and millions of children are in a trajectory leading to disappointment, disillusionment, and other untoward feelings that we know do not bode well for the society. My conclusion was (and is) that the modal American classroom (urban and suburban) lacked almost all of the features of a context of productive learning. The modal American classroom, especially in middle and high schools, is a boring, unstimulating place. I have written much about this, and I will not go over old ground. I mention it here because it is a point Traub does not recognize even though it is crucial for the effectiveness of the kind of program he outlines. I shall have more to say about this later in this chapter because if I am right about classrooms and contexts of productive learning, we are forced to take account of two other factors about which Traub says nothing: preparatory programs for educators and the role of parents in school learning.

The self-scrutinizing process compelled me to confront this question: Why did it take so long for me to come to see that what teachers said about parents was a myth? Granted that myths are not made of whole cloth, whatever bits of truth or experience they may contain are just that: bits. The fact is that professionals whose work requires contact with parents absorb in their training—either from what they have been told or observed when they have been supervised—how they should regard and respond to parents. Undergirding what they have learned in the training process is a conception of the professional's obligations, rights, and prerogatives. That is to say, a professional has obligations both to the profession as well as to those they seek to help. The boundaries of the professional's role are more, rather than less, clear and that is true for teachers, physicians, clinical psychologists, social workers, and so forth. Therefore, to be professional has meant you have something to profess and that something, that knowledge, cannot and should not be superseded by the knowledge of lay people or other types of professionals who do not have the knowledge you have. You do not become a physician so that you can treat illness and disease in the way a sick person thinks is appropriate; sick people do not have the knowledge the physician has. Similarly, you did not become a teacher so that you can teach in the way students and their parents want you to teach. Students and their parents do not have the knowledge and experience you possess and profess. After World War II ended and India was clamoring for independence from Britain, Winston Churchill self-righteously said, "I was not elected Prime Minister to preside over the dissolution of the British empire." Churchill was saying something second nature to professionals. "I did not become the professional I am to deny what I know, to let others who do not have my knowledge and/or professional obligations substitute their opinions or decisions for mine." Within a handful of years after World War II India declared and won its independence and historians then and now began to ask and study why Britain had been so insensitive to and ignorant of the depths of anger and resentment that had been building up in the people of India. The sources of that anger and resentment, the seemingly unbridgeable cultural gulf between the people of the two countries, the British view that the mass of the Indian people were "primitive" and incapable of self-rule, that they were like children who needed forceful direction—all of this and more have occupied historians and novelists.

Something similar has happened after World War II between teachers, physicians, and the populations they served. It's a complicated and fascinating story, but what is most relevant in it for my present purposes is the fact that the authority and stance of the two professions were challenged. Before World War II these were highly respected and even revered professionals whose decisions were, so to speak, law. Patients very rarely challenged a physician's knowledge and prescribed action; they asked few questions, would not voice their frequent inability to comprehend the medical jargon, and very few were secure enough to suggest the advisability of getting a second opinion. The physician was an Olympian figure, the patient was a mortal who followed instructions. To the physician that was the way things should be, the physician presided and decided, the patient obeyed and prayed. The two were not in doubt where power resided; inequality of power was right, natural, and proper.

It was not much different in the teacher-parent relationship, although beginning around the middle of the nineteenth century different immigrant and religious groups challenged, sometimes militantly, the knowledge, wisdom, and attitudes of educators toward them, their children, and their ethnic and religious affiliations. Let us not gloss over the fact that in those days educators very consciously saw it as their responsibility to tame and socialize the children of immigrants, to "Americanize" them, to make them as different from their families as possible. There has never been an immigrant group which initially (and for some time thereafter) was not regarded with disdain accompanied by the fear that the American social fabric would be weakened, if not transformed in very untoward ways. These clashes were between parent groups and educators; there is safety, courage, and power in groups. The individual immigrant parents approached teachers, when they approached them at all, with a mixture of respect, fear, and embarrassment, aware as the parents were that they were talking to a "real" American who spoke with obvious self-confidence, no accent, unalloyed decisiveness, and who expected the parents to take what the teacher said as gospel. If there was any advice the children of these parents heard at home, it was, "Do as the teacher tells you, whether you like it or not." Teacher knew best. There was only one opinion that mattered, that of the teacher who regarded it as right, natural, and proper. Just as in the preunion days the individual teacher was impotent to change salary scales—or anything else for that matter—the individual parents confronted a teacher who had reason to believe that what he or she had said to the parents would be supported by the principal and even those in higher levels of authority.

It was not that I agreed or accepted this traditional state of affairs but rather that I simply did not think about it. Neither of my immigrant parents ever set foot in my schools. In fact, I cannot remember ever seeing a parent there or parents of any of my friends. Matters were not helped any by my experience in a new state training school for mentally retarded individuals, placed charmingly and stunningly in the middle of Connecticut's rural nowhere, and with practically no public transportation. A child could only be admitted through a probate court, which meant that the state was the guardian and parents had no legal rights, they were supplicants. I was "taught" that parents were nuisances, basically ignorant of their child's condition and needs; parents were to be treated courteously, to be informed, but kept at a distance, an unbridgeable distance from any decision making about their child. One third of the residents were from urban ghettos, and their parents were regarded as uneducated, uneducable, simple folk not much above the intellectual level of their offspring.

During the years I carried out research on test anxiety in elementary school children, I rarely saw a parent in the schools. There were PTAs whose members arranged money-raising events for activities school personnel considered helpful. It was *verboten* that the PTA intrude in any way into educational policy and practice. I am referring here only to "middle-class" schools where parents were highly educated and apparently grateful that they were doing something school personnel deemed helpful.

In the case of inner-city schools it was a different story: For all practical purposes there was no PTA; a handful of parents would come to a meeting. Why so few? The answer teachers gave to me went like this: "These parents are uneducated. They don't appreciate the importance of schooling, they are not interested in or able to help their children, to motivate or oversee them. If you ask them to come in to discuss a problem their child is manifesting, many times they will not come in, and give no explanation. We see the children becoming just like their parents. No one appreciates what we are up against." What the words in this message do not convey are two things which set me thinking. The first was their derisory, demeaning import, a total insensitivity to what ghetto residents were "up against," as if they willed the lives they lead, as if the stereotypes employed to describe them should be accepted as explanation, as a dispassionate depiction of social realities. I did not need introductory lectures on racism and stereotyping. As a Jew, I had experienced this way of thinking and had long felt kinship to Blacks. But I had never heard the message expressed so openly, so near unanimously, so insensitively. But it was the second thing in the message that began to open my eyes to something I had never thought about because I had never systematically spent time observing classrooms. My purpose was to observe certain high- and low-test-anxious students, not teachers (except secondarily). It was impossible for me to avoid the judgment that most (not all) teachers were unmotivated, unmotivating, psychologically dense, unable or unwilling even to try to find out what was going on in the minds of their students. In effect, *they were acting and reacting to their students in ways similar to how they said parents acted and reacted to their children.* The message teachers gave to me was an "explanation" for the low performance of students; it excused the poor performance of the teachers. It was an instance of the self-fulfilling prophecy: You start with low expectations, and you respond in ways guaranteed to confirm low expectations. (I will discuss this point when I turn again to Traub's article.)

If I was becoming somewhat more sensitive to these issues, candor requires that I acknowledge that I still was not making "connections" with another development of which I was aware and which came to have an enormous impact on American schools, all schools. I was aware of the development because it was occurring in the field of mental retardation, in which, of course, I had a special interest. It was not a development I predicted. I had too much unlearning to experience for me to begin to see quickly the world of parents and schools in a new light.

In the very early 1950s a very small group of parents of mentally retarded individuals met to create the National Association of Retarded Children (NARC) in order to give voice to their frustration, anger, and powerlessness in regard to the callous attitudes and policies of school personnel affecting mentally handicapped children of school age. It was not unusual for schools to deny admission to many of these children, to segregate them in a room as far from the rest of the school as possible, and to offer a program which was a caricature of "education." Some schools had the chutzpah to label the room the "Opportunity Room." (In my elementary school there was such a labeled room in the basement near the boiler room.) When the spanking new Southbury Training School opened in late 1941, some surrounding towns and cities closed these rooms and happily sent the children to the new institution, not only getting rid of children they never wanted but shifting the costs to the state; they could make "better" use of the money they would save. In its first 2 years after its opening my wife (also a psychologist) and I fought unsuccessfully against this dumping; the standard argument against our efforts—stated boldly in probate court papers—was: These children would be more educable and happier if they were with "their own kind." And the largest subgroup of "their own kind" was Black, and the next largest came from very poor rural areas. To me it was a moral, professional, legal problem because so many of these children were not retarded, they were seen by the schools as behavior problems (an old story). I gave little thought to their parents.

Several years after I left Southbury, the NARC was formed and in little more than a decade became a potent lobby in the state and national corridors of power. The NARC was created by middle-class parents, very highly educated ones. They had come to the conclusion that schools on their own would never change their oppositional stance, they would have to be forced to change by legislative action. And that is what happened, culminating in the mainstreaming legislation of 1975.

The point of this story is that I had been insensitive to the depths of anger these parents felt toward educators. If my eyes were opening wide, I still did not make the connection to what school personnel said about ghetto children and their parents. By the time I started the Yale Psycho-Educational Clinic in the early 1960s I had made the connection: Ghetto parents *had* to view educators with fear and anger which were cloaked in a surface passivity. It reached unambiguous overt expression in the sizzling 1960s in what legitimately could be called a culture war, one that is far from over. Having made the connection before that war truly became hot, I witnessed and participated in that war, aided by as bright, socially committed, activist colleagues as one could find.

Some readers of this book were too young (or not yet born) to understand either the depth and dimensions of the bitter feelings of parents of retarded children or the volcanic explosion of feelings of ghetto parents. And they will have difficulty comprehending how psychologically unprepared school personnel were in reacting to what was happening. So let me relate a long meeting I had with the executive director of a national organization advocating for improved services for children with physical, mental, and neurological impairments. I met him a year or so after the 1975 mainstreaming legislation was passed by Congress. He played a very important role in how that legislation was written, especially the sections having to do with the role of parents in decision making. That legislation was the first time ever that the rights of parents were spelled out in very concrete terms. How come, I asked, that the rights of parents were spelled out in such detail and were approved by Congress? Paraphrased, here is what he said: "You are referring to what we, the different parent groups, called the civil rights section of the bill. There was one thing about which we would not compromise and that was that no longer would school personnel be allowed to make a decision unless (1) the parent had been informed and present at a decision-making meeting, (2) the parent agreed with the decision, and (3) if the parent did not agree, that parent was told that he or she could resort to a series of appeals both within and beyond the school system. Why did we insist on that process? We were not ignorant of educational history; we had no reason to trust school people to act in accord with the letter and spirit of the law, no one was rolling out the welcome mat for us. We were sending a message: no more unilateral decision making for handicapped children, whether or not their parents were White, Black, rich, poor, or any other category."

I had already read the legislation. I made it my business to observe some of these decision-making meetings, and I had talked with numerous school psychologists, social workers, teachers, and principals who had responsibility for and participated in the placement meetings mandated by the legislation. I also knew that a few educational researchers were already observing, recording, and videotaping such meetings (Sarason & Klaber, 1985). As one would expect, school personnel tried hard to observe the letter of the law but in subtle and not so subtle ways were mightily uncomfortable reflecting the spirit of the law. They were not used to sharing power, they were the *professionals*; parents lacked knowledge and experience, they were partisan and subjective, and they had no basis for challenging the methods and conclusions of professionals.

To me, the stance of the educators was historically understandable. After all, the name, rules, conduct, and goals of the game had changed with the strokes of a presidential pen. Unlearning what everything in your professional past has instilled in you is no easy task, but in the type of situation I am discussing little or no unlearning can take place unless a conscious effort is made to be sensitive to what a parent is experiencing in a room of upwards of seven or eight people, an intimidating phalanx of professionals who know and work together, while the parent may know one or two of them. Not many parents have the courage and articulateness to represent their feelings and ideas. And what if you are Black, poor, not highly educated, very much aware of what you feel to be an unbridgeable gulf? You cannot legislate empathy for school personnel who in their training were not exposed for even 5 seconds to how you talk to parents, how you should try to understand the parent who is and should be expected to be "emotionally involved" with their handicapped child.

Thus far in this chapter I have tried to indicate why I had so much to unlearn about the role of parents in schools. I began to write about it in almost every book I have written in the past 25 years, especially in *The Predictable Failure of Educational Reform* (1990b) and *The Case for Change: Rethinking the Preparation of Educators* (1993a). Even so, I felt something was missing in my arguments, some basic principle that went far beyond the educational arena. It is ironic that the principle I was seeking was contained in two events I had discussed in almost every one of my books on education: the Declaration of Independence and the Constitutional Convention of 1787. It would be more correct to say that there was one principle and one fact rooted in history. The historical fact of which the founding fathers were acutely aware (quite an understatement) is this: Those who are given or seize power tend to seek to extend the reach and strength of their power, to ignore or circumvent or run roughshod over those with less power; power is a corrupting psychological virus. How to constrain such an abuse of power? How to structure a government that would protect and preserve the liberty and rights of people? Those two questions were center stage throughout the drama of the convention. The principle was also a political one: When decisions are made that would affect the people, the people should stand in some relationship to the decision-making process. "Taxation without representation" pretty much says it all. The Constitutional Convention is a high-water mark in human history precisely because it enunciated a political principle to counteract what is an indubitable fact in human history: the abuse of power. Here I was referring constantly to the Constitutional Convention and not seeing how the political principle applied to the relationship between parents and school. It was when I made the connection that I wrote *Parental Involvement and the Political Principle* (1995). I should have made the connection much earlier. What I most regret is that when I wrote *The Culture of the School and the Problem of Change* (1971) my thinking about parents and schools lacked clarity and focus. But what if at that time I had made the connection and wrote about it in that book? Would it have made any difference in, had any impact on, the educational reform movement? That question brings me to the question which is the title of this chapter.

I have long been a critic of educators, and by educators I mean those who daily are, so to speak, in the trenches. And I have always, and I do mean always, made it clear that educators were victims, and in several ways. The first, of course, is that like everyone else (including me) they have absorbed attitudes, stances, and ideas reflective of a distinctive country at a particular time in a particular era. They did not will the blatant inadequacies of schools, nor could they examine and understand the possibility that they were part of the problem and not part of a solution. Granted, there are always a few individuals who sense or grasp their victimhood; they are so few in number because of the force of tradition, narrow training, and the culture of schools, all of which combine to undermine the tendency to think "outside of the box." I am reminded (again) of Wertheimer's (1945) account of how in a geometry class the teacher was explaining how to solve the parallelogram problem. When Wertheimer met with a group of these students, he asked if they could think of another way to solve the problem. They could not. He then showed them another way. The students were taken aback and then said that Wertheimer's way was wrong, that the teacher's way is the right way. One problem, one solution, alternatives are given short shrift. The students were not being contentious or oppositional, they were thinking the way they were taught to think. None of us is exempt from this kind of victimhood. That is something that critics of educators seem incapable of understanding, which is why their criticisms are directed demeaningly to the limited intelligence or rigid personalities of educators, as if the problem exists "in" teachers, all else is secondary, noise. Such criticisms have the virtue *for the critics* that they do not have to confront the possibility that *they* may be thinking within the confines of the box, which makes life easier but at the expense of recognition of societal and institutional realities.

Long before I truly understood the issues surrounding parent-school relationships I had already concluded that the educational reform movement would go nowhere. I said as much in all of my books but usually couched in terms that suggested or conveyed to readers some glimmer of hope; not optimism, just hope. It was not until 1997 when I wrote *How Schools Might Be Governed and Why* that my pessimism was unambiguously expressed. The subtitle of that book could have been "Why the Existing Governance Structure of Schools Should Be Abolished."

I had a longstanding dilemma. On the one hand, I did not want to be perceived as a damning, unsympathetic, Ivy League professor who did not have a kind word to say about educators, who was a self-appointed prophet of gloom and doom. On the other hand, I could not bring myself to express the strength of my conviction about how inadequate educators were in thinking about and reacting to the problems they confronted. Over the decades I have had countless opportunities to talk to and interact with teachers and administrators. They would listen respectfully to my criticisms, more than a few would agree with me, but I had no reason to expect that they would ever move to action. They would ask very few questions. I would leave these occasions asking myself, "Why should I expect that what I said would stimulate them to some form of action? I show up, they listen. I talk about student disinterest, the differences between contexts of productive and unproductive learning, the stifling culture of schools, the huge gulf between what educators learn in preparatory programs and the realities of schools, that teachers cannot create and sustain contexts of productive learning for students if those kinds of contexts do not exist for teachers, which clearly they do not. Why should I expect them to absorb, struggle with such ideas? After all, it took me years to unlearn a lot of conventional wisdom and conceptual garbage."

I admit that there were more than a few times when I found myself having semimurderous reactions to the intellectual passivity of the members of these groups, their lack of curiosity, their almost total ignorance of the literature in their field. The minimal conditions simply did not exist for words and concepts to inform action. There is a maxim among psychotherapists: A person does not improve *in* the therapeutic hour but rather *between* therapeutic hours. Absent action, words are but temporary sounds in the air. As I said before, I write because for me it is only when I take pen to paper that I think, otherwise I am only existing. Writing is a form of action for me. I have no reason to believe that my written words lead to action.

I am not (I am told) an aggressive person. I do not like "to take people on." I much prefer to avoid confrontations. I like people, and I want them to like me. I sometimes wonder whether these personality characteristics have prevented me in my talks and writings from being as forthcoming in my criticisms as I should have been, whether I did not have the nerve to say to people that unless they initiated and took responsibility for action they not only deserved caustic criticism but the charge of professional irresponsibility. To understand all is not to forgive all. Was it a failure of nerve on my part that I refrained from stating clearly to educators that if they did not take responsibility for action, there would be others who would, others who had never heard of Mencken's caveat that for every important problem there is a simple answer that is wrong? Was it a failure of nerve on my part? There are days I think it was, and there are days when I think otherwise.

The poignancy of my dilemma was mightily exacerbated once my thoughts about parent-school relationships became clear to me. I am not sure I know all the reasons, but two were clearly at play. The first is that when I personally find myself having to deal with a layered, semifaceless, self-protecting bureaucracy, the members of which seem in no way to understand or even recognize my needs, feelings, or complaints, I have trouble containing my rage. That is especially difficult for me when I am told "rules are rules" and I have to conform. That is what many parents say about their encounters with schools and school systems. The second reason is that I have a short fuse (one that has rarely gotten lit) when school personnel describe a parent in stereotypic ways, thus putting them in categories which make the parent-school interaction impersonal and unproductive.

There is a third reason which derives from my interaction with educators in regard to how and why parents can be valuable resources in schools. Together with Elizabeth Lorentz, I have written three books on how and with what impoverishing consequences people generally—by no means only school personnel—define people as resources. When I have talked to school personnel about this issue, carefully giving concrete examples which I had observed or in which I had been a participant, it was as if I was talking in a foreign language. I stopped talking about it. Why keep banging your head against a wall? They were well-intentioned, hardworking, likeable people. But there was nothing in their experience (past or present) or training to dispose them to examine very overlearned ways of thinking and practicing. For example, I would make the point that parents know their children in ways teachers cannot know them and that that knowledge is or may be very relevant to how the teacher understands, reacts to, and teaches their children. Granted that what parents relate may be slanted, partisan, and even deliberately incomplete, does that mean that what the parents relate is totally irrelevant to you as teacher? Far more often than not, teachers would nod their heads in agreement. But then I would go on to ask: Are not *your* reservations and conclusions about their children also subject to similar reservations, perhaps to a lesser but still important degree? (What I could but did not say was that in too many instances the word *perhaps* did not apply, i.e., there were teachers who were egregiously subjective, partisan, and, yes, prejudiced.) Their heads would not nod in agreement, they clearly did not like what I said; I was another misguided, unsympathetic egghead.

I can assure the reader that there were and still are times when I ask myself: Can it be that I am out in left field in a game I do not understand and grievously misinterpret and judge other players? Am I a do-gooder who by definition wants to do good but simply does not, cannot, comprehend the complex reality such good intentions confront? Have I worn out my welcome? Should I stop banging my head against the wall? Not a wall of indifference, a wall of incomprehension. A wall built by victims who do not know, and would rather not know, the dimensions of their victimhood. Should I in the quiet of the night fold my tent and take off? Should I do what Senator Austin of Vermont said America should do at the height of the Vietnam War: Declare victory and leave? Obviously, I have opted to stay engaged even though I may mistakenly be tilting at windmills.

With all of the previous pages of this chapter as prologue, let me return to where I started: Traub's article "What Schools Cannot Do." Let me begin by saying that Traub's description of inner-city neighborhood life is totally correct (in my experience and opinion). He describes an ambiance schools did not create and about which public policies and legislative actions have been ineffective. In fact, without saying or intending so, Traub's article cannot but have the effect of dissuading any teacher from voluntarily seeking to teach in these inner-city schools unless his or her desire for burnout and masochistic satisfaction is inordinately strong, or they have been promised that after several years they will be transferred to a "better" school. That beginning teachers quickly leave these schools, seek employment elsewhere, or leave teaching as a career should occasion no surprise. Just as parents of these students are dispirited, passive, and overwhelmed, so are the teachers. Teachers can leave, parents cannot. Hopelessness rules, and it has no opposition.

But Traub is aware of two things. The first is that there are classrooms here and classrooms there, a school here and a school there, where hopelessness does not rule unopposed. The second is that urban school systems are not organized on principles that foster the recognition and spread of these classrooms and schools. The urban school system is a particularly clear instance of a non-self-correcting system. Traub does not hold out hope that the urban school system is part of the "solution." His pragmatic suggestions concern the preschool years and after-school programs, all for the purpose of counteracting ineffective parenting and iatrogenic neighborhoods. Why these programs should have their intended consequences Traub says little about, except to emphasize that the personnel for these programs will be well-trained professionals, not the inadequately selected, inadequately trained, and underpaid personnel in past and present programs. As I shall discuss later, his emphasis on professionalization is, by itself, a very frail basis with which to deal with some truly fundamental issues. I am no opponent of professionalization, but I have been too long in the game blithely to accept the assumption that the correlation between paper credentials and quality and effective performance is high.

What if Mr. Traub told me that he was going to write a paper with the title "What Can Schools Do?" and asked me how he might think about it. Where would I start and why? My response would go like this: "When you use the verb *do*, I assume you mean what educators can do to impact on the two groups to whom they have an obvious obligation. I refer, of course, to students and parents. If that is what you mean, you are on the well-paved road of disillusionment because you are identifying parents and students as the objects of change. To most people that sounds reasonable, but it is psychologically and conceptually horribly incomplete, really nonsense, because it requires accepting the assumption that teachers do not have to change, that they are not part of a pattern of causation. Not causation in any witting way but rather in the holding of beliefs they take as true, indubitably so, and in no need to challenge and scrutinize them. They are kin to axioms requiring neither proof or defense. So my starting point—one that educators will mightily resist taking seriously—is in the form of questions to educators: Can you entertain the possibility that you hold beliefs about inner-city students and parents that ought to be examined, not to be kept sacrosanct, as gospel."

So what about inner-city parents whom teachers (and Mr. Traub) see so negatively, so lacking in their ability to contribute to their children's education? Is it possible that such a view is, to a meaningful degree, unjustified? Do teachers unwittingly relate to parents in a way that has all of the consequences of the self-fulfilling prophecy? From what I have said earlier in this chapter and in others, I have concluded that teachers have engaged in the self-fulfilling prophecy, and until that way of thinking and doing begins to change, inner-city schools will not change.

However, having said that, I must go on to say that altering these beliefs, "doing" in a way consistent with new assumptions, is a frustrating, wrenching, patience-demanding, energy-depleting affair. *If that is true for teachers, it is no less true for parents who have never seen themselves as having a role in their children's school.* I observed this process over a 7-year period in connection with Paul Heckman's work in Latino schools in Tucson, which I mentioned in Chapter 4 and discuss later in this chapter. More recently I followed the process in Judy Primavera's Head Start program in Bridgeport. There are many more isolated examples. The point here is that it can be done but only after some unjustified assumptions are examined and unlearned.

Why is this unlearning so painful and difficult? The brief answer is that preparatory programs scandalously underprepare educators for how to think about and relate to parents. I use the word *scandalously* advisedly because the gross inadequacies of these programs guarantee that we will always be devoting our energies and billions of dollars to repair, as if prevention is an unaffordable luxury. As one administrator said to me, "Please don't talk to us about prevention. We cannot keep up with repair." One beginning teacher said to me after her first year, "I was prepared for the realities of this [inner-city] school as I was to go to the moon." I heard variants of that from countless new teachers.

There is a related issue, one that I have difficulty writing about dispassionately. It is no less an issue in suburban schools than in urban schools, but in the former its baleful consequences are ameliorated by the out-of-school pattern of stimulation and existence. Earlier in this book I quoted the poet Yeats: "Education is not about filling empty buckets, it is about lighting fires." Inner-city teachers neither fill empty buckets nor light fires, the minuscule number of exceptions aside. (Those exceptions may be few, but from the standpoint of what can be done their importance cannot be overestimated.) Inner-city classrooms extinguish interest, curiosity, and motivation; they are contexts of unproductive learning. I have written about this in all of my books, which is to say that I have repeated what William James and John Dewey said a century ago. I am a Johnny-come-lately in this matter. And the matter concerns two seamlessly intertwined factors: The psychological world of the developing child and a pedagogy that both recognizes and capitalizes on that world. I ask the reader to ponder this question: Why do parents of infants so eagerly (even anxiously) seek to recognize when the infant is responding to the external world in a more discriminating way than before, a way that bespeaks of expanded awareness and interest? Why do parents go happily bonkers when they see the infant's first smile? Why do parents greet the infant's first recognizable or semirecognizable word? The answer is, very briefly, that parents assume and expect that they have been *given* a window through which to glimpse the mind of that organism and, no less important, they now have a way, albeit a limited one, to capitalize on, to stimulate, to expand the range of the infant's repertoire of response. I italicize the word *given* in order to emphasize that a fundamental starting point in a context of productive learning is "where the child is or is coming from." That is the didactic artistry of the movie *Mr. Holland's Opus*. The first half of the film shows how well-intentioned Mr. Holland creates a context of unproductive learning. Then he has an encounter with one of his students who reveals what is in her head, where she is coming from, why she considers herself a helpless, hopeless music student. Unknowingly, she lit a fire in Mr. Holland's head. The second half of the film shows a context of productive learning. Mr. Holland gave up his treasured, traditional conception of learning. Mr. Holland learned what the British teacher knew and sang to the king's children in the movie *The King and I*: "Getting to know you, getting to know all about you."

I know that sounds corny, sentimental, romantic, unrealistic to many more than a few people, including teachers. Why? The answer is that such judgments are made by people who cannot comprehend, who have never been helped to comprehend, that teaching is an art, that it is not a rehearsed ritual, a set of prescribed rules, or a technical process which eliminates subjectivity, creativity, improvisation, the need to change course in midstream, to stop what you are doing and start all over again. I am, of course, in no way opposed to planning or developing strategies to accomplish goals. But I am opposed to planning and strategizing which renders a teacher insensitive to the possibility that he or she has lost an audience who has retreated to passivity, silence, and disinterest. A visual artist starts with sketches, a kind of "playing around" to work out problems of color, composition, and line that he or she knows will be encountered when beginning to paint. The number of sketches can be many, but it almost always happens that when beginning to paint, he or she sees problems that were overlooked or misunderstood. The visual artist is constantly adapting to what he or she sees "out there." The artistry of the teacher does not inhere in following a script; it inheres in how sensitive he or she has been and is to the individuality of the students who are the audience. How well has he or she gotten to know and to adapt to those individualities? That was what Mr. Holland initially did not comprehend. Parents with one child may have trouble comprehending it. Parents with more than one child have no trouble comprehending it.

Whenever I have discussed the artistry in teaching I get terribly frustrated and sad because I am so aware that language is inadequate to concretize for the reader (or listener) the artistry in teaching. That is why I was so taken with *Mr. Holland's Opus*. You literally could *see* the differences between contexts of productive and unproductive learning. For those who have not seen the film my verbal attempts to describe it are an inadequate substitute.

Teachers are victims of scandalously inadequate preparatory programs. Whatever changes these programs have instituted are, to be charitable, cosmetic and have been and still are mammothly ineffective. Of course, teachers need to have a firmer grasp of subject matter than they now have. Of course, increasing the length of practice teaching is long overdue. But these programs are virtually doing nothing in regard to two interrelated factors which crucially determine whether student learning is productive. The first has to deal with selection. Not everybody who wants to be a psychiatrist should be one. Not everybody who wants to be a clinical psychologist should be one. Not everyone who wants to be a leader, or manager, or administrator should be one. And not everyone who wants to be a teacher should be one. I have discussed this in my book *Teaching as a Performing Art* (1999). The second and related factor is that it is the obligation of preparatory programs to nurture and improve a candidate's comprehension of the personal-phenomenological nature of teaching as a performing art: its inevitable interpersonal features, the personal demands it requires, its respect for individuality, the soul searching it requires and the resistances to it, and above all having the criteria by which to judge whether you are filling empty buckets or lighting fires. In the bulk of American classrooms empty buckets are being filled, somewhat. And those who are filling them are victims. Let us not blame the victims. Not until we begin to take seriously that teaching is a performing art can we expect any improvement in educational outcomes.

Traub says nothing about these issues, leaving us with the impression that he regards urban schools as intractable to any meaningful change, although he is aware of schools where that is not the case. He is certainly correct when he asserts that characteristics of inner-city neighborhoods set very definite limits to what schools can be expected to do. That has long been obvious. But the incontrovertible fact is that these schools contain and are responsible for the education of children. Is he saying that the blatant inadequacies of these classrooms are the result only of conditions outside of schools? That it makes no difference whether teachers in these schools know the difference between filling empty buckets and lighting fires? That even if they knew the difference and were prepared to act consistent with it, it would be to no avail? Mr. Traub rightfully recognizes the stultifying role of the educational bureaucracy of urban school systems. But where did this bureaucracy come from, where were they prepared, why is that preparation tailor-made to administer schools that make a mockery of the concept of productive learning. Violinists say that the Beethoven violin concerto is not for the violin but against it. Preparatory programs are not for productive learning but against it.

Mr. Traub is making a mistake I made 30 years ago, a mistake it took me this long to recognize. I refer to the title of my 1971 book: *The Culture of the School and the Problem of Change*. The mistake inheres in the three times I use the word *the* in the title. The mistake is that it is egregious tunnel vision to think that you can describe and explain any classroom, any school, any local system apart from their embeddedness in an educational system comprised of stakeholders: teachers, administrators, boards of education; the local, state, and federal political agencies; parents; the state Board of Education; and the colleges and universities that prepare educators. The concept of a system engenders imagery of connected parts that work together to achieve an agreed-upon goal. And that imagery has the reassuring implication that if any part or parts malfunction, we will be able to identify the problem and fix it. What we call our educational system not only consists of poorly uncoordinated parts but also parts that are adversaries, on and below the surface. That has been and still is the case in the relationship between schools and preparatory programs. More correctly, that is the case between schools and a higher-education establishment whose opinions of educators and schools is a demeaning one, a variant of the master-peon relationship. What would be comedy, were it not tragedy, is that higher education looks down on its own products. I deliberately say higher education to make the point that it is not only colleges of education who hold teachers in low esteem; that attitude pervades the entire university. That explains why I wrote my last book *American Psychology and Schools: A Critique* (2001). I should have, could have, written that book years ago when the concept of system was becoming clear to me. I regret (very much) not having written it earlier because it concerns one historical tradition and one question. The nature of learning was, up until several decades ago, a dominant area of research in American psychology at the same time that the field had little interest in or relationship to education in general and schools in particular. The question was: How did that come about even though psychology's *potential* contribution to schooling could be significant, especially in regard to the selection and preparation of educators? I say potential only as an example of the more general point that the university has nothing resembling a sincere interest in schools. How can you have an interest in an arena about which you have no knowledge or experience and in which you have no desire to get involved?

Thinking about education in terms of a system is a daunting, even overwhelming, task if your goal is to intrude into it to initiate a change that has percolating effects. But you have to start somewhere on the basis of several criteria: (1) You have direct personal experience and knowledge of the starting point; (2) you know that past efforts, and those currently advocated, have or will fail; (3) whatever changes you will seek to effect center on, rivet on, the distinction between contexts of productive and unproductive learning, on the concrete approach and actions that distinction requires of educators; (4) however convinced you are about the choice of starting point, you know that you will encounter resistance in those whom you seek to help change; (5) you know you will make mistakes, but you are prepared to stay the course.

In the first half of my years of involvement in educational reform my "centering" point, my point of departure, so to speak, was the self-defeating ways reforms were being implemented. I was right, but incompletely so. In the second half I came to what in some ultimate sense is the most important problem: distinguishing clearly between what creates and sustains contexts of productive and unproductive learning. You can require teachers to take all the courses in the catalogue, you can increase the length of the school day and year, you can set standards for promotion, you can institutionalize site-based management, you can initiate a voucher program, you can set up charter schools, you can involve parents, you can reduce class size, you can increase teacher salaries, you can double public expenditures—you can do any or all of these but unless at every step of the way you are judging what you do by a clear picture of the features of a context of productive learning you are shortchanging students. You have to have a first principle, a ruling principle. If you forget that, you are doing, not thinking.

Traub's article is an instance of misplaced emphasis, by which I mean that in riveting on what schools cannot do (and do not do) he cannot explain why, when schools here and there do what he (we) would like them to do, the systems in which they are embedded are unable or unwilling to support the process by which they can spread to other schools. To indict bureaucracy is justified but too superficial. Indeed bureaucracy is a symptom of the bankruptcy of ideas and vision in reaction to which moral imperatives are swamped by pathological concern to appear rational and in control. Damage control becomes the name of the game whose guiding rules are spin and hype. Let me elaborate by an example which I have personally observed over a period of years.

As noted earlier, for 7 years I observed a reform effort by Paul Heckman to transform a school in Tucson that had all of the features of the type of urban school Traub describes. The first published report of that effort is *The Courage to Change* by Heckman (1995) and the teachers in that school. A second report is by Vikki Monterra (1996). A comprehensive report by Heckman will be forthcoming in the next couple of years. What I found both remarkable and inspiring was the radical change that occurred in the relationship between teachers and parents, who had heretofore been regarded as without assets for and interest in the education of their children. There is much more to the effort than that, and the interested reader should read what is already available. The point I wish to make is that school was transformed despite the school system. If it were not for one very atypical administrator who "protected" the school against its critics, it is unlikely that the reform effort would have been as effective as it was. The important point is that the officialdom of the system did not see how or why it was in its self-interest to seek ways to spread the rationale of that effort to other schools. What happened at that school is what Traub would have approved at the same time that he would have had to agree that the poor, dispirited, crime-ridden, immigrant community had assets contradicting the conventional myth of countless deficits. It is when teachers begin to view and act differently toward the parents that things began to happen. I consider it a glimpse of the obvious to say that school systems are not self-correcting systems. But I also consider it obvious that officialdom of school systems are sincere in saying that they spend their days correcting one or another sore spot in the system. *What they are totally blind to is that they are always correcting the ideas, practices, and values of those below them in the hierarchy.* The possibility that "the enemy is us" is alien to their thinking; they are exempt from the ethos of self-correction. *They direct blame to incompetent, or unimaginative, or misguided teachers just as teachers view ghetto parents and their community as mammoth obstacles to the education of their children.*

Let me hasten to say that the kind of urban ghetto Traub describes is, to say the least, dispiriting and psychologically and materially destabilizing. To claim otherwise is more than stupid. But that is no warrant for saying that those parents are without assets in furthering and improving the education of their children. If you *assume* they have no assets, and you relate to them as if they have no assets, they will display no assets: The self-fulfilling prophecy is alive and well! This does not mean that if we unimprison ourselves from certain myths, schools can overcome all or most of the consequences of the deficits of ghetto existence. What it does mean is that we should feel morally obligated to improve what we can to the degree that we can. Traub gives up on these schools, and in doing so he is making two mistakes. The first is he gives support to the myth that ghetto parents are a large part of the problem and have little or nothing to contribute to a solution. The second mistake is that he does not take what he says seriously. If our urban school systems, especially their ghetto schools, are as unrescuable as he seems to believe, what makes him think that they will not subvert the positive effects he assumes will derive from the preschool and after-school programs he proposes?

I have gone on record as saying that schools in their current structure or form cannot serve the overarching purpose of stimulating and sustaining wanting to learn, continuing to want to learn because of the lure of new intellectual horizons. I have no reason to change my mind.

Chapter 9

"Cloning" a Reform Effort

On the first page of the *New York Times* for August 16, 2000, the headlines of a long article is " Seeking to Clone Schools of Success for Poor." The article describes several well-known educational reform efforts. The thrust of the article is clearly stated in relation to one such effort, the story of the Knowledge is Power Program (KIPP).

> As the national political debate focuses on the question of how to raise achievement among poor and minority children, KIPP, founded five years ago by a pair of young Ivy Leaguers, has drawn keen attention from left and right, idealistic do-gooders and entrepreneurial free-marketeers. Honored last year by the liberal Children's Defense Fund, the school was highlighted at last month's Republican National Convention, where its pupils were on stage, rapping, "Read, baby, read."
>
> Now, in an unprecedented effort to turn a boutique school success story into a national network, Donald G. and Doris Fisher, the owners of the Gap clothing chain—who know something about building a franchise—have given $15 million in seed money to create hundreds of KIPP clones across the country.
>
> "If you can replicate the success of KIPP at a bunch of places, and eventually on a scale that cannot be dismissed by lots of excuse-making, do you end up forcing change on the larger system?" asked Scott Hamilton, director of the new KIPP Foundation, which will train teachers to open charter schools in KIPP's image. "Our hope is the answer is yes."
>
> Successful schools for the poor have long been written off as wildflowers in the educational desert that dominates their neighborhoods—mirages or miracles, but dubious prospects for portability. Their outstanding results were chalked up to the local context, support from private donors or the particular brilliance of a dynamic leader.

The article was of special interest to me for two reasons. First, in all my writings I have pointed out that in our educational systems innovations do not spread; the structure and culture of schools are inimical to spread. The reasons are historical, institutional, systemic, attitudinal, and (not least of all) conceptual. It is also a problem that requires taking the obvious seriously, a point about which I shall elaborate shortly.

The second reason the article was of interest to me was that I had seen several videos showing the two young founders of KIPP teaching their classes. I reacted to what I saw in precisely the same way I did to Liane Brouillette's written description (see Chapter 11) of Direct Instruction in the Wesley elementary school in Houston: The two young men were passionate, committed, supportive, and motivating, and they lit fires in their young students. I did ask myself this question: Since the Wesley and KIPP schools were in Houston, and the Wesley school long antedated the KIPP schools, had the latter known about the former or were they unknown to each other, an instance of what the newspaper article said was, so to speak, the $64,000 question for which educational reform had no answer and which had too long been ignored? The odds were, I decided, that KIPP did not know about Wesley.

Let me begin with a personal example because it is one I know best and it is one that illustrates how easy it was for me to ignore the importance of spread or cloning both as a conceptual and practical problem. I started the Yale Psycho-Educational Clinic in 1961–62. As I describe in my autobiography (1988), the clinic was by conventional criteria regarded by many people as an unusually successful venture. However, it took me more than two decades—during which time I was more than an observer of the reform movement—to realize that I had neglected to note in my writings several things which the readers needed to know if they were considering creating a similar type of setting. That I and my colleagues very much wanted others to create such settings goes without saying. We wanted to be influential beyond Yale and the clinic, which was intended to exemplify the potentialities of a community psychology which then did not exist. Now, a community psychology obviously requires a knowledge and understanding of the community in which you seek to be helpful, to make a difference, to be responsive. Despite their many similarities, communities have distinctive and often idiosyncratic characteristics shaped by their history and ecology. New Haven, Bridgeport, Hartford, Stamford, New London are all Connecticut cities, but each is very different from the others in a variety of ways. In short, you have to know the territory. Here is what I failed to say in almost all publications that came from the clinic as well as in what we told visitors or audiences we were invited to address.

1. I came to Connecticut in 1942 as a psychologist in a new state institution for mentally retarded individuals. I met many people and learned a lot about how the state operated. The nature of my position exposed me to the workings of school systems, especially those in cities from which our residents came.

2. I came to have an adjunct appointment in the Yale department of psychology and pediatrics. I learned a lot about New Haven long before I had a full time appointment at Yale. And by knowing a lot I mean that I came to know many people in the human services and medical communities.

3. When I moved to New Haven in 1945, my social and professional networks thus became larger and more varied, including as it did many non-Yale individuals, some of whom "taught" me a great deal about town-gown relationships (mostly conflictful) and New Haven's political culture and power structure (informal and formal).

4. For 15 years before the clinic started, I carried out a research program in the schools in New Haven and surrounding communities. Especially in regard to New Haven my experience in the schools contributed mightily to my understanding of how things did or did not get done, which individuals or groups had formal or informal power.

5. I learned that being a Yale professor had its pluses and minuses if you sought to do anything which could be interpreted as an instance of imperial Yale exploiting the city for its narrow purposes and giving nothing in return. From the standpoint of town people, Yale was in but not part of New Haven. Learning this was probably one of the two or three crucial factors contributing to the quality and quantity of relationships the clinic developed in New Haven. So, when I made contractual relationships with city schools and agencies, they did not include overhead, a budget item Yale (and other universities) add for administrative expenses in monitoring the contract. I was told by a Yale budget officer that the contract had to provide for an overhead item. I balked. I wrote him a two-page, single-spaced letter in which I said that since the contracts allowed us to work with schools and agencies serving New Haven's poverty populations, I considered it monumentally insensitive to require an item for overhead, an addition that would further reinforce negative attitudes to the university and might even cause the schools and agencies to cancel the project. After an exchange of letters, and one not-so-polite meeting, I got my way.

6. The town-gown relationship was of the love-hate variety and that meant that if I wanted to meet anyone in any officialdom, I could count on such a meeting taking place. The fact is that by the time the clinic started I was part of numerous networks among which there was almost always an individual who not only could arrange meetings for me but would testify that I did not meet the stereotype of the socially insensitive, aloof, unknowledgeable professor who did not know what the real world was like. Someone once said I was a born exploiter of personal, social, and institutional networks. I do not buy the word *born*, but it is true that I belonged to a fair number of intersecting networks which I was never reluctant to use for my purposes or for those I sought to help.

7. It was crucially important that Connecticut is a small state. Although it is an exaggeration to say that if you sneeze in one part of the state you hear it in other parts, the fact is that for a person with my interests and extroverted social style I had since 1942 come to know scads of people and agencies in the state. I had a good idea of who was doing what, where, and why. My phone bill has always been on the high side. Staying in touch is important to me.

Without knowledge of the above points it is, in my opinion, impossible to understand how the Yale Psycho-Educational Clinic was created and developed. (There are other points, but enough is enough.) If you had read what we wrote and were of a mind to create a similar setting, you would be in trouble. That does not mean, of course, that what you cloned is not equally worthy and successful. In such a case we should be grateful even though we know they are different in important ways which we hardly understand. But such cases are far less in number than those which are discernibly less successful; they rarely get reported, or if they do, they do not provide the kinds of information which could allow us to explain success or failure, partial or complete.

Is the metaphor of cloning appropriate to education reform? It is appropriate as long as we keep two things in mind. The first is that unlike cloning in lower organisms, it is impossible literally to clone what was demonstrated with one organized group in one place embedded in a larger surround to which it belongs. The demonstrated reform may have taken place in one classroom, or one school, or one school system. In each instance I shall assume the demonstration has been judged successful and that an effort will be mounted to spread or apply the reform to other similar settings. No educational reformer seeks, so to speak, to hide his or her light under a bushel. They want other settings to benefit from what they have demonstrated, and well they should. But I feel secure in stating categorically that no reformer expects that his or her attempts at cloning will be other than an approximate replication, not literally cloning. In the course of the *initial* demonstration, the reformer has already and quickly learned that not everyone in that demonstration contributed equally to outcomes. Reformers do not see themselves as cloners but as approximaters. And in the quiet of their nights reformers are not satisfied with their approximations. And they have good reason to regard cloning as a metaphor for the spread of reform as inappropriate, a reason wrapped up in the question, How come it became possible to clone sheep?

The answer has several parts. The most obvious part is that it took more than half of a century to achieve the goal. The second part, implied in the first, is that these decades were marked by countless efforts, most of them failures, to clarify and test knotty theoretical and technological problems and issues vital to understanding failure and giving directions to subsequent research. Understanding failure was a prerequisite to visions of success; failure was not disparaged, it was a spur for unlearning and new learning.

The third part of the answer I regard as instructive for educational reform; more specifically, why cloning is an inappropriate, even mischievous, metaphor for how reforms will or should spread. *I refer to the fact that the biological researchers—whether their efforts were failures or successes—always had control over choice of the substances they were studying, the techniques they employed, the manipulations they devised, and the organisms they used.* No educational reformer has ever had anything resembling such a degree of control if only because no one person or official or public agency or community would give the reformer such control. Indeed, there are laws which were enacted precisely to limit drastically what any researcher can do to and with people they seek to study, help, or change. Those laws reflected a backlash against research with humans where their rights, beliefs, interests, and preferences were not taken into account and respected. These laws aside, the reformer is always dealing with people embedded in organized systems within systems, people differing widely in power, personality, experience, age, and more. To talk about cloning an educational reform is to reinforce the imagery of an impersonal engineering process. It ludicrously oversimplifies what is involved in an effort to spread a reform. It mammothly obscures the fact that any noncosmetic reform in one site will inevitably engender resistance when applied to another site. And even if the resistance is weak or even absent, one can expect that because no two sites are anything like identical, the process and outcomes in the second site may be quite different in small or large ways; it may be the difference between success and failure, relative or absolute. And it is for the purpose of understanding and learning from success and failure that the history of cloning is relevant for educational reform.

In discussing the cloning of sheep, I emphasized the role and frequency of previous failures. Those failures were known and described, which is another way of saying that the role of this or that variable (and their interactions) contributing to success or failure gradually became more clear. A researcher may have reported a failure which then spurred him and other researchers to ponder whether it was due to some aspect of his method, mode of analysis, or faulty or incomplete interpretation of relevant theory and literature. The crucial point is that without adequate description of what was done and why, the chances that the failure can be scientifically meaningful and productive are very slight. Failures are expected, they are far from inherently worthless, they stimulate criticism and new thinking. The researcher who failed may never benefit from it; he chalks it up to the category "unproductive" failure. To another researcher who reads the published report, the failure may have a theoretical significance of which the failed researcher was and is unaware, a significance that opens new vistas. The crucial point is that without adequate description of what was done and why, the outcome of research is not interpretable. Let me illustrate this crucial point by a recent article about an educational reform that had polar opposite outcomes in two sites.

The article by David Hill appeared in the August/September issue of *Teacher* (2000). The title is "Punching Out." In bold print next to the title is the following: "Edison Schools Inc. offers its workers big paychecks and perks galore in return for long hours. But teachers in San Francisco say that the deal is no bargain and they are calling it quits. A report on the classroom culture of America's No. 1 for profit school company."

It is mystifying why Hill says he is reporting on the "classroom culture" because it is crystal clear that he is describing two cultures: A school culture and the corporate culture housed in New York. It is a clash of two cultures. The Edison company took over an abysmally chaotic and low-performing school; 2 years later all but 6 of 31 teachers resigned en masse because of a host of grievances the article discusses. The turnover rate for all Edison schools is 23%, while the national average for teacher turnover is 14%. For my present purposes it is not necessary to give the litany of teacher grievances contained in the article. Suffice it to say the school is a mess that no one in the school or corporate headquarters wanted or predicted. The article describes aspects of the disaster but does not attempt to identify the factors which might explain the disaster. Yes, from the standpoint of the teachers the hours and workload were horrendous, although it was made clear to the teachers that their salaries, higher than in other San Francisco schools, were compensation for longer work hours; and the teachers made it clear that corporate officials were grossly insensitive and unresponsive to the teachers' grievances. Interviews with the officials contained little or no explanation for why their relationship with the teachers went steadily downhill.

Hill was invited by the company to visit an Edison school in Denver which serves the same kind of poverty population and which opened at approximately the same time as the San Francisco school. Here is part of what Hill observed and reported.

> McCown suggested that I visit a school where Edison's vision of teaching is working, so I spent some time at Wyatt-Edison Charter in Denver. The school, housed in a beautifully restored 1887 building, opened its doors in 1998, the same year San Francisco turned over Edison Elementary to the Edison company. Both schools serve a predominantly poor, minority student body. But

when it comes to the teachers, the schools couldn't be more different. Most of those I met at Wyatt-Edison gushed about the company and its school design. We work hard, they all agreed, but there are ample rewards.

"It's a demanding school," third grade teacher Tera Gottbrath told me. She was sitting at her desk in her basement classroom the day after the school had closed for the summer. When I walked in, she was using her laptop computer Edison provides for them free of charge to teachers and students in grades three and above to tap into the company's Internet bulletin board for teachers. Edison has high expectations, she told me, and the workload is much heavier than at a regular teaching job.

This sounded like what I had heard in San Francisco, but then she added: "They treat you like a professional, and that's why it's worth it. Teachers have always gotten a bad rap for having it easy, for working just eight or nine months a year and being able to leave at 2 p.m. I feel that if we want to improve the reputation of the profession, we need to be putting more into it."

David Hill is an educational reporter, and a good one. He does not hold himself out as a diagnostician of the clinical or etiological variety. He describes what he sees and is told. He refrains from judgment. The questions we, the readers, ask about the article depends, of course, on our particular interests and experience. For example, if a geneticist stumbled on the article he might be reminded of research with twins: The two schools were born at the same time by the same parents; they should look like each other; they should have developed in highly similar ways; and if it is too much to expect that they should look more like identical twins than fraternal twins, clones so to speak, it is not too much to say that their differences as fraternal twins are far greater than one would have predicted. It is as if one of the fraternal twins is developmentally arrested, and the other, experiencing normal growth. What etiology could explain this? When did this developmental arrest begin, and what contributed to it? We know, the geneticist would say, that no set of fraternal or identical twins literally have the same environments or that each responds to each other or to the parents in the same way or that the parents respond to each of them literally in the same ways. Even so, how do we explain such vastly different offspring? What do we need to know to begin to clarify the puzzle?

Then there will be readers who will feel confirmed in their belief that just as church and state should be kept apart so should the private sector and the public schools be kept apart. It has been, they would contend, an old story that the private sector has been a baleful influence on how schools are organized and judged. We know, they would say, what the bottom line of the for-profit sector is and that it is no respecter of views that are not crassly materialistic and utilitarian. That one of the two schools seems educationally viable and productive is likely to cause that reader to pause and then to agree that, albeit it is one school, it does not confirm that reader's expectation. Does that not suggest that we should endeavor to find out why that school appears to be consistent with educational purpose with which that reader probably would agree? More to the point, the difference between the two schools are differences which have by no means been absent when card-carrying public educators from within and without the school arena have sought to apply a presumably successful reform from one site to another. On what basis can one assume that these reformers will succeed more often and fail less often than reforms carried out by a for-profit company?

It will be recalled that this chapter was stimulated by a newspaper article about how crucial it was to "clone" a number of educational reforms (including the Edison project) considered worthy of cloning. It has been historically the case that the educational reforms rarely spread, and the newspaper article contained statements of educators asserting that spreading those reforms was a top-priority policy and action issue. I did not read Hill's article on Edison until a week later and after I had begun writing this chapter. I immediately saw the connection between the two articles, and a number of questions raced through my mind, questions I had raised in most of my writings but which I had never really pursued or answered in concrete ways even though I had monotonously raised the questions. Let me now ask the questions using Hill's account.

Has it been the explicit intention of Edison from the start to collect data of diverse kinds to allow it to determine the problems encountered in implementing its educational rationale? Even without Mr. Hill's article, I and any other thinking individual can assume there were problems. Were some of these problems a consequence of an incomplete, or faulty, or unrealistic educational rationale? Were they a consequence of faulty aspects of its rationale for implementation? What has Edison learned, and what changes did that learning bring about? At present, Edison has 79 schools. Can Edison show that what it learned in its first 10 schools demonstrably lessened in the next 10 schools the frequency and gravity of the problems previously encountered? Can Edison show that quality of growth increased and the occurrence of serious problems or failures decreased as the number of schools steadily increased? If there is anything we know from the organizational literature, it is that the management of growth is a ubiquitous and serious problem, especially when the organization is new and under pressure to show results. What did Edison learn about organizational growth? What lessons, if any, did Edison learn about *that* predictable problem?

Edison, like several other well-known reform efforts, is in a number of schools around the country. In fact, Edison is in far fewer schools than other reform programs mentioned in the "cloning" article. Nevertheless, Edison had the inevitable problem they all have: the center-periphery problem. The center is in one place, what constitutes the periphery may be all over the map. It is an unavoidable problem for the obvious reason that it is the stated obligation of the "controlling" center to know what is going on in the periphery; at least to know it well enough either to prevent departures from its theoretical-constitutional rationale, or to prevent small problems from mushrooming into large ones, or as a basis for considering a change in that rationale. Put it another way: Unless an organization has a self-correcting stance and process, it learns little or nothing. What I am saying here about the center-periphery problem is no less applicable to the relationship between teacher and principal in one school, and even more obviously true between those in the central office of a school system and the schools they administer. (To take an extreme example: New York City has 1,100 schools. Need one say more?) In the specific case of Edison, we cannot understand or judge what Edison says it has accomplished (or will accomplish) unless the reports we assume they will someday make public speak directly to how and why they altered the way they handled the center-periphery problem, if indeed they altered it at all. For the purpose of spreading educational reform, the geography of an organization is the opposite of a minor variable. It is not only a practical matter but an awesome conceptual one or theoretical one as well. It is not a matter solved by hiring people who have "communication skills" or who are willing to spend their lives on the road.

On what basis do we expect that advocates of *any* educational reform, whether in a public or for-profit agency, should provide us with a credible report allowing us to judge whether it should be given approval and support for adoption generally, for spreading its outcomes? One answer is moral in nature: We do not want to encourage and support a reform unless we are convinced—which does not mean that we are 100% certain—that it has the desired effects on those who are the object of reform—students, school personnel, parents. That is to say, it *approximates* "success" to a sufficient degree to warrant its spread; it will do much more good than harm, it will help far more people than not; it may not be the best thing since sliced bread, but it is nonetheless worthy to be applied. The second answer, the basis for the first, is scientific in nature: We need to know when, where, and why the reform will be effective or ineffective, the self-correcting process that needs to be developed, the role and the problems with personnel selection, the factors that disrupt an intervention, and how the center-periphery problems were experienced and dealt with—in summary, what factors increase or decrease the level of approximation of success one should expect from the reform, factors which anyone who passes judgment on the reform or wishes to employ it should be told. It is not enough for the report to restrict itself to outcomes in terms of scores because replication of such outcomes does not tell us about the developmental context which give meaning to those outcomes. Test scores are important, but from the standpoint of spread or replication, those scores can be uninterpretable or misleading. They can be undisputably valid, but only if we know how they are manifestations of the developmental context and what is required to replicate that context and those outcomes. *If we are to learn and benefit from an educational reformer, we have to know what the reformers learned.* I shall return to this point shortly.

That Edison is a for-profit company is no basis for criticizing it. But precisely because it is a for-profit company, that places on it the special obligation to describe and explain to what extent, if any, its goal to become profitable (it is not now) has not undermined its educational, organizational rationale. That rationale should not be summarily dismissed out of hand. Such a dismissal ignores the fact that Edison is responding in its distinctive way to the brute fact that efforts to improve American schools have not spread beyond their initial demonstrations. What we should require of Edison is no more than what we should require of any serious, noncosmetic effort.

We hear much today about standards and accountability. There is, in my opinion, a prior question about standards and accountability which I failed to pose clearly in my writings: What kind of data and description should reformers provide when they present us with their accomplishments? What should they tell us about the story of what they did and learned; of when and why they were successful in one site and failed in another; of why they conclude (if they do) that their accomplishments are as good as one can expect, or what future efforts to increase the level of accomplishment will be necessary? For example, Edison is seriously considering developing its own teacher preparatory program. Why? What in Edison's experience leads it to such a radical consideration? Has Edison concluded that the preparatory programs from which their teachers came and still come ill prepare them as teachers and, therefore, set limits to what their reform program—or any reform program—can accomplish? Has Edison concluded that the defects of existing preparatory programs were not only in how they prepare their students but also in their criteria for selection of would-be teachers? Is Edison satisfied with the preparation of its principals and other administrators necessary for its geographically dispersed schools? How would Edison respond to the criticisms that it is blaming teachers for some of its major problems and ignoring the role of those who are at central headquarters? These are questions I for one would want answered by Edison when and if it issues a report. The fact is that I

know of no leader of a major reform who will not agree that existing preparatory programs are a major, perhaps decisive, obstacle to education
reform. However, unlike Edison none of them has, so to speak, seen fit to
"take on" the school of education establishment, or even to articulate publicly what they say privately.

Anyone familiar with my writings will know that I have been a vehe-
ment critic of teacher preparatory programs. That is why I applaud the fact
that Edison is even considering developing its own program. I may not
agree with what Edison comes up with, but that will not be a warrant for
me to ignore the fact that Edison is saying out loud what reformers have
long concluded. That Edison is a for-profit company is in regard to this issue
irrelevant. What is relevant here is that what Edison is planning is part of
the story they should be obliged to relate if the public is to have a basis for
judging the level at which Edison has approximated the level of accomplishment it may claim.

What should be the standards by which we judge a report of the pur-
ported accomplishments of any major reform program? What do we want
to know, what do we need to know? Because someone comes up with a
drug for this or that disease does not mean that he or she is permitted to
market it; there was a time when a person could do just that. When it became clear that such license was not in the public interest, standards were
developed to prevent such marketing unless that drug went through a
number of developmental steps demonstrating when, for whom, and
under which conditions the benefits of that drug far outweighed untoward
side effects. Those standards did not spring full-blown like Athena from
the head of Zeus; they changed and became more detailed as experience
dictated.

We do not have standards, formal or informal, for reports purporting
to demonstrate the accomplishment of an educational reform project. In
that sense each reformer is accountable to him- or herself, not to any agreed-
upon standards it is hoped reformers will feel obliged to report in telling
their story. It is beyond my purpose here to attempt to state what those
standards might be, although I confess that I should have explicitly dealt
with the problem more forthrightly earlier. I am in no way suggesting a
governmental role. There is a sufficient number of reformers and critics of
reformers who are knowledgeable about the issues, who have been through
the mill, so to speak , who recognize that quantitative data are not interpretable except in a context containing qualitative factors, who know the
difference between fact and opinion, and who respect the rules of evidence.
And they know that the standards they seek will increase the complexity
of the reformer's task in terms of time, money, and personnel. Telling an
action-research story is no easy job, but not to respect that difficulty is tan-

tamount to resigning ourselves at best to a guessing game and at worst to a perpetuation of predictable disappointment. It will not be easy to get agreement on standards. We are dealing with an awesomely complicated problem we have not been forced to deal with before. I say "awesomely" advisedly. I feel secure in saying that only a few readers of this book have ever attempted to carry out a serious educational reform which began by a demonstration in one site and then sought to replicate (or approximate) it in several or many more sites geographically separated from each other. I know of no such effort for which the reformer has described the complexity and problems one inevitably confronts. Those problems are personal, practical, logistical, predictable, *as well as unpredictable*, semicontrollable as well as uncontrollable, all demanding of limited time and resources, all increasing internal and external pressures to be consistent with stated purposes, all contributing to the necessity for guilt-producing compromises and short cuts. I have said that the major satisfaction these reformers derive from their effort is the gratification of pain required by masochistic needs.

Every reformer knows that the story he or she told or will tell is woefully incomplete. How incomplete is only known when the writing of the story begins, and truly known when he or she is finished writing and recognizes that to have written the whole story would have put him or her in the tradition of the Tolstoy who wrote *War and Peace*, the Joyce who wrote *Ulysses*, and the Proust who wrote *Remembrance of Things Past*. Educational reform has caught the public's attention as never before for many reasons, one of which is its incomprehension of why reforms have failed or why presumably successful reforms not only do not spread but in cases where they do spread the outcomes are less than expected. What I have emphasized in this chapter is but one aspect of a complicated answer: We do not have that kind of comprehensive account of any reform effort that allows one to begin to identify those factors (and their interactive nature) which play a significant role in the development, implementation, and sustaining of the reform effort. It makes no difference whether the reform failed or was moderately successful in terms of outcomes. What we want and need to know is what can, should, and must we learn from the study of these efforts so as to make for better outcomes. Outcomes are just that: outcomes. Outcomes tell us whether we should relax, be satisfied, and thank God, or whether we need to seek to improve. If we seek improvement, the source to which we initially should go is a comprehensive account of the history of the reform effort in order to identify those conceptions, processes, and events that need attention, rethinking, revision. If such an account is not available or skimpy or largely consists of isolated anecdotes and personal opinions hardly explained, how can you learn from what was done? What basis do you have to alter rationale and implementation? It is understandable if the reformer, consciously or not, wants to make the best case for the outcomes achieved. But there is more at stake than the reformer's need to appear to be successful, which at best may be self-serving (wittingly or otherwise) or at worst an irresponsible professional scientific failure to give clear direction to possible and necessary future improvement.

When people die in a hospital, their records are scrutinized by a committee of knowledgeable colleagues in order for them to determine (1) if treatment mistakes were made and (2) if mistakes were made how can their reoccurrences be prevented? It is that kind of process which led to a national study—reported in the national media—indicating that the number of these mistakes was alarmingly large, especially in regard to the intelligibility of a prescription for medication and/or sloppy communication between the attending physician, the hospital pharmacist, and the ward personnel who give the medication to patients. The bulk of people who go to hospitals do not die there. On a percentage basis the number who die is small. However small, the public expects that efforts will be made to make that number smaller, that hospitals cannot relax, that they are obliged to learn from mistakes, that they should and must improve, that the fact that the outcome of hospital stays is statistically beneficial is a fact that in no way excuses glossing over the need to improve outcomes.

It is a glimpse of the obvious that none of the major educational reform efforts has had levels of outcomes that lessen the need for reformers to determine why their outcomes are not that robust or compelling or consistent as to justify claiming that improvement is a minor problem. In fact, none of the major reformers makes such a claim. Strangely, however, they have told us little or nothing about how they or others could improve outcomes. Unless and until we, the readers of their publications, are provided with a more comprehensive, dispassionate, and forthright account of the problems encountered in the implementation process, we do not know what the reformers have learned and we, the readers, do not know how to pass judgment on whether the reforms in their present state should be encouraged to spread. A major reform effort is expensive in terms of time, money, and energy. Spreading that reform adds to the expense. Is it being a carping critic to say that unless a reform has built-in ways for learning and self-correction, we should be wary of supporting it? Are not the societal stakes too high to justify the lack of discussion of this problem?

I first became sensitive to this problem when after 25 years my book *The Culture of the School and the Problem of Change* (1971) went out of print. I reached an agreement with another publisher to reprint it if I could add about a hundred pages discussing what, if anything, had happened in that quarter of a century that confirmed or disconfirmed my basic arguments. The book was titled *Revisiting "The Culture of the School and the Problem of*

Change" (1996). Because the escalating cost of publishing books was so high, I was asked to eliminate a chapter from the original book. It turned out that the least costly and noninterfering way I could do that was to leave out the chapter on the school John Dewey started at the University of Chicago in 1896. It saddened me to do it because that school had a major influence on educational reform in the first half of the twentieth century. Soon after the republication I realized I had made a mistake, and for two reasons. The first was that people who had read it earlier, or used it for teaching purposes, wrote or personally told me that the chapter had helped them understand how the context of the school reflected Dewey's ideas in actions and organization, and in a way later reform efforts did not emulate. I was told what I had long known about post–World War II reforms: the developmental history of reform efforts was superficial, unsystematic, and, to say the least, unrevealing about how to judge outcomes.

The second reason I regard excising that chapter as unforgivable is because it emphasized a point that goes far to explain why Dewey's conceptions—which I regard as both seminal and crucial—would be distorted and misapplied by educators in the public schools. Dewey wanted to influence the reform of public schools, but it took him a long time to acknowledge that his ideas had been misinterpreted and even grievously misapplied.[1] Dewey very much wanted to see his ideas and practices spread, just like reformers who have come after him.

The point I stressed is this: *Dewey had the freedom, support, and resources to create a school; he did not seek to reform an existing one.* Dewey knew a great deal about schools, more than enough to conclude that their inadequacies and inequities were many, longstanding, systemic, conceptual, and self-defeating. But Dewey never took on the task of reforming one of those schools. As a consequence he never tested his ideas in a school organized according to principles the polar opposite of those he espoused. That, of course, does not mean that his ideas were wrong but rather that he vastly underestimated the obstacles that would be predictably encountered if he or others sought to reform an existing school. Creating a new school and reforming an existing one are not totally different processes, but from the stand point of implementation their differences are dramatic, they are differences which make a difference, a very big one.

---

1. It is an understatement to say that Dewey wrote a lot. If you want to read all he wrote, you need at least a year's sabbatical to read and digest the corpus of his writings; and Dewey's writing style is not a felicitous one. In any event, it is my impression that Dewey had difficulty criticizing those who lionized him, and his later criticisms and disappointments were expressed in muted and indirect ways. Of the people I knew who knew Dewey, I got a picture of a gentle, sensitive soul who very much tended to avoid hurting the feelings of others.

In this chapter I have been emphasizing that when a presumably successful reform has been achieved in one site, its transfer to another site is no simple matter. Aside from the obvious fact that no two schools are the same, there is the omnipresent problem of identifying and describing the significant factors contributing to whatever degree of success the reform achieved in the initial school. Replicating outcomes requires replicating a complicated developmental context and how to do that, how to respect that scientific obligation, has hardly been done in the history of educational reform. *Dewey could have done that if he had recognized the problem.* The chapter I wrote on the Dewey school was stimulated by reading a large book about the school by two of its teachers (Mayhew & Edwards, 1966). It was immediately apparent to me that those (and there were many) who were influenced by Dewey and sought to capitalize on his ideas had no published basis for comprehending what life was like for students, teachers, and parents in the Dewey school. The book by the two teachers was published decades after the school was no longer in existence. Yes, many articles and books about Dewey and his school were published, but they certainly did not add up even to a semi-integrated description. There was no basis for Dewey or those who sought to emulate him to expect anything resembling replication.

But the story does not end there. In 1997 Laurel Tanner wrote a book *Dewey's Laboratory School.* In the foreword of the book Philip Jackson states that Tanner spent months "digging through old records and teacher reports from the Dewey school, many of which currently are housed in the archives of the University of Chicago's Regenstein Library. It became evident as the year wore on that Laurel Tanner had come upon a treasure trove of both primary and secondary material" relevant to life and practice in the school (p. x). In her preface Tanner says:

> What we do need, particularly if we are teachers or teacher educators, is to know more about the workings of his experimental school (1896–1904). That is something I emphatically decided as I read the teachers' reports from a century ago in the marvelous Regenstein Library at the University of Chicago. What those teachers were doing was so current (they could be our colleagues), the problems they were trying to solve so contemporary, and the theoretical basis for the school so remarkable that I had to make these ideas more widely available. There are lessons for today from the school, lessons about child development and learning, school administration and supervision, curriculum development, and character education. The theory behind the Laboratory School—the idea . . . —is remarkable for it embraces all that we, who as a people demand so much of our schools, could want for our children. So much was accomplished in those 7 short years to develop a consecutive curriculum to match the theory. It really was amazing because Dewey

had such a hard time getting his school and the curriculum in shape. We give up too easily but I think there is a reason: We fear that if we stay with a plan we will go down with the ship. The point is that he did not give up; he followed his experimental philosophy and kept on trying until he came up with a form of organization that fit his educational theories. Because of his experimental philosophy the concept of planning was flexible. Without the experimental philosophy his school probably would have failed and closed after 6 months because his first plan of organization did not work out. The school moved to a departmental form of organization but the curriculum was not compartmentalized. How on earth did he do it? There are lessons to be learned from which we can profit.

Dewey's chief interest, like our own, was educational reform. When he established his experimental school, the purpose, as he put it, was "to discover in administration, selection of subject matter, methods of learning, teaching, and discipline, how a school could become a cooperative community while developing in individuals their own capacities and identifying their own needs" (Mayhew & Edwards, 1936, pp. xv–xvi). If ever the term "school restructuring" was appropriate to describe a reform effort, it was in the instance of Dewey's school. A century prior to the recent restructuring movement, Dewey insisted that school administration and curriculum development were organically related activities and should be approached as such. The old autocratic ways of working with teachers would never do.

Dewey and the teachers put into practice some of the ideas that we are trying to implement today: relating the curriculum to children's life and experience, integrating the curriculum, teaching critical thinking and problem solving, stimulating creative thinking, supporting collaborative decision making by the school staff. Dewey saw his school as a laboratory for studying how children learn and for identifying the possibilities and problems of the schools in view of the information gained. One hundred years later the problem still exists but so do the possibilities. (pp. xi–xii)

Tanner did not write her book as an addition to history but rather to demonstrate the relevance for today of what the school stood for. It is a book worth reading. The excerpts from the book had a special relevance for me because I knew that Dewey was not only a philosopher and educational theorist and activist but also a very sophisticated person concerning the history of science and the canons of science. And one of these canons is that you keep a clear and comprehensive record of what you did, the mistakes you made, errors of omissions, and so forth, so that others can judge whether your conclusions are justified. The Mayhew and Edwards book suggested to me that Dewey indeed sought to keep records of what was going on and/or what was changing in the school, that his experimental stance was not empty rhetoric, that those who wanted to apply his ideas and practices had to understand the context of the school, a context without which those ideas and practices lose meaning. I venture the opinion that with one exception I know of no reform effort that could begin to match the accounts and description apparently available about the Dewey school. The one exception is the Eight Year Study (Aiken, 1942), conducted by people who knew, worked with, and were mightily influenced by Dewey.

There are two reasons why what I am saying about how a reform effort should be viewed is not likely to be heeded. For one thing, I am not aware of any agency that recognizes the necessity of asking an appropriate group of individuals to think through and get agreement on what a report on a reform effort should contain. As I said earlier, they will find that the task is more complicated than envisioned, which is precisely what reformers learned in their attempts to make a difference. But getting such agreement cannot be avoided if we want to get a better understanding of why outcomes vary from total failure to less than compelling. Is it asking too much to want to be in the position of knowing what was learned from a reform effort before deciding that it should be encouraged to spread the program with the expectation of better outcomes?

There will be resistance to what I have proposed because it will require that the reform effort have more staff and resources. The account or story we want from the reformer has to be based on carefully and timely recorded events, processes, obstacles, crises, compromises, misunderstandings, personnel changes in the school and the reform staff, and more. I have used words like *story*, *record*, *account*, *report*, but none of these words captures or suggests the awesome, if not bewildering, diversity of data that has to be understood and integrated. (The reformer has much to learn from the anthropologist.)

The second reason is related to the first. What I propose will require a level of funding that agencies will shrink from, if only because they are woefully ignorant of how complex a reform effort is and that why and how the reform is written up is a problem that cannot be glossed over, but probably will continue to be glossed over. I say that because over the decades I have countless times met senior staff of funding agencies, public and private. With practically no exceptions I found them serious and sincere people who wanted to improve schooling. None of them had had a direct, sustained experience in schools. They were profoundly risk-aversive to any idea that was not mainstream or which they regarded as radical. They certainly had no way of comprehending the complexity of what a reformer confronts and experiences, and their conception of the rules of evidence for judging a reform was less than rudimentary.

For example, it is rare that a report about a reform project funded and circulated by these agencies does not emphasize the need for better trained teachers. But I know of no agency that (1) has taken the initiative seriously to determine why teachers are not better trained, (2) what is meant by better trained, (3) how the criteria for selection to preparatory programs might or should be altered, and (4) what obstacles and resistances (attitudinal and institutional) these efforts of program reform will encounter. As near as these reports come to concrete suggestions is advocating that teachers take more subject-matter courses and that their practice teaching experience should be lengthened. No one is or should be opposed to such advocacy. To be opposed is kin to being against motherhood. But should not these agencies feel obliged to determine how much of a difference those suggestions will make? Are they content to depend alone on hope and good intentions about problems they have identified and seek to clarify? Is it possible that their suggestions, however appropriate, may be woefully incomplete and misleading? The last question is one that none of them can entertain if only because none of them has ever had direct and sustained experience in preparatory programs. I am sure there are exceptions, there always are, but none come to mind at the moment.

Am I inexcusably venting my spleen here? For a period of 15 years I was directly involved in teacher training. For half a century I have been writing about it. For 20 of those years I never succeeded in obtaining grant support, after which point I gave up and never again sought support. So, I can understand if readers familiar with my writings may conclude that I am allowing personal frustrations to color and distort what I have said here and elsewhere.

The fact is that what I have said here was by way of returning to the question I asked at the beginning of this chapter: How come it took so long to clone sheep successfully? There is a general answer, which is in several parts. First, the researchers knew precisely what outcome they desired, and they did not underestimate the gulf between that outcome and their ignorance; they respected the complexity of their task. Second, they knew there would be many failed attempts; that there would be many techniques, conceptions, and theories that would have to be discarded or significantly altered, that what was achieved in the past could be a hindrance if that past goes unexamined and unchallenged. Third, they believed that regardless of whether ongoing studies were considered productive of new knowledge or they failed for one reason or another, each effort should be reported in ways that allowed peers to learn from and pass judgment on what was being reported. Fourth, the complexity of the task precluded setting a timetable for achieving the goal. When, for example, in his inaugural address President Kennedy said that by the end of the 1960s this country would put a man on the moon, he had been assured that almost all scientific and technical problems to achieve that goal had been or would be clarified; the margin of error was acceptably small. Fifth, problems, obstacles, and failures, are predictable; when and from whom breakthroughs are reported is unpredictable. The history of science is replete with examples of breakthroughs which did not follow conventional wisdom. Conventional wisdom is not to be taken lightly, but neither is it to be given iconic status.

As I said early in this chapter, successfully cloning sheep, however complicated the task and process was, was a relatively simple affair compared to reforming schools, and for two reasons we should never lose sight of. The first is researchers of cloning had a degree of control over what they did that no reformer has or should have. The second reason is that our ignorance about why reform efforts have been disappointing can hardly be considered a subject of serious discussion suffused as that discussion is with a bromidic conventional wisdom that is more sloganeering than it is unfettered thinking. In addition, as I have emphasized in this chapter, we have no secure basis for judging the different degrees of success or failure, for identifying those factors which point to the ways reform efforts might be improved. When I read the reports about major reform efforts, it is as if each reformer has not been influenced by other reformers. There may be times when intellectual anarchy is understandable, but when that anarchy does not evolve, however slowly, into a more integrated picture, the state of anarchy should be labeled for what it is: a catastrophe, a Tower of Babel.

What I have said in this chapter I said or alluded to in a more gentle, muted way in my previous writings. I did not want to offend this or that reformer, or segments of the educational community, or funding agencies. That was a mistake. Just as I have criticized reformers for not being able to present us the complicated story of their efforts, I refrained from expressing my true feelings. I am seen as a critic, but the fact is that I was not critical enough. I have said in these pages that reformers have not been revealingly self-critical of their efforts. Let me note that they are not critical of each other, a remarkable fact that is scandalously antiscientific. If researchers of cloning had such a stance, they would never have been able to demonstrate cloning. I can assure the reader that I am quite aware that a reform effort cannot be carried out in a strictly scientific way. But that is no excuse for not trying to approximate it as seriously and as best as one can. And let us not forget that of distinctive features of science one of them is quintessentially moral: The obligation to describe and report as clearly and as comprehensively as is practically possible what one has thought, done, experienced, and how one's efforts relate to what others have reported.

I should have written far more extensively about these issues, but I did not want to give further ammunition to a scientific community whose criticisms of schools, educators, and educational research expose an almost total ignorance of what life in school is like and why. In the post–World War II era there have been more than a few "hard" scientists and academics who indulged their rescue fantasies and who tried to implement their ideas. No one has as yet seen fit to chronicle the story of what they tried to demonstrate. It would be a very important chronicle from which we can learn much about how to fail. Learning what not to do is crucial for educational reform (and living generally).

We have learned certain things about conceiving and implementing a reform effort but they are far from enough. We are at the beginning of a journey that will take a long time before we can say that we are approximating our goal. Reaching our goal is impossible because in the realm of human affairs and relationships we are not dealing with problems that have a solution, as $4 \div 2$ has a solution. We are never dealing with issues that have a once-and-for-all solution. There are problems that we have to solve again and again and again. To expect otherwise is indeed utopian.

Chapter 10

Film, Language, and Context

When I started to write this chapter I read the manuscript of the book *The School Choice Wars,* by John Merrifield (2001). I recommend reading it, if only because of the extraordinarily clear way he exposes the fuzziness and ultimately self-defeating consequences of such labels as vouchers, school choice, charter schools, privatization, and competition. He makes a very compelling case that, given the way partisans of the reforms use this or that label, there is no reason whatsoever to expect that our school systems will be affected and changed in intended ways. These labels are words referring to concepts and goals which, Merrifield demonstrates, have generated a great deal of heat and no light. The problem is not linguistic, it is conceptual. Partisanship is inherently neither evil nor virtuous, but it carries with it the obligation to be as clear as possible about what your ends are and why they will be achieved by the means you have chosen. And that obligation does not exempt you from being logical and respectful of data relevant to your ends and means. Partisanship is no excuse for sloppy thinking or glibly oversimplifying a complex set of issues. The emotional strength with which you adhere to your advocacy is a two-edged sword: At the same time that it is a barometer of your commitment, it should be a warning sign that good intentions (like love) are not enough to achieve your purposes.

The above is by way of prologue to a discussion of the meaning of a word whose frequency in the literature is enormous at the same time that its meaning varies as wildly as responses to an inkblot. I say word rather than concept because this particular word rarely is used in a way to suggest that it has conceptual underpinnings. We utter the word with the greatest of ease, unreflectively assuming that we know what we are talking about and so will our listeners or readers. I have been guilty of it, and so has the reader. I refer to the word *learning.* What do we mean by it? That question took on a certain urgency for me about 30 years ago when I stepped down as director of the Yale Psycho-Educational Clinic and began writing on what I had "learned," again using the word as if it were a conceptual map by means of which I could answer questions about the substance of what I had learned, how I had learned it, as well as why, where, and when I learned it and with and from whom I learned it. I quickly realized that I was faced with a mammoth phenomenological jigsaw puzzle, for which the more I pondered, the more the number of pieces increased, and the strength of any secure feeling that I could answer any question decreased. Of one thing I was absolutely sure: From the time the idea of the clinic came into my head to the time I began to reflect on the intervening years, I had experienced a great deal (quite an understatement!); I had changed as a thinker and person; my sense of my past, present, and future had been dramatically altered. Intuitively and inchoately I knew that, just as two people who marry or live together know it, or when the first child is born, or when they get divorced. We say we know that, but only after subsequent experience exposes to us how inadequate that intuitive knowing was as a predictor of what you would later experience and say you now know. I said "exposes to us" and that implies the processes of memory and reflection, and the motivation to explore the past. Why did things work out as they did? What did I learn about myself? What should I have learned? People differ widely in how they approach these questions. Some people hardly ask or pursue the questions; others seriously pursue them with the goal of formulating an answer or principle that encapsulates what they have learned, an answer in the present that explains the past and will be utilized in the future. That answer may be right, wrong, or misguided, but it is accompanied with the feeling that one has learned something personally important one did not know or appreciate before. Let me get at this in another way.

Imagine a study in which the same test of memory was given to three groups of freshmen: To one group the researcher said that he is going to give them a test of intelligence. To another group he said that he is developing a test of memory which has several flaws he is trying to remedy. To a third group he said only that he will give them a test of memory. After he had given the test, the researcher asked the subjects to relate what thoughts and feelings they had about the test while taking it. Then he debriefed them. The researcher reported that the most significant result was that unlike the first and third group, the middle group (the flawed test) reported nothing suggesting curiosity or any other special reaction, and they had the lowest memory scores. The intelligence test group had the highest score.

What if anything did the students learn before the purpose of the study was revealed to them? That, of course, depends on your concept of learning. I am not aware of a conception of learning that, given the conditions I described, would suggest that the students learned anything worthy of note by them or others, anything that would suggest they had changed in some way. But what about the "intelligence test" group which had been challenged and energized by the stated purpose of the task? Had not they learned that taking an intelligence test was important to them and others? No, because their reaction to the instruction was a manifestation of countless previous experiences from which they had distilled the principle that how you did on an intelligence test was a difference that made a very big difference in how people regarded you and, therefore, how you regarded yourself. They already had learned *that*, and it is most unlikely that their reaction increased by more than the tiniest of smidgeons the strength and consequences of the reaction. In a word they had learned nothing. That does not mean they were meaningless experiences, but rather that we gain nothing by saying it was a learning experience and recognized as such by the students.

But let us indulge our imagination in another direction. What if we were able closely to follow each student and listen in on his conversations with others at dinner that night? My prediction would be that in relating his experience in the study some of these freshmen students would say, "You cannot trust what a researcher tells you about what he is after." And it is likely that upper classmen sitting at the dinner table will laugh and say, "You had better believe it." The freshman student knows he has learned something he may not or does not want to forget. He has acquired a personal stake in remembering even though it is based on one experience. A single experience, however short in duration, may or may not change a person, cause him or her to know something has been learned that will influence their thinking and makeup over a long period of time, even a life time. Sheer experience is no guarantee of learning.

What about the research psychologist? Did he learn anything? He was primed to learn, for him the personal stakes were high, he wanted his ideas to be proved valid, he gave little or no thought to what he would think and do if he was proved wrong. So he was delighted with the results, he published a paper, he added another item to his list of publications, he started to think of follow-up studies. He knew he had learned something worth knowing that would have productive consequences. But what if the results had not confirmed what the researcher expected? He would be more than disappointed. He would be in a quandary. He would ask (plague) himself with questions: "Did I design the study poorly? Was my 'theory' incomplete and did it mislead me? Are there factors that are important but I was not aware of them? Maybe I am not as bright as I thought I was." When you have thought through a complex problem and you are convinced about what you learned, the possibility that you may have to start *unlearning* what you learned is, to say the least, unsettling and very difficult. Some people never can confront unlearning, for others unlearning becomes a step in new learning. What do children learn about themselves (as thinkers, knowers, persons) over their school years? Every reader will agree that the question is a crucial one. But there is another question I would contend is no less important precisely because it inevitably should be recognized in the substance of your answer to the first question, but is not. What do children have to *unlearn*—cognitively, socially, and affectively—before and during the school years? When, if ever, does learning take place unencumbered with the necessity to unlearn? Can you explain the difficulties, small or large, without invoking the relationship between learning and unlearning?

A familiar example is what happened back in the 1960s when in countless workshops around the country math teachers were helped to learn the new math. I sat in on some of those workshops and observed teachers struggle mightily with a new math so different from what they had previously learned and taught. The anxiety, anger, and frustration they experienced were obvious, so much so that we did not have to be sages to predict that the new math would never achieve its purposes. Sitting in those workshops reminded me of what I experienced in England when after an hour of instruction I drove a rented car in which the steering wheel was not where it is in an American car and the rules of the road were no less strange. I am sure the readers will have no difficulty coming up with examples from their own experience.

It is not my intention in this chapter to sketch what a comprehensive conception of learning should encompass. The purpose of the chapter is (1) to indicate why I shied away from dealing with a problem I considered crucial, and (2) why I dealt with it in a restricted way. I shied away because I knew that to do justice to a comprehensive conception of learning was first and foremost a mammoth scholarly and analytical endeavor requiring reading a vast literature on theory, research, and applications of conceptions of learning. In addition, such an endeavor should be embedded in social and intellectual history because changing conceptions of human learning and capacities are barometers of how societies change. For example, today in terms of learning (its nature, speed, limits, and so forth), we do not regard women, minorities, old people, people with disabilities, and preschoolers the way they were regarded in past centuries. That is a very important point because it should, although it does not, require us to be skeptical about our tendency to believe that we know all that is needed to be known about human learning, as if future societal changes will not cause us to think differently. For most of human history schooling for the masses was an alien, subversive concept because it suggested that the masses could learn, or be trusted to learn, to be mature and responsible in matters too complex for them to comprehend; you do not throw pearls to swine, so to speak.

I am not by temperament disposed to spend years reading, pondering, analyzing, integrating a vast literature and relate it to school learning.

If I knew that task was long overdue, I also knew I was not one who could do it justice. For the first 6 decades of the twentieth century, theorizing and researching the process and dynamics of learning was a very dominant problem occupying some of the best minds in American psychology. But it had little to do with human learning, let alone school learning. It was largely laboratory research using the Norway rat as subject. The long-term vision was that by taking the route it did, it would provide the principles of learning that would illuminate and be applicable to human learning. It was not a total loss, but it illuminated very little. After those six decades the field of animal learning lost its dominance compared to what was, and that field became semimoribund. Why? The world had changed, America had changed, students entering the field were not interested in animal learning, they were not interested in problems of memory for a series of words each of which was exposed for one second on a screen. "Rat Psychology" was less than unattractive; it was seen as trivial and a conceptual dead end. And this sea swell change was both reflected in and handsomely funded by the federal National Institute of Mental Health which was responding to presidential and congressional mandates as well as the society at large. This is a clear instance of how changes in a society impinged directly on what a field like psychology would consider important and unimportant problems. In regard to that change, animal learning had little to offer. I go into this in greater detail in my previous book *American Psychology and Schools: A Critique* (2001).

There is one instructive and confirming exception to what I have said, and it concerns the work of B. F. Skinner, who before World War II was already a major figure in competing conceptions of learning based on studies of rat learning. Unlike other leaders in that arena Skinner was drawn to the applications of his conception of learning to human problems. You only have to read the first few pages of his 1962 *Walden Two* to conclude that Skinner was on the road to social activism. There are few major social problems our society confronts today that are absent in those pages. Although Skinner wrote about school learning, his influence on classroom learning was minimal. It was the many hundreds of graduate students around the country who embraced his principles of learning and applied them in the clinical relationship between patient and psychotherapist. They were little interested in schools or animals or the laboratory. They were interested in learning in the therapeutic relationship. They have made some important practical contributions to the treatment of a few types of incapacitating personal problems (e.g., phobias, physical pain). Why were Skinner's progeny uninterested in school learning—a problem no less fateful for our society than clinical ones, and I have argued in my last book, they are more fateful? For one thing, what Skinner wrote about schools and classrooms exposed his unfamiliarity with both. More important, there is nothing in graduate training in psychology that exposes students to what passes for learning in the classroom and why psychology potentially has a great deal to offer there. Skinner did not understand that, his students did not, and the field of learning is no less narrow in scope today than in its heyday when rats were run in mazes to get pellets of food or to pull a lever to get the pellets. Different eras, different conceptions, different consequences for one of its most important institutions.

There was another reason I shied away from pursuing a problem I considered of bedrock importance, and again it is revealing of my temperament, ambitions, values, and a need to make a difference in the world before I left it. "Making a difference" sounds presumptuous and arrogant, and that well may be the case, but I must remind the reader that I am talking of the time when I was in my midthirties, I had started a research program on test anxiety in elementary school children, and my fantasies of making a difference in the world were, if not florid, expansive. (I trust the reader will agree that there is more than a modest negative correlation between expansiveness and arrogance, on the one hand, and the passage of time, on the other hand.) The point here is that in the course of spending scores of hours in classrooms, I was both appalled and puzzled by the passivity and conformity of the students and the lack of any air of excitement. In general the classrooms were pleasant, humane, even nurturing, but there were no sparks indicative of curiosity, propelling interests, eagerness, or signs of an active inner life. I did not then, as I do not now, expect students to display the degree of youthful piss and vinegar they display in venues outside of school, but I also did not expect them to be devoid of spontaneity and liveliness. There were exceptions, of course, there always are exceptions; they were very few in number but they had the compelling virtue of telling me that what I was ordinarily observing and concluding had validity, I was not "making it up."

How to explain it? Why did it occasionally bother me to the point almost of anger? Why was I so ready to blame the teacher? Those and similar questions plagued me. I felt that not only did I have to answer these questions, but if I did, I could play a role in transforming schools. That would be making a difference in the world. So where and how and with whom do I start the process of understanding? Fortunately, this came at a time when I was working most closely with an anthropologist, Thomas Gladwin, who had returned from several years of studying the culture of the people on the islands of Truk in the South Pacific (Gladwin & Sarason, 1953). One thing Tom helped me see was that however you define the thinking, behavioral, interpersonal, and social regularities of a people, culture is not a *willed* phenomenon. People do not create a culture, they

unreflectively and inevitably inherit it and become transmitters and rein-
forcers of culture. Cultures do change, of course, but people do not see it
as a cultural change until *after* the new regularities are general, pronounced,
obvious, and cannot be ignored.

That meant that I should not try to explain what I had observed in classrooms and schools in terms of individual characteristics and personality
but rather in terms of conceptions and axioms that are shared and socially
and institutionally inherited. You could say that culture is a way not only
of teaching a people what "reality" is but why they should conform to,
respect, and transmit it. Culture defines what is considered right, natural,
and proper. What is designated as counterculture is a rejection of what is
right, natural, and proper. I was rejecting what I had observed, and I sought
to understand why people in the school culture considered what they did
as right, natural, and proper.

It was not because I was a member of the Yale department of psychology—known for its emphasis on learning theory and research—that I focused
on the concept of learning. In fact, I had already concluded learning about
learning by running rats in a maze was a fruitless endeavor. Observing classrooms only confirmed that such an approach was barren of fruit. Besides,
from a conception of culture, I had to understand where and how people in
the school culture acquired a conception of learning that produced an amazing degree of similarity among classrooms in all schools I had visited—
schools that varied in appearance and population served, size, resources, and
more. It was trying to understand those amazing similarities that led me over
the decades to explore and write about this, that, and the other aspect of
school culture, with the result that the more I thought that I was understanding, the more I saw that there was more yet to understand. That explains
why I shied away from dealing directly with conceptions of learning, admittedly a fundamental problem but one that had far less attractiveness to a
person like me than describing and fathoming the culture of the school. It
was with a sense of relief and guilt and inadequacy that I went in the directions that I did. And yet, ironically and not surprisingly, it led me to the
conclusion that schooling will fall far short of the mark unless and until the
current conception of learning is replaced by one that can distinguish between contexts of productive and unproductive learning. That is an assertion which I state explicitly or is clearly implied in everything I have written
about education, beginning in 1965 and with ever-increasing feeling and, I
must add, despair as I see the current reform scene come up with nostrums
that confuse symptoms with cause, labels with new knowledge, good intentions with achievement, opinion with fact, and action with progress.

I finished writing the above in the evening of December 7, 2000. The
next morning I was reading the *New York Times* and came to the op-ed page

where there was a piece with the title "The Problem Ain't the Kids" by Louis Gerstner, CEO of IBM, and Tommy Thompson, Governor of Wisconsin. Both men have long had a deep interest in educational reform. Gerstner had earlier convened a national conference comprised largely of business executives, some governors, and a few educators. Governor Thompson was there. The conference got a good deal of play in the mass media, and the conference report outlined what needed to be done to improve educational outcomes. The use of technology was emphasized, but the tenor of the report concentrated on a not-so-subtle warning that school personnel had to be held accountable for the inadequacies of schools and, therefore, those which could not achieve better outcomes deserved criticism and more. It is not unfair to say that it was a shape-up or ship-out manifesto. The conference gave rise to Achieve Inc. As the op-ed piece states:

> Through a collaboration called the Math Achievement Partnership, 11 states, ranging geographically from Washington to North Carolina, are already pooling their resources and political capital to attack this problem. They are working with mathematicians and educators organized by Achieve Inc., the nonprofit organization, created by governors and corporate leaders, of which we are the co-chairmen.

In our 1992 book Lorentz and I presented our argument as to why the conference report was an egregious example of the excesses of do-goodism. Our scorn was such that the publisher politely insisted that we tone it down, which we did because it was the case that Gerstner's and the hearts of the other participants were in the right place even if their heads were not.

Why the op-ed piece now?

> The new results, from the Third International Mathematics and Science Study, in which 38 countries participated, show American eighth graders about where they were four years ago—average, putting them on par with students from Bulgaria, Latvia and New Zealand. They came out ahead of those in 17 countries, including South Africa and Thailand.
>
> It's especially troubling that four years ago, when today's American eighth graders were in fourth grade, as a group they ranked better—well above the international math average on an earlier version of the same test, scoring behind their peers in only seven countries. The message here is extraordinary and irrefutable: Every day our public schools are open, the gulf between our children and the world's top performers grows wider.
>
> The problem isn't the kids; it's what and how they are taught. What American schools consider eighth-grade math is barely sixth-grade math in countries like The Netherlands and Singapore. Most eighth-grade math exams in the United States emphasize arithmetic, computation, whole numbers and

fractions—topics that students in top-ranked nations are expected to master well before middle school. These countries' eighth graders are getting the fundamentals of algebra and geometry.

I predicted the new findings when the initial ones on fourth graders were made known, accompanied as they were with expressions of satisfaction and delight that finally American schools were back on the right road. And I predicted it on the same grounds that I predicted in the 1960s that Head Start would not demonstrate robust effects, that once these children experienced classroom learning in the school the cognitive benefits of being in Head Start would wash out, which is what largely happened. In regard to the international math testing results my prediction had two sources. The first was based on personal experience and available studies indicating that as students go from elementary to middle to high school their interest in and motivation for school learning steadily decrease. That decrease is more obvious in regard to math and science, but it holds for all subject matter. The second and related source is that the modal American classroom is a context of unproductive learning and that is clearly the case in middle and high schools. This is only in small measure a consequence of size: Elementary schools are significantly smaller than middle schools which in turn are significantly smaller than high schools. Size does not explain why so many elementary school classrooms are contexts of unproductive learning.

Are there exceptions to what I have just said? Of course there are, and I have observed some. But people like Gerstner are not asking and pursuing that question. They are so riveted on group data that it does not occur to them to locate and study exceptions, even if they are in urban areas where you would not expect to find them. What are the characteristics of these classroom exceptions? Do the teachers of these classrooms think about students differently? Relate to them differently? Learn about them differently? Recognize and adapt to the individuality of students differently? Relate to and utilize parents differently? Is it unbridled fantasy to hypothesize that exceptions may tell us something important about teachers and the contexts of learning they create and sustain? Will we learn nothing about selection and preparation of teachers, of student learning? Or why the exceptional classroom has no impact on other classrooms in the same schools?

So what is the first step Gerstner and Thompson are taking? "The first step is using what we can learn from top-performing nations to agree on what our kids should know before high school." And the next steps?

These expectations will be made public early next year. Next, the math partnership will develop more rigorous lessons in math, better training and support for teachers, and a common measure for comparing results annually, not every four years. The partnership is open to any state that wants to join.

Gerstner and Thompson are ignorant of the new math debacle of the 1960s, and I assume that is true for their educational advisors and math consultants. One goal they will for sure meet: They will present us with group data, and quickly, because, after all, this is, as Gerstner has previously told us, the wondrous age of technology. That unlearning is a factor in and precondition for learning is an alien thought in Gerstner's and Thompson's thinking. With friends like that, educational reform need never worry about enemies.

So what is a context of productive learning? I have discussed this in all of my writings, but as I have indicated in previous pages I do not pretend that I have answered the question well or comprehensively. But there are a few of its features I want very briefly to state again and give examples.

The first example is what William James said 100 years ago about what he learned and had to unlearn from his talks to teachers over the years. The negative way is to say that if he oriented his course to a presentation of the abstractions and findings of "psychological science," it would be of little or no help to teachers in understanding and appropriately responding to real children in real classrooms; not only are they real children but children each of whom has an individuality. They are all subsumed under the label "children," but *this* Tom is not *that* David and *this* Mary is not *that* Catherine. They are psychologically and interpersonally similar and different in small or large ways. You do not have to tell that to teachers, they know it, you can bet the ranch on it. As James said, the art of teaching does not derive and cannot be derived from psychological science. Teachers do not and should not teach on the basis of labels and generalizations, both of which have meaning but neither tell the teacher in any concrete fashion what it means for action with the Toms and Marys who are before her in the here and now. What James tells us is that as a result of his experience with teachers he will focus on what teachers experience and confront as conduits of all that we mean by and surrounds subject matter. The positive way of putting it is that the teacher's task is to understand where the learner is and is coming from. You start there, you capitalize on it, for the purpose of enlarging horizons and skills. The teacher has goals and end points, but she will fall short of the mark if her starting point is other than where the learner is and is coming from. The starting point serves the purpose of coalescing energies and interests for a self-sustaining voyage of intellectual discovery that is as personally rewarding as it is unpredictable. The teacher should have a clear picture of where she would hope her students will be at the end of the phase of the voyage she oversees, but if her starting point is other than what William James emphasized, her students will be glad when that phase is over and they can turn to a much more interesting world of meaning. James wanted for students what had been provided him in his life: lighted fires.

The second example is a recent book by Bensman, *Central Park East and Its Graduates* (2000). The school began in 1974 serving students from east Harlem. The first follow-up of its graduates was also by Bensman in 1987, published with the title *Quality Education in the Inner City*.

> The result was *Quality Education in the Inner City* (Bensman, 1987), which identified two keys to Central Park East's success. The first involved its philosophy of education. "Unlike almost all schools in America," I wrote, "CPE begins not with what outside experts have predetermined that the students need to learn, but with the students' own ideas and interests. The staff listen carefully to what children are saying and observe what they are doing. But most important, they respect those thoughts and actions" (p. 8). Respect was crucial not only in teacher-student relationships, but in administrator-teacher relationships, and school-family relationships as well. "By demonstrating consistent respect for children, parents and teachers, the CPE schools are able to get the best from all three—teachers give more of their time and devotion, children give more of their energy, parents give more of their concern" (p. 9).
>
> But CPE's educational outlook was clearly not enough to explain the school's success, I argued, for a close reading of the school's history indicated that it had made many mistakes, including some that generated internal conflict severe enough to call the school's continued existence into question. What made CPE unusual, I argued, was it had survived its predictable mistakes and had done so for three reasons: It started small; it enjoyed staunch support from District 4 Superintendent Anthony Alvarado; and most teachers and parents felt that they had made such a large investment in the school's success that they wanted to give it a chance to grow and improve.
>
> Before *Quality Education* was published, CPE's reputation grew exponentially as a result of Deborah Meier's winning the MacArthur "Genius" Award in the spring of 1986. Using the prize money she won, Meier founded the Center for Collaborative Education and began sending *Quality Education* to those expressing interest in school reform.
>
> Ironically, at the time I wrote *Quality Education* in 1986, I did not consider it the full-out study it could have been—after all, the project was already behind schedule when I came aboard. Yet, here I was, hearing from people all over the country how helpful this study was proving to their efforts to improve local schools.
>
> The magnitude of this response made me realize that the school reform effort was engaging the dedicated effort and concerted attention of people concerned with social justice, and I began to wonder about how I could aid their efforts. The chance came in 1991, when Deborah Meier proposed that I follow up on the early graduates of CPE, to evaluate the school's long term impact on their school careers and personal lives.
>
> Deborah's proposal appealed to me because writing *Quality Education in the Inner City* had not satisfied my curiosity about CPE's success. I knew what

CPE's staff had done to reach their students, but I didn't really understand how. How could a teacher keep track of what 30 students were thinking and doing? How could a teacher encourage and nourish such a large and diverse group of children? Finally, what did quality education mean to inner-city students in the long term? Would the strengths gained in nurturing classrooms enable students to overcome challenges posed by broken families, poverty, and discrimination? (Bensman, 2000, pp. 2–3)

If you read both of the follow-ups, you will be impressed, even inspired, by the ways CPE positively influenced and shaped the subsequent careers and lives of its graduates. In the most recent follow-up Bensman makes a valiant effort to do something with language that is literally impossible: to convey the concreteness, immediacy, and complexity of context. *Words about a context are far from a good substitute for the experience of being part of the context.* (Bensman had been in and a part of the context, as was true for the graduates he interviewed.) If you relate to friends that the previous evening you had the best dinner ever in the most charming restaurant you had ever been in, and you relate this experience in great detail and with much appropriate feeling, your friends will conclude that you had an encompassing experience at the same time that they are not in doubt that your words do not arouse in them the experience of the context you are describing. They will listen respectfully, they may say they envy you the experience, they may have a "sense" of the total context in which you had the experience, but they know that that sense is incomplete and inevitably so; they may even be bored by your efforts to arouse in them your sense of context. And if some of your friends regard you as someone who exaggerates in judging food and restaurants, they may seek to steer the conversation in new directions. Take another example: Your friend has just come back from a trip to China and is showing you, one by one, scores of photographs and describing each of them with the enthusiasm and delight intended to arouse in you something similar to what your friend experienced. Friendship requires that you dutifully look and listen even though your interest and patience are wearing thin. At best, you may decide that you would like to take a similar trip and see and experience what your friend did.

That is the problem Bensman was up against. He did as well as I would have hoped. But I have learned over the years that the descriptions of school contexts should be taken with some grains of salt, and for two reasons. First, knowing schools (as I think I do), I find the descriptions of contexts less than satisfactory in engendering in me the sense that I more than superficially understand the relationships between context and outcomes. My skepticism is not because I am a perfectionist or a glutton for detail or suspicious of the partisanship of the describers but rather because of my own attempt to describe a particular complicated context: the Yale Psycho-

Educational Clinic. I was dissatisfied then, as I have been by my elaborations in subsequent writings, including pages in the present book.

The concept of context is a way of saying that understanding of the thoughts, actions, and feelings of discrete individuals are an inadequate basis of explanation of how they are influenced by and are an influence in their circumscribed surround. So, for example, the leader of the site is unquestionably crucial: his or her values, personality, style, conceptions of self, stated purposes, motivations, and more. But knowing *that*, we are far from knowing in a clear way why, how, and to what degree that knowledge has become part of the psyches of others in the site. You can reverse that sentence by asking how, why, and with what consequences was the leader changed (or not) by the thoughts, feelings, and actions of the others in the site. We say that a site has an ambiance, by which we usually mean that if you spend time in it, you get a "sense," a "flavor," a "feeling" about it that may or may not be consistent with what you had been led to expect. You may be favorably impressed and conclude as an act of faith that it accomplishes what it says it does. You may be unimpressed and puzzled and come to be skeptical of what it says it accomplishes. There is, I believe, one criterion by which to judge the adequacy, comprehensiveness, and utility of the description of a school context: It has been replicated by others and with similar outcomes or, at a minimum, you believe that it is capable of replication to a discernible degree. Why, then, was I so favorable to Bensman's reports of a school I had never visited? The answer is in three parts, the last of which is most crucial.

1. I knew Debbie Meier and knew what she thought about how and why young children learn what they do. Nobody needs to convince a Debbie Meier that young children are explorers, curious, with interests and assets that propel them in the service of a need to feel or become competent. She would agree with every word William James and John Dewey said about learning and children. She also does not have to be told that capitalizing on those interests makes possible over time the learning of academic skills and subject matter as well as a working knowledge of resources that exist outside the classrooms and schools. Debbie Meier does not regard passing an achievement test as synonymous with critical or creative thinking, although she in no way devalues skills and subject matter. It is bedrock to her thinking that the relationship between school and family is not a matter of foreign affairs but of a symbiosis crucial to the needs and purposes of both parties. And, finally, she takes for granted that whatever makes for productive learning in children must also be created and sustained for teachers. My one question about Debbie was whether she suffered the defects of her virtues: She is a strong-willed, street-smart

person who is unlikely to suffer fools gladly. What role, if any, do her virtues play in clouding the story Bensman tells? He does say that "serious mistakes" were made early on at CPE. He does not say what the nature and sources of those mistakes were or what their consequences were. The ups and downs of a leader are not irrelevant to outcomes, good or bad. It was an act of faith on my part not to discount the possibility that her leadership was as consistent, productive, and inspiring as Bensman's accounts suggest. But in matters of school reform I always feel uncomfortable with *my* acts of faith.

2. Although I never visited CPE, there were several occasions when I met and interacted with members of its staff. I used these opportunities to try to intuit and gauge these individuals' opinions of the uniformly positive accounts of the CPE "story," some of which had appeared in the mass media. They said nothing to contradict those accounts. They talked about CPE with missionary zeal. It was as if they were clones of Debbie Meier in terms of practice and articulated principles. I was impressed, but I would be less than candid if I did not confess that I was still somewhat skeptical. As a student of school reform efforts over the decades, I had become a skeptic of what I read and was told.

3. Frederick Wiseman is a producer-director of film documentaries. The first of his documentaries that I saw was back in the 1960s: *Titicut Follies*, which was about a state hospital in Massachusetts. It played a role in the deinstitutionalization of such human warehouses, dens of injustice and human degradation. From my personal visits to and observations of these institutions I thought I knew the game and score. That documentary convinced me I was wrong. Watching the film was unsettling in the same way the movie *One Flew Over the Cuckoo's Nest* was unsettling (if not unbelievable) to viewers who had no experience with state hospitals. That movie was unsettling but believable to me because it did not contradict but rather exposed how incapable I had been—how internally resistant I had been—to pursue the implications of conclusions I had drawn from personal experience. *Titicut Follies* was a similar experience for me. Now, there are two characteristics of Wiseman's films. First, there is no narrator to tell you what you are seeing and how to interpret it. There simply is no narration. What you get are sequences of people interacting and talking in circumscribed spaces in nonrehearsed or uncontrived ways: talking and doing what is usual in terms of their usual roles and relationships. Each sequence lasts several minutes, sometimes much more. It is jarring as you go from one sequence in one site to another with no obvious rationale. But as you continue to watch, you find yourself forming strong impressions of what life is like in the overall setting: how people think and act, their values, the problems with which they cope, their hopes and fears. Those impressions derive from the second characteristic of Wiseman's films: they run 3–4

hours, no commercials, on public television stations! That is one long physically exhausting, intellectually rewarding experience but at the end you feel secure in the conclusion that you have far more than a superficial understanding of the psychological-social dynamics of the setting.

A few years ago I saw on PBS channel 13 in New York Wiseman's film on Central Park East. It started at 9 P.M. and ended near 1 A.M. Whatever doubts I had about what CPE was doing and accomplishing faded away. I had seen what I needed to see. I needed no help from a narrator. So, when Bensman's recent book appeared, I read it with the background of having seen the film. The book and the film complement each other. It is in no way to devalue Bensman's contribution to say that the film had a greater impact on me. His book deals with what happened to CPE graduates and the film did not. What the film allowed me to do was to make the results reported by Bensman very believable.

If I tried to explain to the reader why the film was so important to me, I could be faced with the same impossible problem that Bensman confronted: Language, written or oral, is far from an adequate tool for conveying to the listener or reader the imagery and complexity of what the speaker or writer experienced and intended. We like to believe that our words arouse in others the imagery they aroused in us. I can write pages about the kind of individual my grandson is. But what readers are very likely to conclude is that I think Nathaniel is unusual, lovable, and bright, and what else do you expect a doting grandfather to say, to try to describe? They will not, if asked, say they now know him or me. If that is true in the case of describing an individual, it does not hold a candle to the complexity of describing a context. If the reader wants to understand what I mean by a context of productive learning, they should see Wiseman's film and then read Bensman's book.

The third example is similar to the second. In 1996 a new, small high school was created in Providence, Rhode Island, with an initial cohort of 52 almost exclusively minority students, the majority of whom could be labeled "at risk." The two leaders of the school were Dennis Littky and Elliot Washor. I have discussed that school in my book *Charter Schools: Another Flawed Educational Reform?* (1998a). I shall not repeat what I have written in that book. Suffice it to say that what Debbie Meier stands for is in every respect identical to what Littky and Washor espouse. In June 2000, that initial cohort was graduated. All but two have been accepted into a college. A book about the school (called the Met) has been written by Eliot Levine (*One Kid at a Time*, 2001). As in Bensman's book, Levine has made a valiant attempt to convey the Met context and outcomes. And those outcomes are as impressive as those for CPE.

Why is it that when Littky told me that the Met would be opened several months hence, I would have been willing to bet any skeptic, and I would have given handsome odds, that the school would meet its objectives—to create and sustain a context of productive learning—and would most positively shape and influence the lives of its students. Why the lack of skepticism?

1. I first got to know Dennis Littky 25 years ago when he was principal of a middle school on Long Island in a middle-to-upper class community. I visited the school several times, and he visited me. From the standpoint of pedagogy, ambiance, innovativeness, support from and utilization of community resources it was by far the most stimulating, instructive middle school I had ever seen. In my book *You Are Thinking of Teaching?* (1993c) I devote a chapter to a description of one of its programs. That description contains long excerpts from a book written both by the students in the program and the supervising teacher whose idea the program was (Vlahakis et al., 1978). There were obstacles to initiating that "community service" program, but they were overcome, a fact understandable only if you know and observe Dennis Littky who initially struck me as a bearded hippie with an Indian skull cap whose hold on the realities of the culture of schools was wildly unrealistic. He said all of the things a person like me wanted to hear, but given what he appeared to be, I feared that what I would observe would be, to put it mildly, disappointing. Like Debbie Meier, Dennis has strong, passionate convictions about what students are and can learn and become, and he never hides his criticisms of school contexts that are for students stultifying and boring, and see students as empty vessels having no assets for critical thinking. And, he would say, those schools— by which he meant almost all schools—inhibit and impoverish the ability of teachers to think for themselves. So, when Mr. Vlahakis told him about the program he wanted to develop, Dennis went into action and helped obtain the necessary parental and community support. What to most people seems an out-in-left-field idea will be seriously considered and supported by Dennis if it has the potential to enlarge and deepen the *personal and intellectual* horizons of students. Dennis is a very serious thinker. He is not intellectually soft.

2. We stayed in touch by phone. One day I got a call from him that he was accepting a position as principal of a disorganizing and disorganized, very inadequately performing high school in an economically poor, blue-collar town in New Hampshire. I became anxious. The middle school on Long Island was in a community of very highly educated families who had learned to trust and support whatever Dennis said was the educationally right thing to do. The town he was describing could not be more different.

If I conveyed my anxiety, Dennis conveyed his usual enthusiasm and optimism: He had no doubt he would prevail. I was not reassured. What happened is contained in a thick book (Kammerand-Campbell, 1989) that was to me as reassuring and instructive as it was as fascinatingly dramatic. How and why Dennis lived through the years at Thayer High School I cannot explain. Persistence and courage are inadequate words of explanation. The next point is another story, to me the clincher, the kind of "data" that convinced me as words could not that Dennis had done in that high school in that community what he had done in the middle school on Long Island.

3. I got a call from Dennis telling me that in the next week there would be a 2-hour film on the National Broadcasting System about the Thayer story. It was not a documentary, he said, but it well reflected what took place with what outcomes. The two leading actors were Jill Eichenberry and Michael Tucker from the long running TV series *L.A. Law*. The title of the film was *A Town Torn Apart*, based on the 1989 book. Commercial film makers have long been castigated for playing loose with facts. If you do not expect them to adhere even semislavishly to the facts, neither do you condone introduction of theme, characters, and events that are major sources of distortions that violate what took place and why. Having read the book, knowing Dennis as I did, and having him relate what he had been up against and experienced, the different forms of prejudice he had to confront, my expectations were foreboding in nature. NBC, I predicted, would make a mockery of Dennis, the high school, and the community of Winchester. Roll the film and weep! I was very wrong. The film was engrossing, surprising in the degree to which it was faithful to the book and in depicting how much the school, its students, and the community changed, and Dennis' way of thinking about and implementing a context of productive learning. What I was viewing was what I had observed years before in the middle school on Long Island. And it is what I have observed in my visits to the Met. It is relevant to note that over the course of observing what was happening and being accomplished at the Met I was a consultant to a foundation devoted to the creation of charter schools. I conveyed my enthusiasm to its director and staff on several occasions and urged them to go to Providence, spend at least 2 days there, see for themselves. For several months they did not choose to go from Chicago to Providence. I was quite aware that my descriptions of Dennis, Elliot, and the Met were inadequate. Finally, the head of the foundation agreed to go and spend 2 days there. He came away convinced and inspired. Over the next year he had members of his staff make two visits, with similar reactions. This is not to say they got the whole picture or that they comprehended in any secure way the personal, intellectual, social dynamics of the school or how and

why its history was contained in the present or that they had no questions about what would happen to the students after life at the Met. (Those visits took place before the students were graduated and all but a few accepted by a college.) But one thing is for sure: They had gotten a compelling "sense" that my description of the school was not the hype of a missionary who saw only what his beliefs determined he would see, blotting out evidence to the contrary. If they did not become mindless converts, they had no doubt whatsoever that what they witnessed was very important in its implications for educational reform. It could not, should not, be ignored.

I said earlier that the litmus test of a description of context is the basis it provides for replication. Replications can never be total, a glimpse of the obvious. But when I read the educational reform literature, there are pathetically few descriptions of context that can be a guide even to semi-adequate replication. That is why I have said what I have about CPE and the Met. If you go only by written description, I contend, you cannot assume that the words are doing justice to the complexity of your own experience of the context, a complexity that had for you compelling and propelling features. That does not mean that written description is of no value; that would be a truly stupid conclusion. For the need to convey concepts, ideas, purposes, and values, we have to resort to language. You cannot *see* an idea, a concept, a value, or a theory. We do need language, and I do not want to be interpreted as derogating language for the description of context. There is a difference between derogation and a recognition of the limitations of language for the purpose of influencing readers and listeners to replicate what you have experienced, done, and concluded.

Am I recommending the use of film, not as a substitute, but as an additional way of comprehending context? I do recommend it, whenever the purpose of a serious effort of educational reform is intended to be a means of spreading to and/or requiring other sites to adopt the reform. How best to determine how and to what extent films should be employed are questions I am not competent to address. There are films, and there are films, just as we know that not all filmmakers are equal in their artistry. Films are means, they are not ends in themselves. It will take exploration, creativity, and study to begin to understand the *benefits and limitations* of these films for the purpose of increasing our determination of context. These kinds of film will certainly require the reformer to state as comprehensively as possible what he or she means by context, in itself a methodological virtue; you make films for a purpose and that is the moral and scientific responsibility of the reformer. For me the significance of the films of Central Park East and the Met is the force they give to what I have said in these pages. It can be done and has been done, and I have no doubt it can be done better. I do not view this kind of film as a gimmick, a sales pitch, or a luxury.

In my previous writings I never gave the concept of context the scrutiny it deserved even though all of my experience in schools, and reading the reform literature, left no doubt in my mind that it was a crucial concept. But the seeds of what I have said about films go back to the mid-1960s when Jacob Kounin came to the Yale Psycho-Educational Clinic and showed us a film of two elementary school classrooms in the same school. I have discussed that film in my previous book *American Psychology and Schools: A Critique* (Sarason, 2001). It was a revelation: children of the same age in the same school in classroom contexts that could not be more different. Years later I saw the movie *Mr. Holland's Opus* and marveled at a portrayal of a teacher and a high school which no educator ever told me was other than realistic and valid; I discuss that film in almost all of my books. Then I wrote the book *Letters to a Serious Education President* (1993b), in which I told the fictional president why he should support research on employing films that would demonstrate the difference between contexts of productive and unproductive learning. Then came the film about Dennis Littky and Wiseman's film on Central Park East. It was not until I began writing this book that I finally confronted the fact that depending solely on language to convey context was part of the problem in clarifying why educational reforms do not spread, or if they do, we are at sea about why they fall so short of their mark or are outright failures; we are left with speculations, opinions, and intuitions. A colleague of mine once said of a person, "Deep down he is shallow." That is the way I judge the descriptions of contexts by reformers. And it is also the way I judge myself when I used the concept of context. I do not pretend that I have discernibly advanced in understanding and employing that concept.

Let me try one more time to illustrate what I have intended to say. Freud can be criticized about many of his theorizings and therapeutic practices. But there is one thing even his most articulate critic would be hard put to deny: He gave us a picture of the family drama in its interpersonal complexities. Understanding any family member required seeing that person in the context of his family. It took 75 years before two questions could be asked. The first was, Why were the outcomes of psychotherapy nothing to crow about? The second was, How come, despite his illuminations of the family drama, Freud riveted on treating individuals and not the family in which the problems of the individual had incubated and became manifest? It was in the effort to answer those questions that gave rise to a family therapy in which all members were present at the same time. Then as now psychotherapists trained in and comfortable with treating individuals do not look with favor on family therapy, even though there is reason to believe that family therapy can claim some success (I say that largely, but not exclusively, on the basis of having seen films of family therapy).

No one denies the significance of context, but there is little recognition of the fact that conveying context through written language, despite its other virtues, has its limitations. Films are not substitutes for written language, they are additional ways of illuminating context. It is our failure to recognize that that adds to my pessimism about educational reform. It should not have taken me so long to recognize the implications of that failure. After all, I have spent a large part of my days writing, always agonizably aware of the discrepancy between the words I write and the welter of ideas, relationships, and experiences I want to convey. I envy novelists. They do not have to describe an existing context, they create one. Then again, novelists like reformers have to be believable, and if they are not, we are not likely to buy their next novel.

This chapter has implications for some other educational issues, historical, political, ideological, I initially intended to write about here. The substance of these is and has been a source of controversy. I have written relatively little about some of these issues but not with the depth of feeling I had. I, so to speak, pulled my punches. I regret that. What is going on today in policy discussions about educational reform is not only inexcusable but a disaster.

Chapter 11

What Constitutes a Case History of a Reform Effort?

One of the consequences of thinking about and writing a self-scrutinizing memoir is confronting the fact that you have personal characteristics that antedate and influence how you have dealt with particular substantive problems to which you have devoted your adult years. That is to say, the personal characteristics would have become manifest regardless of the substantive or professional problems that came to occupy me. So, before my attention and energies turned to matters educational, I had thought and written about what, broadly speaking, were psychological issues powered by those personal characteristics. I use the word *powered* advisedly in order to make the point that strong personal needs determined the style of my attack on these problems. Here again I use the word *attack* advisedly because I needed to feel that I would come up with something that would require others (= the world) to change their thinking and actions. You may label it unrealistic ambition, or grandiosity, or narcissism, and I would not disagree if you wanted to convey that I had an inordinate need to be recognized, respected, acclaimed: I wanted to be numero uno; I would see the "truth," others were, unfortunately for them, in "error." I know how that sounds to the reader. I too cringe when I read what I have just said. The fact is that I did not choose to have these personal characteristics. Having said that, let me assure the reader that I have always possessed another characteristic: I know that I do not know all I should know, that there are others who know more than I do, that I am not God's gift to the improvement of logical thinking, and that in my foreshortened future I will, as in the past, commit errors of omission and commission. I would love to be perfect, but I know damned well that I cannot and will not be perfect.

That I am aware of my limitations is not apparent in my writings. On the contrary, I have been a relentless critic of the reform movement. I acknowledge the good intentions of reformers, but I leave no doubt that I regard their efforts as doomed because they do not conceptualize the problems the way I do. There are several sentences that appear frequently in my writings: "The more things change the more they remain the same," Mencken's caveat "For every major problem there is a simple answer that is wrong," and "It is hard to be completely wrong." Almost always I am pointing out either what I see as the Achilles heel (or heels) of a reform effort, or I am predicting that the future results will prove me right. There are critics who, aside from implying I am a hopeless utopian, seem to see me as someone unable to see or admit that perhaps things are not as bad or hopeless as I seem to believe, I am set to see what is wrong, I am allergic to seeing what may be right. I can understand why some people would come to such a conclusion. I have never really attempted to deal with such criticisms until I wrote *The Predictable Failure of Educational Reform* (1990b). That was the book in which I pointed out that in 1965, orally and in print, I predicted that as it was being conceived and implemented educational reform would go nowhere. I was, I said, 100% correct, which is why I had been such a critic of reform: It reinforced the validity of the conceptual underpinnings of my prediction in 1965 and thereafter. What I should have stressed was that I knew it was possible that I was right for the wrong reasons. But no one was pointing out what those reasons might be. That is why after the 1990 book my criticisms continued.

Let me give an instance of the personal-stylistic dilemma I confront when I read about a reform effort. It was reported in the *New York Times* of August 1, 2000, that a charter school was opened for first graders in 1997, new cohorts were added in the next 2 years, and on August 1, 2000, the school was welcoming the fourth cohort. It is an 11-month school housed in what had previously been a Christian Science Church in Newark, New Jersey. It will now have 250 students drawn from a poor area containing Italians and Hispanics.

1. "We found out that we needed 25 percent more time in the day, and so we run from 7:30 a.m. to 5:30 p.m.," said Stephen N. Adubato, one of the guiding forces behind the academy's creation and the executive director of the North Ward Center, a publicly financed social services agency in this mostly Italian and Hispanic neighborhood. "And we found out that we didn't need to have the kids out there hanging out in these dirty streets. They need structure, and this charter school is a lab with a license to innovate and test those things."

2. "Research by the Center for the Social Organization of Schools at Johns Hopkins University adds some scientific weight to Mr. Adubato's view that time spent on city streets in the summer is wasted or even harmful for many students from poor families. The research found what it termed a 'summer slide' in which poor students who were learning at the same pace as their affluent counterparts during the regular school year fell much

further behind over the summer, and tended to forget more of what they had learned."

3. "Teachers received for eleven months what they ordinarily would get for ten months. The teachers chosen when the school opened in 1997 willingly agreed to the eleven months of the year."

4. "The academy's principal, Michael A. Pallante, said the school got about $7,500 per student a year from the Newark school system—about 90% of what other public schools get per student. That money is supplemented with donations from foundations, corporations and the North Ward Center, he said."

5. "This year the school, with its first fourth grade class, will administer the statewide assessment test for all fourth graders."

I did not approach reading the article dispassionately. Two years before I had written *Charter Schools: Another Flawed Educational Reform?* (1998a). In that book I detailed why I predicted two things. First, most charter schools would fall far short of their intended goals. Second, we would never be able to ascertain why some charter schools failed and others did not. (I make it clear that as a concept, symbol, or principle I am very much in favor of charter schools, a fact some critics fail to acknowledge.) I began reading the article with the "here we go again" expectation. I was right and wrong. What initially caught my eye was the name and role of Mr. Adubato whom I have never met. But I do watch his program on the New York–New Jersey PBS channel 13 devoted to the New Jersey political scene as well as to the state's social problems. He is a very bright and sharp, articulate and forceful individual who is politically and socially knowledgeable and well connected. He has an independent mind and a keen sense of social responsibility. He has a challenging but not abrasive interpersonal style. As the article suggests, he is a driving force behind the charter school. And I would be mightily surprised if he has not played the major role in attracting financial and other resources to the charter school. Also, he probably should be credited for creating a school that is in and of a particular community, not an alien body in it.

On the basis of this long newspaper article I am able to perform an act of faith and say that if I had to bet I would give odds that this charter school will in the future be judged as a successful one, a judgment I have rarely made about charter schools I have known. Yes, there are many questions I would ask about the creation and development of the school which might make me change my mind, but those are not questions a newspaper article should be expected to answer. Nevertheless, when I finished reading the article, I was pleasantly surprised that I would bet as I indicated.

But, I asked myself, what if I had read the article when I was writing the charter school book? The answer is that I would have been critical of the significance people would draw from its hoped-for success. In the context of the history of the charter school movement, it is of very limited significance that this or that charter school succeeded or failed. Of course, the people who can demonstrate the success of their efforts deserve praise, just as people who failed or fell short of the mark deserve no commendation. There are reasons a school is given charter status: (a) It has an innovative rationale, (b) it has tailored appropriate methodologies to that rationale, (c) it will employ appropriate and credible descriptions and assessments of accomplishments, and (d) it will provide the chartering agency with a basis for increasing or decreasing the number of charter schools and/or changing its criteria for giving schools a charter. The reader should not gloss over the fact—and it is a fact—that charter schools rest on the assumption that if you seek to innovate, you have to be independent of the school system. And precisely because of their innovations it is hoped and expected that charter schools will have a positive impact on schools in the traditional school system. In other words, charter schools were not conceived as isolated sites or events, as if each exists in a world of its own, of its own making.

To meet such an objective requires a careful, detailed, candid, longitudinal account of the process, issues, and problems encountered and how and to what degree they were dealt with. It is essentially a case history of how a group of people (by no means homogeneous) thought, changed, adapted, and even compromised in experiencing and doing as they did. In the absence of such an account we have no basis whatsoever for identifying those "variables" (individuals, leadership, events, problems, conflicts, and so forth) which contributed to success or failure. That is by way of saying that we have no basis for replication; it is, so to speak, a "private experience" from which the surrounding world will learn nothing or will draw unjustifiable conclusions.

On December 29, 2000, the *Washington Post* contained a news article with the headline "Texas Charter School Moratorium Urged." There are 193 charter schools in Texas. "In the past two years, at least seven have closed because of problems ranging from declining attendance to financial mismanagement to embezzlement. Only 59 percent of Texas charter school students passed a state skills exam in the 1998–99 school year, compared with the state average of 78.4 percent. And this summer, the state education agency gave an 'unacceptable' rating to nearly one-fourth of 103 charter schools it studied." I could say the article is grist for my mill of predictions. The fact is that I do not know what were the criteria for "unacceptable" or how to interpret the achievement test scores (e.g., in terms of past performance or in comparison to scores in similar noncharter schools). It is apparent from the article that we will never know how to judge why some charter schools are failing or succeeding. What the article says about Texas has also been reported about Arizona which has a far greater number of charter schools. We are dealing with a conceptual and methodological mess motivated by good intentions and abysmal ignorance. By any criterion of accountability, the Texas legislature and those with the responsibility to initiate and monitor the charter schools get an F.

I know of no charter school which was prepared to keep track of its creation and development, and I would bet (again) and give very handsome odds that such a longitudinal account is not in the picture of the school Adubato and his colleagues created, and that is why the praise of them that I can muster is very lukewarm. My severest criticism is of those elected state and federal officials who in a self-congratulating manner pass reform legislation which does not require or provide funds for keeping that kind of a record from which we can learn why a success is a success and a failure is a failure.

I feel compelled to reiterate that keeping such a record would not be required if each charter school was not expected to have significance beyond its walls. But that is the opposite of what charter school advocates said and still say: Charter schools are expected—at the least, hoped—to be influential on changing school systems from which they were "freed." And that influence would be based on credible evidence demonstrating what contributes to differing degrees of success or failure. Rhetoric and personal opinion alone are not in the category of credible evidence. The Food and Drug Administration will not approve drug or medication for public use unless there is credible evidence that it is safe and effective even though it may have side effects of a degree and kind that does not contradict approval. The first cohorts of charter schools should have been similarly scrutinized before passing legislation dramatically expanding the number of new charter schools. There are several reasons no proposal of mine has ever been taken seriously. First, each proposal derives from a criticism of the quick-fix mentality. Second, the proposals are not cosmetic and are seen by diverse vested interests and stakeholders as, so to speak, preventing them from going their own way. Third, there is and cannot be a guarantee that any noncosmetic reform will, initially at least, not require correction in conception and method; we are not dealing with simple problems in uncomplicated institutions which have been immune to changing old traditions and ways of thinking about learning and education. Fourth, I am seen, at best, as impractical and, at worst, as a utopian.

Yes, I have had little to say of positive nature of the educational reform movement; please note that I did not say *nothing*, I said *little*. The reader should bear in mind that I have lived through all but two decades

of the twentieth century. For the past 60 years I have been either a participant in or an observer of what seems (to me at least) to have been countless reform efforts. For a number of years (perhaps 10–15) I got caught up
in the fads and fashions, the "new" thinking and programs that came and
went on the educational stage. The Federal Office of Education, its succes-
sor, the Department of Education, and numerous well-heeled foundations
became factories supporting a myriad of reform programs. They, like the
charter-school movement, were suffused with optimism, promoted with
Madison Avenue–like hype, had their 15 minutes of celebrity, and then left
the stage. This, I hasten to add, does not mean they were all mindless affairs.
As I like to say, it is hard to be completely wrong, although many of them
were just that: wrong, superficial, mindless, and utopian in their utter insensitivity to the complexities of schools and school systems. There were a
few efforts which deserved to be taken seriously, more on the level of
conceptualization than implementation, but they were written up in ways
that simply did not allow me to distinguish between important and unimportant causal values. Far from becoming a utopian, I was steadily becoming a somewhat disillusioned realist trying to make sense of a congeries of
efforts whose major characteristics met not a single criterion on any list of
what constitutes credible evidence; they were worse than impractical, they
obscured or distracted attention away from basic issues.

    I know that writing up the substance and history of a reform effort is
no easy task, as professional historians well know. Such a write-up is not
just telling a story in a chronological way; there is a cast of characters differing in age, education, experience, values, power, personal style, and
more. It is especially complicated and thorny in a reform effort because it
is crucial to determine, with some degree of clarity, why goals of the effort
were not as robust as one had hoped and how subsequent reform efforts
have to be altered in small or large ways. *I am not the one who is imposing the
task on the reformers; it is in the nature of the way the reformers have defined
their goals and how they wanted their efforts to be interpreted and used by others.*
As a reformer, if you do not assume and discharge that obligation, why
on earth did you and your colleagues devote so much time, energy, and
resources to the effort? If you do not intend to give us as complete an account as possible—and I know that completeness is impossible—of what
was done and why, and with what predictable and unpredictable results,
we are left with personal opinions as well as scores of unanswered questions. Strongly held personal opinions are crucial as sources of motivation
for implementing a complicated reform effort, but does it make me a carping critic when after reformers write up their findings they have not provided me other than personal opinions about why things worked or didn't
work, what errors of omission and commission others should avoid, what

compromises they had to make as they experienced the brute fact that they were operating in an arena they did not and could not control, one which is far from predictable, and what they would do differently if they were to do it all over again? The name of the game is context, and if I am not provided with a sense of that complicated context about which I am knowledgeable, it should be understandable if I have to conclude that I cannot accept the interpretations and conclusions of the reformer. I am not being oppositional; I am like the matron in the Wendy's commercial who plaintively asked, "Where's the beef?"

Let me give two examples of the point I am trying to make. The first is very recent, the second goes back 50 years. Taken together they confronted me with one of my errors of misplaced emphasis. It was not that I was unaware of a particular and important point, but I did not do justice to it in my writings.

In August 2000, I received a manuscript of a case study (a longitudinal account) of a segregated elementary school in Houston which for decades served the children of poor Black parents. The manuscript was authored by Liane Brouillette, formerly of the University of Houston and now at the University of California at Irvine.[1] It is a fascinating account in which observation, interviews, and archival data are skillfully used to convey a sense of context. The central character is Thaddeus Lott, a man who when he became principal of this dispiriting school began to change the world of the school, with the result that test scores for that school exceeded those of schools in the affluent parts of the city. Far from being greeted with relief, approval, or praise, the educational authorities looked for shenanigans. "One possible answer ('They cheat') fell by the wayside after numerous investigations and even a few classroom shakedowns in search of pre-test subterfuge."

At the center of the resistance to the acceptance of the elevated test scores was the school's use of Direct Instruction. I have many reservations about Direct Instruction, and Brouillette fairly presents those criticisms which have in common the point that Direct Instruction is a form of ritual which reinforces mindless rote memory and a subversion of learning how to think independently and creatively; that is to say, it is rampant rote learning, a shortchanging of children's potential to be the thinkers we want them to be. It views students as recording devices able only to play back what others want them to play back, it is regimentation.

So how do you explain the superior test scores? If all I knew was that Direct Instruction had been religiously employed, it would not have altered

---

1. I highly recommend Brouillette's *Charter Schools: Lessons in School Reform* (2002).

my criticism of it. But prior to her description of Direct Instruction Brouillette had given a stirring, poignant, longitudinal account of the ambiances of two interrelated contexts: within the school and local community. That explains why when I read Brouillette's description of a Direct Instruction classroom what popped into my mind was what I had seen in religious services in Black churches: features of evangelical revival meetings in which ministers and audiences willingly, happily, and spontaneously play mutually reinforcing roles. The teacher was not demanding responsiveness, or fostering a ritual in which students *had* to participate. The students *wanted*—and that is the key word—to do what they were doing, it made cognitive and emotional sense to them, they were engaged, they were not dutifully going through the motions with no sense of purpose. And that was as true for the teacher as it was for the students. As Brouillette implies, this was not like a play but a musical, a potpourri of personal expressiveness. The teacher was not performing as a traditional teacher, but as a galvanizing performing artist always alert to what captures an audience, what will make that audience willing and even eager to return for more. I am, therefore, not surprised that the students at Wesley Elementary School have the test scores they do. But it is missing the trees for the forest to attribute them to Direct Instruction, as if that tool and its rationale suffice for an explanation. Absent the kind of teacher and a most unusual principal Brouillette describes, and the cultural religious similarities between students and teacher as well as between teachers and parents, Direct Instruction by itself cannot be expected to foster one of the most important criteria of a context of productive learning: *wanting* to learn but not because learning is externally demanded. In the restaurant business they say success depends on three things: location, location, location. In schools the three things are context, context, and context. If you do not know the context, your explanation or judgment of what you see or what has been reported can be misleading or wrong.

As I said, if all I knew about Wesley Elementary School was that Direct Instruction was being used, my reservations about that tool and rationale would not change. I would be puzzled, to be sure, by the elevated test scores, but I would have no basis for altering my reservations about Direct Instruction. I still have those reservations, but in the process of reading Brouillette's paper I was reminded that over the decades I had observed teachers, albeit relatively few in numbers and almost all in the ghetto schools, who created and sustained an ambiance in their classrooms that made for productive learning. They did not use Direct Instruction, but they engendered in their students a wanting to learn that was reflected in elevated test scores. *In none of these instances was there another teacher in the school who could claim similar accomplishments.* In fact, in all of these instances the teacher was in a school where other teachers created context of *unproductive* learning, the kind of context I found very difficult to observe without feeling sorry for the students. Considered as a whole the Wesley Elementary School is a context of productive learning both for students and teachers.

What I am saying here is something of which I was aware but did not write about in terms of its theoretical and practical import. Let me make the point by analogy. Two things have long been acknowledged in the psychotherapy community. First, there is no one type of psychotherapy that is effective with all clients and all sources of personal stress and misery. Second, by virtue of personality and interpersonal style some psychotherapists are inadequate and ineffective with the approach they were trained to employ. More generally and the way I have previously put it: Not all psychologists should be psychologists, not all physicians should be physicians, not all social workers should be social workers, and so forth. The "tools of the trade"—the way they are employed and their effectiveness—are never independent of whatever is meant by the user's personality, nor is the user's personality totally independent of and uninfluenced by the context in which the user is a member.

If I have had reservations about Direct Instruction, it was not because I believed that there were no conditions and context for which it was appropriate but rather because it was being promoted as if it was the answer independent of teacher style and characteristics. Like it or not, ignore it or not, the obvious fact remains: Outcomes are a consequence of teacher and context variables. It would be nice if it were otherwise but that is not the way the human and social cookies are constructed and crumble.

I judge any educational reform by (1) how clearly it has addressed the task of how you reinforce and sustain a child's wanting to learn, and (2) how well it can demonstrate that there is evidence (other than personal opinion, mine or any one else's) that the task has achieved its goal, or (3) if it has not achieved its goal for a significant number of students, whether we are provided an explanation that will serve as a basis of altering the approach. For me, wanting to learn more is crucial, a fire that will spread beyond the confines of a particular lesson or subject matter. The artistry of the teacher inheres in his or her ability to help spread the student's fire to new domains. That will sound idealistic, utopian, or romantic only to those people unable or unwilling to recognize that until we can establish the differences between contexts of productive and unproductive learning—the criteria for identifying them—we are dooming ourselves to disappointments in the future no less than in the past. I have posed the problem, but I do not pretend to have done more than clarify it *somewhat.* I have my limitations as diagnostician and theoretician. Nevertheless, what I think I understand about a context of productive learning has been the basis of my depressing predictions about why reform efforts have near totally failed in the past and will continue to fail in the future. Unfortunately, my track record for accurate predicting has been very good. I say "unfortunately" because although I take intellectual satisfaction from my track record, I take no satisfaction whatever for what it portends for the society's future.

I used Brouillette's paper for the purpose of illustrating the bedrock importance of stimulating and supporting a student's wanting to learn, to learn more, willingly to experience how such wanting takes him or her to domains of knowledge and actions that had been, understandably so, not in the ken of the student. Wanting to learn is a door opener to heretofore unknown worlds. A teacher lights that kind of fire with the hope that it will rage and spread. That is why I have chosen another real life example, one involving literally millions of adults and many thousands of teachers. *What I shall describe had nothing to do with educational reform, it was not powered by any theory of learning.* What these millions of adults were told went like this: "We will make it financially possible for you to obtain any kind of education you decide you need and want which will allow you to do what you want to become regardless of the level of education you previously obtained. If you want to go to graduate school as preparation to become this or that kind of professional, if you are already such a professional and want to switch fields, we will provide you with funds for tuition, fees, books, and a monthly learning stipend. All this (and more) will be possible. The only thing you have to do is gain admittance to an approved educational or vocational institution appropriate to your goal. In no way will we play a role in what you decide. Our sole obligation is to provide the funds that will support you in whatever direction your interests have taken you."

That is the message contained in legislation we know as the GI Bill of Rights of which several million World War II veterans took advantage. Two considerations explain why that legislation was enacted. First, it was a reflection of the sincere gratitude the society felt toward veterans, a gratitude that carried with it an obligation to compensate for disrupted lives, separation from family and loved ones, psychological and physical trauma, and predictable problems veterans would have in returning to civilian life after a long war in which they were scattered all over the planet. The second consideration was memories of the Great Depression which ended only when it was apparent that we would have to enter the war. Would the return of million of veterans to civilian life bring about another depression, a possibility that would add insult to injury in what veterans had experienced? It was a scenario for civil strife.

I have written about how the GI Bill changed lives, the university, and the society. I began my teaching career in 1945 when cascades of veterans were flooding college campuses. What I experienced and concluded in the next 15 years is part of my personal story. How many times have I over the years schmoozed with colleagues of my age from diverse colleges and universities about how rewarding it was to teach and be with the veterans? Many scores of times. Those veterans were not passive, they asked questions, many could voice disagreements, they did not want to be treated as empty buckets to be filled, they were full of fire. They wanted to learn, change, grow; they were intellectually hungry.

What I am suggesting, of course, is that they contributed one of the hallmarks of a context of productive learning: *they wanted to learn*. But there was another feature that has received little or no attention. The teachers of these veterans appreciated and respected them. We understood why they were there, which is to say that we knew where they were coming from and that labeling them as "students" was institutionally correct and psychologically wrong. That was especially true in my case because many of the veterans were my age or older, and I was quite aware that they had spent months or years in the military, a fact that exacerbated my insecurity as a fledgling teacher. Our relationship very quickly became one of friendship that endured over the years. At the center of a context of productive learning is a quality of relationship between students and teacher in which students feel safe, recognized, and understood. I am referring to classrooms which were in university departments which in turn were in a larger institutional ecology. Saying that allows me to identify another feature of a context of productive learning: For a decade or so after World War II it is fair to say that all layers of the university seemed to acknowledge that veterans were a breed apart, not the students of the prewar years. They had to be understood as individuals who had had special experiences and had unusual needs, pressures, and goals. Teachers and administrators were not impersonal figures bureaucratically discharging their obligations to "rule." I am not trying to convey an idealized picture in which everybody, or even most people, became born-again humans. I am reporting what I observed and experienced. Let me give one example. In prewar Yale, students had to wear a tie, buttoned shirt, and jacket at dinner. When the veterans arrived, and in very short order, it was as if the only thing the dress code prohibited was nudity. Nobody complained, no one said anything. In my later years at Yale I became friendly with John Perry Miller who had become dean of the graduate school. We were reminiscing about the "old days," and I brought up the change in the dress code. He said, " When people looked at veterans and thought about foxholes, prisoners of war, Kamikaze bombing of aircraft carriers, Guadalcanal and Iwo Jima, who wanted to say anything about a dress code? Who really cared?"

I began this chapter discussing a charter school in Newark which its creators obviously believe is on the way to meeting its goals. I explained why from my standpoint I was not being a perverse contrarian in saying that there was no expectation that there would ever be presented a description of process and context. Attaching as I do such importance to the differences between contexts of productive and unproductive learning, I need more than personal opinion or scores on a state test to be able to conclude that whatever the outcomes they are consistent with prior statements of goals. And that is no less the case if that charter school is not as successful as was hoped. Yes, I assume that the creators of the school did not create it only to demonstrate that students could pass the state test. That is to say, they would not be satisfied if fires had not been lit in the minds of the students, however much what was poured into their mental buckets they were able to pour out on a test. The creators of the school want more than that. But, as I predict, we will not be provided with a description of context giving us even a semisecure basis for judgment; we will remain in the dark.

So why did I respond so favorably to Brouillette's account of a poor, Black, Houston elementary school where the test scores were consistently and amazingly high and where a teaching program was employed about which I had long been critical because it was based on a conception of learning that struck me as rigid, narrow, and fact oriented? In fact, on my initial reading of her paper, when I came to the part on the Direct Instruction program, my unreflective response was, "Is this going to be another instance of filling buckets and extinguishing fires?" I was wrong. I was not taking seriously the crucial significance of context. Brouillette provided a description of context that caused me to think and see the issues and the outcomes in a different light. Those children obviously, unmistakenly, enthusiastically wanted to learn, and everything and everyone in that school context reinforced that wanting, not the least the principal, Thaddeus Lott. Without knowledge of context, explanation becomes a guessing game or, in my case, an unjustified negative judgment.

The GI Bill story is for me the most significant for the purposes of this chapter, even though the context relevant to its educational consequences has never been studied. So how to justify the importance I attach to the GI Bill? There are several reasons. The first is that the GI Bill was intended to have positive educational consequences for a mass of veterans. Second, those consequences were never spelled out because concrete outcomes would be a function, initially at least, of decisions veterans would make about what they wanted to do, what they wanted to learn and become. Third, I and thousands of teachers were part of the context, and I have never known any of them to disagree with what I and Ambrose have described or concluded. Being part of the context is a mixed blessing when it comes to description and explanation, but when you can find no one in the teaching role, in very different colleges and universities, who does not agree with what you experienced and concluded, you are justified in the belief that something special was happening. Fourth, while that belief is confirmed time and again by what recipients spontaneously report of the impact of the GI Bill on the trajectory of their lives, you can assume that your beliefs are not out in left field or the products of your imagination and distortions of memory. You are justified in describing the educational context as I have. Fifth, when the number of veterans entering higher education became smaller and you became aware that a number of features of the learning context had changed—characteristics of students, a dramatic increase in the size of educational institution , a younger faculty, an obvious increase in layers of an administrative bureaucracy—it was hard not to note that the learning context was changing in diverse ways, none of them conducive to the high level of wanting to learn.

Wanting to learn—have I emphasized that too much as if it were a magic bullet which alone determines trajectory and outcome? Am I subject to the same criticism directed at John Dewey who a century ago said many of the things I have said? He is one of my heroes. Many years ago I saw a magazine cartoon in which a young child in a Dewey "progressive school" plaintively asks the teacher, "*Must* I do what I *want* to do today?"

In the course of writing this self-scrutinizing memoir I think I know why I give wanting to learn so much emphasis. Although no one has ever disagreed with the way I have put and emphasized it, I have been both puzzled and discouraged by how the bulk of these people are unaware that their *practice* violates what they presumably believe. There are several factors that play a role in this disconnect, but there is one about which I have not been all that clear. Briefly put, assuming that there is much that any child wants to learn about or do, and that not all students want to learn about the same things, the task of the teacher is awesomely difficult, and for most teachers, overwhelming. As schools and classrooms are conventionally organized, as preparatory programs train teachers to conform to that organization, it is an impossible task. The would-be teacher learns to articulate the usual, high-sounding rhetoric: Each child is a distinctive individual, each child can learn, the mission of the school is to help the *individual* fully realize his or her potential. It does not take long at all for that would-be teacher to understand that rhetoric is one thing, acting consistently with it is quite another thing, much like the difference between *your* fantasy and *your* reality.

Yes, as things are now, it is an impossible task. But the *practical* problem is not how to solve what, as a teacher, you know in your heart of hearts to be impossible but rather to what degree you can approximate your goal.

As I have said many times, it is not sinful to fall short of the mark, it is sinful not to have a mark. There is a difference between compromising your beliefs and caving in to the easy way out.

What I have just said is based on the fact that over the decades I have observed teachers, relatively very few in number, who by my criteria fell short of the mark but who in comparison to most other teachers approximated the goal of lighting fires in students; most of their students wanted to learn, they were active, alive, and eager to learn. I could describe what their teachers did and the quality of their relationship to students. *But if it occurred to me at the time to explain the assumptions and beliefs that determined why they did what they did in the style they did, I could not have done so.* They varied in terms of personality and style. In short, I could not explain their artistry. My thinking about teaching had not developed to the point where I truly understood that teaching is a very complicated art. That came much later in my book *Teaching as a Performing Art* (1999), and I was posing the problem, I was not explaining it. I regret that it took me so long to see the obvious because it would have influenced some important issues in my earlier writings. At the least, I would have been obliged to say that we know precious little about the artistry of teaching and how it engenders or stifles a student's wanting to learn. In the past 2 decades we have become used to hearing from educators and elected officials how important it is to train more or better qualified teachers. I have yet to hear any of them define *better qualified*. Aside from saying that teachers should take subject-matter courses, what they mean by better qualified has the clarifying features of a poorly reproduced ink blot. I wish I had been able to say that years ago. I was not an especially slow learner, but it took me too long to see what I now regard as obvious: Teaching is a very complicated performing art which has hardly been recognized or studied.

If you take seriously the importance of wanting to learn, how should a teacher capitalize on such a belief or assumption? I cannot answer that question, I have no recipe book. Speaking only for myself and knowing how I learn and what I want to learn, there is only one way I can conceivably come up with a beginning answer: *I would have to teach in a school and experience what is involved in taking seriously what I believe.* I know I would make mistakes, commit errors of omission and commission, question my sanity and endurance (let alone wisdom), and experience for the umpteenth time the difference between giving advice based on abstractions in contrast to using concrete experience gained over time. I am too old and infirm to act out such a fantasy. Of one thing I am certain: Not until a variety of investigators study teaching as a performing art will the conceptual skies begin to clear and, as I predicted in my book, will the selection and the preparation of teachers stand a chance of being radically and appropriately transformed. The current conception of teaching is as inimical to educational reform as is the quick-fix mentality because both are obstacles, mammoth ones, to the recognition that we have met the enemy and it is us.

Finally, there is another reason it took me so long to realize the importance of seeing teaching as a performing art. It is a reason inherent in what initially attracted me to the arena of education reform. It is an instance of what I said at the very beginning of this chapter: I came to the arena with strong interests determining how I would approach school reform, what my focus would be. It was not that I dispassionately, rationally, systematically explored whether to start with this or that problem and method. If, back then, you would have asked me what I was going to do, I would have given you a professorial lecture on why it was so important to understand the culture of schools. It was and is an accurate answer. If the answer is phenomenologically valid, it was an uncomplicated one, certainly a too global one. Today as a result of writing this self-scrutinizing memoir, I realize that long before I came to think about educational reform I was always interested in *contexts:* their structure and boundaries, the behavioral regularities they fostered and reinforced, and how people's behavior varied depending on the contexts which you observed. In *Teaching as a Performing Art* I give two examples. One was the internationally respected child developmentalist, Charlotta Bühler, from whom in 1943 I took a seminar in graduate school; the other was Henry Schaefer-Simmern (1948), an art teacher, historian, and theorist I encountered shortly after graduate school. Both were émigrés, imperious, arrogant, and intimidating. I interacted with them in different contexts. I cannot exaggerate how astounded and flabbergasted I was the first time I observed each of them relate to children. Each was amazingly sensitive, supportive, even tender. The lesson I learned went beyond "different contexts, different behavior." What got seared in my head was something not emphasized in my training either as a clinician or researcher: If the conclusions you come to are based exclusively or primarily on observations in one context, you may be drawing some very incomplete or misleading conclusions. That was not a lesson I learned in any conscious, thinking-through manner. But in ways I cannot describe or account for, it powered how I approached the culture of schools. Whatever is meant by the school culture, it refers to, among other things, contrasts within it: classrooms varying in terms of age of students, the gymnasium, the principal's office, the teachers' lounge, the school cafeteria, faculty meetings, parent's night, and so forth.

Contexts are what Roger Barker, the founder of ecological psychology, called behavior settings because they have what are called demand characteristics: they set boundaries on what people say and do in a particular behavior setting, for example, in a school assembly. A school is part of a system of schools, but it is not a system in which contexts in one school ever have anything to do with contexts in another school. So, for example, I was puzzled that no school (or any context in it) interacted with a similar school several blocks away. How could I account for that? How did school people account for that ? Did the two schools have nothing to learn from each other, nothing to give and take? Those questions got connected in my mind with the obvious feature of the classroom as the sole turf and responsibility of the teacher, and just as he or she does not want to tell another teacher how to think, he or she does not want another teacher or even the principal to intrude into his or her turf.

My interest in contexts prevented me from recognizing what I now believe is a bedrock problem: achieving a better understanding of teaching as a performing art so that we will be better able to *select and train* teachers by criteria and methods vastly different from and more appropriate to the creation and sustenance of contexts of productive learning in classrooms. I know I am right, and at the same time I know that the self-convincing process can have the unfortunate and unintended consequences of self-deception.

Chapter 12

Math, Music, and Learning

When do you say nothing about an issue which you believe to be crucially important for the cultural life of the country but which receives the most superficial discussion by practically everyone else? Do you remain silent because you are convinced that what you have to say will be neither understood nor appreciated and at best will cause you to be seen as an idealist unable to adapt to realities? To whom are you obligated? To yourself and your ideas? To a future which may come to understand your ideas and suggestions or to a present so beset with seemingly intractable problems that you should put the ideas on your intellectual back burner and try to be "practical"? This chapter is about issues of human development about which I chose to remain silent, and I very much regret my lack of courage to say what I believed even though it would be met with silence or a kind of patronizing respect given to an aged person who does not know he has shot his bolt and is no longer in touch with the world of ideas and practice. Since, as I like to say, it is hard to be completely wrong, I cannot assert that those who will criticize me are completely wrong. Enough of this prologue of musings—let me put my cards on the table, if only because the self-scrutinizing process which stimulated this book requires it.

What are the activities to which preschoolers are exposed to, interested in, and enjoy? One of them is music. They hear sounds from day one, but as the days go on, almost all parents sing to the infant, sometimes to soothe, sometimes to express joy. Parents are often surprised and delighted when the child seems to respond differently to music (melody, rhythm). There are pregnant mothers who believe that exposing the fetus to music may condition it later to be more receptive to music. (Apparently there is some evidence for such a belief, but it is still very much an open question.) The ways, occasions, and frequency with which parents use music in their interactions with the very young child have hardly been studied. To the parent it happens "naturally," unreflectively, it is "one of those things" that the parent "just" does. There comes a time when it is obvious to the parent that the child not only responds differentially to music but hugely enjoys it and seems to seek to get the parent to repeat the music, and the parent willingly, even enthusiastically obliges. The parent conditions the child, and the child conditions the parent; neither is indifferent to music, it is both a means and an end. There are households where popular and classical music are being played for long periods of time on records, radio, and TV for parent pleasure, and it is the rare parent who will say that their 2- or 3-year-old child displays no preferences or differential attention and interest. Interest is the point to be emphasized because it connotes curiosity and motivation, not simply a fleeting response. Even before the child can talk, the world of sound and music is taking on shape, context, interest, and emotion. Even before the child can talk, the world of music is not only "out there," but "in there" as well.

That TV has changed the world is a gross understatement, which is very clear in regard to preschoolers' hearing and singing music. There were and are many parents who as soon as their child could securely sit up in a high chair or locomote would plant the child before the TV set to watch children's programs or cartoons, all of which contain a good deal of music. You do not have to be an astute observer to see how actively they become engaged. Let me give one representative example. During the years when the Mouseketeers were watched by millions of preschoolers, many of those children could not read, but they could spell Mickey Mouse: "M-I-C" (pause) "K-E-Y" (pause) "M-O-U-S-E," just as they heard it sung on the program. Many doctoral dissertations have been done on less important topics, but I have no doubt that studies of TV children's programs, language acquisition, and self-initiated singing would be very revealing and instructive. Singing and music become the child's way of internally mastering the world to which he is exposed. It is not a passive kind of mastery but an active one that, so to speak, feeds on itself; it motivates, propels. I have known preschoolers who could not read who by age 4 could sing perfectly "Rudolph, the Red-Nosed Reindeer." And I could say the same for "I'm Dreaming of a White Christmas." When children do this, it says a great deal about wanting to learn and the importance of the relationship between music and the concrete interests of preschoolers.

Relevant here is the series of TV concerts for children Leonard Bernstein conducted approximately 50 years ago. The audience in the concert hall was comprised of young children some of whom by visual inspection were preschoolers. I watched it on TV with my wife and preschool daughter. Bernstein was Bernstein: Flamboyant, a virtuoso storyteller, he had an amazing sensitivity to the nature of his audience and, in this case, spoke with and not down to the audience. His objective was to employ concrete imagery as a means to explain and appreciate music: the composer's intentions. Anyone who watched our family of three would have seen what we saw on the faces of Bernstein's live young audience. Fascination tells only part of the story. It was as if a new world was being revealed, as if the familiar world of music took on new meanings. It was as if we (they) did not want the program to end, there was more to learn and enjoy. We are used to hearing that music is abstract, whatever personal meaning it has depends on the listener, a kind of inkblot you respond to depending on the kind of person you are. There is a kernel of truth to that but it is just that: a kernel. The genius of Bernstein as teacher, composer, and conductor was to demonstrate convincingly to young children that music has structure, intent, and organization, which when we comprehend it enlarges our understanding and appreciation of aspects of a world about which we had not known. Popular songs are popular because the words and music reinforce each other and are easily assimilated by our own imagery, feelings, and fantasies. In addition, singing popular music is something the child wants and is capable of *doing*; the child listens but then *acts*. Music has become for the child a personal activity. When children hear classical or chamber music, the absence of words is a barrier to relating the music to concrete ideas and experience. It is not surprising that so many people go through life hardly ever listening to such music; for them the music is not comprehensible in any concrete meaningful way. Bernstein's concerts for young children was his way of demonstrating that such music can be concretely meaningful, a source of pleasure, and a goad to exploring such music. The several programs were a kind of crash course, an introductory one at that, to make the point. Bernstein was planting seeds he knew could sprout if the appropriate soil was provided and sustained by the appropriate fertilizers.

Without denying its learned aspects, I have argued that the human organism is "wired" to be attracted to and influenced by music, and the musical experience (passive or active) becomes a force in the organization and expression of feeling, thinking, and fantasy. It is a pleasurable experience, a propelling one that feeds on itself. I said it is pleasurable, but in the case of the preschooler it would be more correct to say that it is a joyous one, and that point should not be underestimated because it is inextricably part of the child's need for self-mastery, personal expression, and ways of influencing and even controlling the behavior of others. Music is also a stimulant to and reinforcer of curiosity and seeking. As parents we readily assent to the assertion that music is of great interest to our preschoolers, but our assent does not do justice to its encompassing, percolating, organizational, motivational, and cognitive dynamics. We learn to do more justice to the role of music when we observe the magnetic quality that it has for our adolescents and teenagers. Some parents are bemused, some puzzled, some aghast at their teenager's obsessive interest in the popular music of the day and its social, age-graded, cultural aspects. It did not take long after World War II for parents and others to become aware that the younger generation was turning away from, if not rejecting, what had for decades been the popular music. There is no simple explanation for the change, and it is not important for the point I have been emphasizing: the force and role of the new music in the lives of the younger generation, and how it became connected with other calls for social change. The now legendary Woodstock happening was about far more than music even though the music was visually center stage.

It was on these and other grounds that I have long been asking myself several interrelated questions. Why is it that in many schools music plays little or no role as an activity or a course? Why is it that when budgets are cut, music is a sitting, unarmed target as if it is a luxury or frill, the absence of which will not affect "real" school learning? How do school personnel explain and what conclusions do they draw from the fact that outside of school students display an obvious and intense interest in music, and yet as they go through the grades their interest in learning steadily decreases? I have asked these questions of teachers, administrators at all levels. Their answers can be paraphrased in this way: "Certainly there ought to be more exposure to music in the curriculum. Kids love to hear and sing music, and many of them would jump for joy if they had the opportunity to learn to play an instrument which, of course, for a lot of them coming from poor or economically borderline families or from homes where music is not especially valued is impossible. There are two problems. The first, of course, is money. Try selling the argument to officialdom and the community that the school budget should be increased so as to support more music education. For example, during an economic turndown a decade ago several school systems in Connecticut decided to cut the football program because it is expensive. All hell broke loose, and the schools backed down. Even when there is no economic turndown but a resistance to higher property taxes, asking for money to have a respectable music curriculum is dead from the get-go. The other problem is that the curriculum is already crowded. There is little or no room for additions now and in the foreseeable future. Where do you cut to make room? We are criticized for not doing a better job in the core curriculum courses, and we are under pressure to do more, which means more time for that core. We are aware that outside of schools students are galvanized by popular music, not classical music, but we can't compete. I do not know how we can compete. I am not sure we should try. Beside, no one is asking us to try."

Let me present my position by a personal example. During the summer before my last year in graduate school (1941–42) I worked for a well-known consulting statistician. My job was to crunch numbers; nothing fancy, just crunching numbers. I had taken an introductory math course in college and a statistics course in graduate school. In the graduate course I had learned that plus and minus one standard deviation from the midpoint of the normal probability curve contained 68% of the scores of the particular variable that had been studied. We had been offered no explanation why that had to be so; it was a "law" that had many applications. One day during a conversation with Dr. Franzen, when he was going over the numbers I had crunched that day and he was talking aloud to himself about what the numbers meant, I told him that I did not understand what was for me the "plus and minus one standard deviation law." I was emboldened to ask him because I had already learned that he was a frustrated teacher and, very important, he liked and respected me, another fact that puzzled me. The long and short of it is that over the next several days he taught me enough calculus to begin to sense (not really to know) the derivation of the normal probability curve. That explains why years later when I was writing the school culture book (1971) and was aware of (a) how students did not enjoy math, (b) how teachers did not enjoy teaching math, and (c) how the "new math" was proclaimed as a semipanacea for a and b, I began to ask my highly educated friends this question: In the years since you took math—and I do not include arithmetic—how many times have you had occasions to use calculus, geometry, or trigonometry? I asked that question of social scientists (including psychologists from the "hard" part of that field), physicians, friends in business and industry, and people in the humanities. If it was not a random sample of highly educated people, at least it was not a small sample. Not one person could remember a time when he or she had used math. I would bet and give very attractive odds that the number of readers of this book who could say that they used the math they learned in school and college would be minuscule. Before going on let me say that the most influential course I took in college was taught by Herbert Woodward on the history of science. And by *influential* I mean that I learned about ideas, cultures, individuals, eras, and the canons of science things I have never forgotten and, more important, draw on today. And because of that course I then took Woodward's geology course in which in the most detailed and masterly way he disabused me and the other students of the possibility that the core of our planet was hard. That was the second most instructive course I ever took.

The third most instructive college course I took was Richard Henry's introduction to mathematics. He, like Woodward, considered logical thinking to be the most important thing which he wanted his students to appreciate, not in the abstract but via newspaper articles and columnists where our job was to examine the relations between premise and conclusion, between fact and opinion. Henry did not neglect the conventional substance of math but of that substance, with but one exception, I remember nothing. The exception was on the second or third meeting of the class. He started the class by saying, "You are going to make a choice today. On the first day of next month you will get a million dollars. Or on the first day I will give you a penny, on the second day I will double it, and on the next day I will double that, and that doubling will go on each day until the end of the month. Which option will you take? Think about it for 5 minutes." Our first impulses was to take the million dollars and run. We had already learned that by reputation Henry was a humorist but the polar opposite of a fool. So with pencil and paper we quickly began the doubling exercise and in short order understood the workings of the law of compound interest. We learned a lot, including the vulnerability of the human mind to the world of appearances.

How do we explain the infrequency with which we use the math (not the arithmetic) we were taught? How do we justify requiring students to take at least one math course? It certainly is not because of the overwhelming interest of students in math. We do not say that students have a literature, or history, or social studies anxiety but we do say that many students have a math anxiety as a result of which they stay as far as possible from math after the first course. One reason for justifying making math mandatory is the argument that one cannot understand the role of science in the modern world (or the world of the past) without some foundation in math. It is certainly the case that without the contribution of the advancements in math the contributions of science to understanding and changing the world would have been dramatically less than it has been. Scientists and mathematicians know that in a way that no other groups do or can. But that does not mean that these others cannot be helped to grasp in a relatively nontechnical but meaningful way when and why the symbiotic relationship between math and science became enormously productive. For example, even though I tried hard and read a great deal about Einstein's theory of relativity, I never understood it. Then, several years ago, Stanley Glazek of the Warsaw Institute of Theoretical Physics, entered my life via the good offices of another friend, Kenneth Wilson, a Nobel Laureate in physics at Ohio State University. Stan was interested in educational reform and wanted to find out if Einstein's $E=mc^2$ could be taught to and understood by high school students. Stan persuaded me—and he had to persuade me—to be his first "pupil." Aside from the obligations of friendship, I thought I could be helpful in forcing him to be as concrete as possible, to provide in a step-by-step visual fashion Einstein's basic ideas, to avoid abstractions which had meaning for him but which had no meaning for a person like me or the students he wanted to teach. We met twice a week for 3 weeks. I gave him a hard time. What was clear to him was a puzzle to me. The long and short of it was that I began to understand about space-time, clocks, synchronicity, and the role of Einstein's imaginative "thought experiments" which were as concrete as they were imaginative. Toward the end we had a major disagreement. Stan argued that if I wanted truly to understand $E=mc^2$ I had to know why the "Lorentz transformations," a mathematical achievement by Lorentz, became so important to Einstein. Stan said he would help me comprehend the mathematics. I said, "No way." It was sufficient for *my* purposes to know that the Lorentz transformations were recognized by Einstein as a crucial brick in the edifice of theory he had developed. I could live with the knowledge that the intimidating formulas were important, period. I saw no point in knowing more. I had already learned more than I had ever expected.

Under far from accommodating circumstances, Stan went back to Warsaw and taught $E=mc^2$ to six high school students who volunteered for the experience on their own time. It was Stan's judgment that only one student understood Einstein's theory, including the Lorentz transformations. But what floored me was what the students later wrote about their experience: They had learned things about the puzzle of space-time that were stimulating and for which they were grateful. No one mentioned math. Stan was disappointed that he could say that only one student seemed to comprehend it all. (Stan never learns anything in a halfway fashion, whether it is math, physics, mountain climbing, or educational reform.) From what the students wrote, I consider what Stan did a roaring success: They had changed, they knew it, and were grateful. They were a self-selected group and generalizing to the population of high school students is not justified.

What is justified relates to the questions I raised earlier about math. Again I will use personal experience. It is 2 years since I learned what I did with Stan, which is not to suggest that when we finished I had a firm sense of competence about what I had learned. It was an eye-opening experience. Of that I was sure. But to say that it was accompanied by a feeling of competence would not be warranted. Two years later as I write these pages my memory of what I learned is very blurred, and I realize that the logical relationships among the ideas I learned are hardly retrievable by me. There has been no occasion whatsoever when what I had learned about $E=mc^2$ became relevant to my personal and professional life. It is as if what I had learned had succumbed to the magnetic force of the "file and forget" mental category. It simply was not relevant to my preoccupations. I had no reason to rehearse what I had learned. The ideas and their relationships were orbiting somewhere in my head, but their orbits were, so to speak, light years away from the intellectual and personal orbits I was daily tracking. That, of course, is what most adults feel about the math courses they were required to take in school. But they do not feel that way about having had to learn addition, subtraction, multiplication, and division. From the time we get up in the morning and look at the clock, until we look at the same clock when we go to bed, we use arithmetical, not mathematical, knowledge and skills. Glazek spends his days with math and physics; they are what powers his thinking, motivation, and actions. As a percentage of all adult, highly educated people, the Glazeks of this world are minuscule in number. Why, then, must everyone take a math course in school? Some will say that learning math sharpens one's ability to think logically and precisely. That was the same argument put forth by advocates many decades ago for mandating that students learn Latin, which they dutifully learned, did not use, and then forgot.

There is another reason math is required and that is colleges and universities (most of them, at least, and all of the prestigious ones certainly) look with more than disfavor on applicants who never took a math course in school. Wrapped up in that attitude of disfavor is a conception of what a student should already know if he or she is to benefit from a college education. The irony is that the university has good reason to know that most of its students have little or no interest in math and that if they can avoid taking a college math course, they will do just that. And if they cannot avoid it, they suffer through it. That is especially true in large universities where the instructors of introductory math courses tend to be those with the least amount of teaching experience; they did not get their doctorate—in some cases they have not yet finished their degree—to spend their academic degree teaching introductory math to students for whom math is not seen as relevant to their future careers.

How much of what I have said can be attributed to poor teaching? Very little, depending very much on what you mean by teaching. I say that because the word *teaching* conjures up imagery of one person telling students what and how to think about subject matter, to acquire skill in applying it. That imagery is grossly misleading because it does not deal with several questions. Why and what are students learning? Why do some children not learn or have difficulty learning the subject matter? What is the teacher learning or not learning in the process of teaching? Is the teacher's conception of learning applicable only to students and not to what and how the teacher learns? The conventional imagery obscures such questions, which is why too many people regard teaching as far from a very complicated task and are puzzled why some people (like me) unnecessarily make teaching into a rocket science. The ancient Greeks conceived of the world as comprised of discrete, undefined, irreducible atoms, but it took millennia to find out how horribly complicated the atom is. One part of us knows how psychologically complicated a human being is, and another part of us resists taking that complexity seriously. We know that we are very complicated organisms who at any one moment, hour, or day in our surround are aware of aspects that we categorize, label, simplify, and justify. We employ concepts like learning and teaching as if their relationship to our internal and external reality is clear and bounded.

If by teaching you mean that the teacher has an interrelated set of conceptions that require him or her to be knowledgeable about the psychological stage and characteristics of students—what for shorthand I call "knowing where the student is and is coming from"—then what I have said about the state of teaching math is very much a function of poor teaching. This is not because teachers are intellectually inferior or not well motivated but rather because of the way they were taught. I have written at length about this in almost every one of my books and will not repeat them here. What I will do in very brief fashion is to give examples about learners and their teachers. I do so in an attempt to indicate that the conventional imagery of the teacher is a gross oversimplification.

I shall assume that no reader will dispute that parents have a teaching role. So let us examine how a parent thinks about and approaches the task of toilet training her child. We know one thing for sure: Parents differ widely in how they think about helping the child realize the goal. On the one extreme is the parent whose understanding of the young child is such that it leads her to adopt an unrealistic time perspective which, when it clearly is not going the way she expected, is flustered, disappointed, and resorts to ways of heightening incentives or threats of withdrawing "goodies" and even love, or both (and more). For this kind of parent the "cause" resides in the child, not in her own understanding, her "theory" and style of action. She may say she does not understand the child's uncooperativeness, but she does not entertain the possibility that the child does not and cannot understand her.[1]

On the other extreme are parents whose stance it is that when the child is "ready" to be toilet trained, the process will not take very long, there will be no battles. This does not mean the parent does nothing, she may do a lot, but she avoids making toilet training a "big deal," she knows that she plays a cause and effect role in the interaction; she may inwardly be very impatient but she tries to control displaying it. It may appear to be a laissez-faire stance with its pejorative implications but that ignores the fact that the parent has a "game plan," just as the parent on the other extreme had a game plan. Both have scripts arrived at neither impulsively nor at random. Both scripts reflected very different conceptions of how parents

---

1. I trust the reader will understand that for my present purposes I simplify matters and do not do justice to the psychological understanding of the phenomenology of child and parent. I have no doubt that readers who are parents will fill in the gaps in my simplified presentation.

should teach and how children learn. I am not passing judgment here. I am not saying that one script is inherently good or bad. I have clinically seen instances from both extremes where the results were untoward because the parents were so rigid in following their scripts that they were unable to see the percolating, negative consequences for the child's action in other activities and interactions, or for parental harmony.

In between these extremes are permutations and combinations that defy easy categorization. But overall, several generalizations are justified, to which almost all parents will give assent even after they may confess they wish they had a better understanding of these generalizations (especially with their first child).

1. If by teaching you mean using language (telling, describing, repeating) as a means to influence a child's behavior, then of course parents are teachers, inevitably so.

2. No. 1 is only a part of the story and in some ways the easy part. What parents learn early on is that articulating in some way or signaling intention to change some aspect of the child's behavior does not mean that the child comprehends in the way we expected or hoped for. We think we understand the child, and in many respects we truly do, but there are many times we are jolted into recognizing that the child sees us and the world in ways we should have recognized but did not. It is easy to say that we understand our child, but when his or her world of thinking, acting, and feeling is so different from ours, getting understanding is no easy matter. We can read books, talk to other parents, but we are still left with our child in our situation. In the abstract we are told that no two kids are the same; and no two parents are the same. We know that from concrete experience, but we are still left with the question: How do we gain that degree of understanding that has the intended consequences for us and the child? For parents and teachers, that is the important, bedeviling question. Understanding is the means by which we as teachers think and do what we do to and with our children.

3. Understanding is no simple process. In fact, it is a combination of several processes. One is the degree to which we are observant of and curious about the child's behavior and the meaning of that behavior in the developing mind of the child. Those are meanings we project onto the child, as if to say that "if I did what I see my child doing, this is how I would be thinking or feeling." It is both a projection and an identification with the child; we go from overt behavior to what we think is going on in the child's mind. Unreflectively, we want to know what is "under" the "standing" we observed. The second process involves how sensitive we are to the quality of the ways the child responds to us and how that may be a function of the

quality and ways we convey feelings. If we as parents are at our wits' end about our child's behavior, one can assume that the child's sense of safety and security will be affected. The principle is that the parent-child relationship is one of mutual influence, for good or for bad. Physically the child is separate from the parent. Psychologically, that is never the case. It is not that the child learns, period. It is that both parent and child are learning from and in relation to each other, although more than a few parents act as if they are totally unaware of the principle. The third process centers on mistakes, those occasions when parents recognize that they misunderstood the disconnect the child's actions and the meanings placed on it. As one mother said to me, "I made a lot of mistakes with my first child. But the worst mistake was that I was so anxiously self-absorbed with my incompetence that I would try to undo the first mistake in thoughtless ways. The chief beneficiary of my mistakes was my second child. By the time he was born, I was more relaxed. I could watch and think about *him* (emphasis hers) in a way I never could with my first child."

The concept and process of understanding is complicated, fuzzy, even mysterious because it is not observable, it refers to internal cognitive and affective processes, and it is in relation to at least two people: the "understander" and the person who is the object of the understanding. Nevertheless, in their role as teachers, shapers, and influencers, parents are understanders not because they want to be—they have no choice—but rather because they have pedagogical goals the attainment of which depends on what to the parents is justified as valid understanding of their young child. Clarity about goals and techniques to achieve them is preceded by and based on what the parent considers necessary and sufficient understanding; they may be very superficial, have features of a cookbook, and hardly be tested by reflection. On the other extreme it can be an obsessive concern with understanding that becomes an end itself.

Over the decades I have participated in many meetings at which a fair number of well-known child psychologists were participants. Some of them had written texts on child development, acclaimed texts and deservedly so. As teaching texts they tell us what generalizations about child development are permissible from research. If most of the texts are about these generalizations, the authors will always note—too often in a passing fashion—that (a) there were exceptions to each of these generalizations, and (b) applying them ritualistically to your child requires a secure feeling that you understand your child well enough to decide whether application to your child is appropriate.

But I brought this matter up to point out that every writer of a child psychology text that I have ever met responded with a mixture of humor and chagrin to my question: "What did you learn about child rearing from your children that you said little or nothing about in your book?" Paraphrased, their answers can be summed up in this way: "I may have expert knowledge of the research literature, be a loving and conscientious parent, but it did not take many weeks after a child's birth to realize that what I knew conceptually in no way exempted me from all that is involved in trying to understand what was going on in that complicated, ever-changing and active little character. Initially, between me and that child were generalizations about what to look for and what to do. What I was faced with was a concrete picture, so to speak, that was not in my text or anyone else's; there were similarities, of course, but they were organized differently. What I had written did not emphasize the pressures, anxiety, and need that parents experience in trying to figure out how best to respond to the young child. It is easy to say that every child, context, and parent-child relationship is unique but that is no help in deciding concretely how to respond to your very concrete, palpable child."

When I earlier asked how we can explain what I described about how math is taught and how students experience, regard and utilize it, I said that it depended on what you mean by teaching. It will come as no surprise when I now say that a significant part of the explanation is a conception of teaching in which understanding of the learner is ignored, or short-circuited. Do not take my word for it. If you, as I have over the years, observe what teachers are taught about understanding real children in real classrooms in real schools, you will conclude that why and how you understand children is pathetically meager. And, in addition, if you study the process and consequences of how new teachers are socialized to fit into the school culture, you will conclude that understanding as a means or precondition to attaining educational goals is an alien concept. Generally speaking, parents understand this far better than teachers do. There is more to teaching than having clarity of goals, a one-fits-all pedagogy, a calendar-driven conception of the learning process, and good intentions and strong motivation. Parents know all that because they have had to deal with the problematics of individuality as they try to understand their child and themselves in relation to the child. Parents do not label themselves as teachers in a conventional classroom sense of a teacher precisely because they know and have experienced something difficult to put into words and yet crucial for explaining why and how a child does or does not achieve the goals a parent has in mind.

A hundred years ago William James published his *Talks to Teachers and to Students* (1900). My literary skills cannot match his, and, therefore, I shall give an excerpt of what he said which may give the reader a better sense of what I have tried to convey about teaching, learning, and understanding. I feel compelled to say that of the thousands of educators I have known, hardly a handful have read his book.

> I say moreover that you make a great, a very great mistake, if you think that psychology, being the science of the mind's laws, is something from which you can deduce definite programmes and schemes and methods of instruction for immediate schoolroom use. Psychology is a science, and teaching is an art; and sciences never generate arts directly out of themselves. An intermediary inventive mind must make the application, by using its originality. . . .
>
> The art of teaching grew up in the schoolroom, out of the inventiveness and sympathetic concrete observation. Even where (as in the case of Herbart) the advancer of the art was also a psychologist, the pedagogics and the psychology ran side by side, and the former was not derived in any sense from the latter. The two were congruent, but neither was subordinate. And so everywhere the teaching must *agree* with the psychology, but need not necessarily be the only kind of teaching that would so agree; for many diverse methods of teaching may equally well agree with psychological laws.
>
> To know psychology, therefore, is absolutely no guarantee that we shall be good teachers. To advance to that result, we must have an additional endowment altogether, a happy tact and ingenuity to tell us what definite things to say and do when the pupil is before us. That ingenuity in meeting and pursuing the pupil, that tact for the concrete situation, though they are the alpha and omega of the teacher's art, are things to which psychology cannot help us in the least. (p. 6)

Teaching is an art! And by that James means that the teacher knows or seeks to know where the learner psychologically is and is coming from and to use that understanding to enlarge, direct, or redirect the learner's interests, motivation, and curiosity. John Dewey says it in another way: You teach children, not subject matter, by which he meant that understanding where the learner is and is coming from is both a precondition and concomitant of productive learning. James is aware that not all teachers (and people generally) adopt or are adept in employing such a stance. But it is too easy to gloss over a crucial point that has special significance for the learning of math. Unless the subject matter has concrete meanings—it fits in with personal imagery and experience—it is an exercise in memory. That is what Glazek had to learn in his effort to teach $E=mc^2$ to anxious, heretofore-bewildered me. It reminded me of the time in my high school geometry class when on the 2nd or 3rd day the teacher drew two connecting lines on the board and said, "This is an obtuse angle." What does obtuse mean? What does geometry mean? To what in my world is this relevant? Truly, I sat there in a semipanic. I looked around at the other students, but they were not manifesting my panic. I found out later that many of them were in the same experiential boat I was in. It was a boat encased in a deep fog which never lifted. But I "learned" two things: (a) the teacher knew geometry, and (b) I wanted absolutely nothing to do with math, any math, anywhere, anytime. Math had no concrete, personal meanings for me. What about Latin which, like geometry, I was required to take? When I saw the text for the course, I expected the worst: another memory game. But the teacher, God bless her, taught Latin as a way of understanding the English language! Latin, I learned, may be regarded as a dead language, but a lot of its descendants were alive in the English language as she taught us how to use an English dictionary. I found it, and still find it, fascinating. My personal world had expanded in a concrete, meaningful way. My math course had effectively constricted any expansion of learning in and through that arena. Even though I was a straight-A student in all my other courses, I barely passed geometry. No one noticed, least of all my geometry teacher, who undoubtedly concluded that I did not have the kind of mind necessary for math; blaming the victim is an old story.

Now let us return to music which, as I said earlier in this chapter, is a source of interest, motivation, and enjoyment for all people from their earliest days. For example, the reader may be familiar with the Suzuki approach to starting to play the violin as early as 2–3 years of age, and with obvious success. Another example: On October 19, 2000, a segment of the TV program *60 Minutes* was devoted to a Venezuelan effort, almost exclusively and deliberately for students in schools in poverty areas, in which very young students are given instruments to learn and which they study and practice in groups which become rather large orchestras. There are now over one hundred such orchestras in the country. The results are more than impressive, they are inspiring. But they are not surprising. They did not have to be cajoled to learn and do what they do. It was assumed, and correctly so, that they had experience hearing music and would wish to achieve a sense of mastery in regard to it, especially if the learning and playing would take place in groups of children they knew.

How could you use music to illuminate aspects of math, physics, biology, and history? As long as we regard each of these standard subjects as special and bounded, that question cannot arise in our minds. But the fact is that no musical instrument produces sound which is explainable without math and physics. The coiled metal strings inside a piano do not vary in length for mysterious reasons. Their length as well as the spacing of the black and white keys were developed over time in order to produce certain variations in sound, variations that reflected principles of laws of math and physics. That, of course, does not mean that someone (young or old) who is learning to play the piano should be exposed to the math and physics of the piano, unless of course the individual manifests curiosity about how and why the piano can produce such a variety of sounds. It is when the individual has a sense of mastery over and competence with the piano that such exposure becomes a possibility (and only a possibility). But look at it from the standpoint of the teacher of math and physics, courses so many students find boring or worse. How can he or she use music to convey the math and physics of sound? Granted that math and physics are about more than music (or sound), the fact remains that the interest of students in music is a means for learning that math and physics are very basic to human behavior, and vice versa.

Why is it that when the first time we hear our voice on a tape recording, we are surprised because it does not fit our image or conception of how we "normally" sound? A major reason is that when we normally talk, what we hear is not only a function of the external sound of our voice but also of stimuli from our voice box conducted through facial bones to our brain. When because of disease, the voice box has to be surgically removed and replaced by a mechanical one, we begin to understand how much of the human body (especially breathing) enters into the production of sound and what we call music. Someone less ignorant than I of physics, math, and human biology could, I am sure, come up with more pedagogically instructive and compelling examples. The point here is not when or how these interrelationships are presented to, discussed, and experienced by students. *The point is that it is our obligation as teachers (and researchers) to determine how we can enliven and enlarge the interest and competence of students in subject matter they dislike or find boring and to do this via a subject matter one knows is of much interest and enjoyment to students and everyone else.* This is not in the nature of a "forced marriage" among seemingly unrelated subject matter, a gimmick, an employment of means that waters down or dumbs down presumably more desirable ends. It is not primarily for enjoyment, a time-limited experience whose consequences have few or no cognitive consequences, no sense of discovery, no sense that one has learned something important and lasting about self and the world. Enjoyment is not to be sneezed at, but when I say enjoyment I mean it as a consequence of propelling interest and curiosity.

What I have said above I have known for a long time but largely in the abstract. Yes, I knew it from my experience which left me ignorant of and incompetent with matters quantitative, a source of feeling intellectually inferior, the feeling that if I was really smart I would have been able to understand such matters. What I did not and could not know until midlife when I became immersed in schools and their classrooms was that my inadequacy was a direct consequence of the blunting of a personality characteristic that has always marked what I think and do. I refer to curiosity: how and why things and people are what they are. I am not saying that the strength of my curiosity was more or less than that of others when I was growing up. I am only saying that my curiosity, for reasons conscious and unconscious which I cannot explain in any clear fashion to myself, required that I had to understand what my curiosity had aroused. I use the words "had to understand" advisedly. It was psychologically not a matter of choice. And for whatever reasons I did not understand, my reactions could vary from flight to panic (certainly anxiety). That explains why the word *curiosity* appears with such frequency in my writings. It all came to the fore back in the late 1950s and the early 1960s when the new math was proclaimed and introduced. Its advocates said that math need not be experienced as at best a bore and at worst a mind killer. It could be an enjoyable experience. So my wife and I (E. K. Sarason & S. B. Sarason, 1969) did an observational study of students being taught the new math. As we concluded, joy was the last word in the English language that an observer would use to describe the students; confused, perplexed, and with little animation, yes. Similarly, curiosity was not a word I could use to describe students in the many scores of classrooms I have observed. And when a Yale doctoral student (Susskind, 1969) then did a study on the frequency and quality of questions students ask, their rates were scandalously low. I still find it amazing that his study was one of 15 on question asking that he could find in the literature. Although his was the most rigorous by far, they all agree that classrooms are not places where students ask questions. Ponder the following questions:

> Why is the sky blue?
> Where is the sun at night?
> What keeps an airplane in the sky?
> Where do pictures on the TV come from?
> How come we hear voices on the telephone?
> How is rain made?
> How come we can hear voices on the radio?
> Who started the world?
> Why do boys have a penis and girls don't?
> How are babies made?

The list of questions every preschooler asks is, to say the least, not short. They may be about people or the natural world. Humans are quintessentially question-asking organisms. As more than a few parents have said to me, "I'm glad my child asks tons of questions, although there are times I could strangle him, shut him off." Parents differ markedly in when, how, and with what frequency they stimulate and reinforce question asking. They also differ in the quality and substance with which they answer questions. But there are three things that we as parents tend not to recognize: How we answer questions very much influences the number and content of questions our answers bring in their wake; the questions a child asks are only a sample of the questions he or she is verbally able or feels safe to ask; what we think are appropriate answers may not be understood or accepted, in which case the child privately answers the question, almost always inappropriately, in ways understandable to him or her. The cognitive world of the child is not that of the parent at the same time each is in the other's world.

I am laboring the obvious only to make the point that when you observe preschoolers as they go through the grades, *curiosity* and *question asking* are, to indulge understatement, words you will only very rarely apply to student behavior. And it is most apparent in the middle and high school years. You get a very different picture if you observe and get to know these students outside of school.

I have alluded to and briefly discussed all of this in my previous writings, always aware and even feeling guilty that I was not conveying what I truly believed. Let me explain the sources of my feelings. On more than a few occasions I presented the basis of my point of view to small groups of teachers and administrators. On an abstract level no one seemed to disagree with what I said about the curiosity and question asking of preschoolers. A fair number of the participants were parents and said that of course what I was saying was valid. But when I would then contrast preschool with school behavior, they became defensive. They questioned whether it was justified to make sweeping generalizations on the basis of a small research literature. I said that unless I was way out in left field the scores of classrooms I had observed fit the picture, the usual minuscule number of exceptions aside. But there was almost always someone who would say something like this, "You are overlooking something very important. You expect teachers to know each student extraordinarily well, to be aware of facial expressions and body language indicating puzzlement, or there are questions in his head that he cannot or will not give voice to whatever the reasons may be, or to be especially aware of the not-so-few students who never ask questions. That is all well and good, but the fact is if you take seriously what you have said, we would never cover the curriculum. We do not have that luxury. We are under pressure to cover that curriculum. If all but a few do well on the final test of the year, we are satisfied and relieved. We don't have time to explore why they are interested or disinterested in what they have learned, what questions of importance to them were in their head, or whether what we teach them has personal significance for them. Teachers teach under pressure, and kids learn under that pressure. We know it and they know it."

What would then happen was that the participants would describe their role and status. Not describe, really, but vent strong feeling about the different aspects of the school culture which prevent teachers from teaching the way they like and should. They felt misunderstood and underappreciated by their superiors as well as by the general public. They were largely right, but that is not my point here. They were not aware that they were now confirming what I had told them at the beginning about curiosity, question asking in the classroom. If in the context of the classroom the teacher cannot afford to satisfy her curiosity about students, the curiosity of students is locked in an unwanted privacy. Just as teachers feel that higher powers are not interested in what they think, so do students feel about teachers whose overarching concern is subject matter, not the personal world of the student.

Those meetings (and more) both depressed and angered me. It depressed me because although they were confirming what I believed to be the case, they felt totally helpless to do anything about it. As individuals such a feeling is understandable. My anger was stimulated by the realization (again) that they were in a profession in which there was no leadership to galvanize and coalesce them for action that at a minimum would put into words the realities of teachers, teaching, and the culture of schools, realities that teachers are unable or unwilling to state publicly. Publicly they will agree with the slogan that schools have the obligation to make it possible for the intellectual potential of each child to be realized, at the same time they know how hollow that rhetoric is. How they were prepared in colleges and universities to be educators, plus their socialization in the school culture, have made them conformists, their own worst enemy; they have no proactive stance. It is a form of learned helplessness.

Chapter 13

What I Want for Students and Why:
Or, We Have Met the Enemy and It Is Us

What have I learned from this effort at a self-scrutinizing memoir? When I give my answer the reader may regard it as blatantly, unjustifiably personal, an answer that suggests that I wish to impose my values on others, that I ignore the obvious fact of individual differences in temperament, pattern of cognitive abilities, background and family influences, and expectations for work and career. But if I were to say that regardless of the sources of these individual differences I advocate that all students should be encouraged and supported in learning to obey the law, to refrain from assaulting others, to help others who can benefit from their help, the reader is not likely to criticize my advocacy. Why not criticize me for wanting others to try to be the way I try to be? The reply of the reader would go something like this: "Our society is not a jungle, at least no one truly wants it to be a jungle. There will always be people who know what is right and wrong and yet violate the rules of behavior. Even so, we are obliged to influence and help them change although what we do is frequently ineffectual and counterproductive. But we have to try and learn by our mistakes. We have to believe that everyone possesses the seeds of conscience, and it is our job to try to fertilize those seeds. We owe it to ourselves and others. And if we do not pay that debt, everyone is shortchanged. If as individuals and a society we are far from perfect, there are rules of social living everyone should want to observe, indeed, do want to observe these rules, and when they do not, it says something about them and us. And by 'us' we mean that we have to ask ourselves if we did all we could to prevent what we know to be wrong. That in no way means that we take the individual off the hook and accept blame, but rather that we should ask whether we did all we could or should have done. So, we have no moral alternative to what you are advocating. We have to believe several things. The first is that there is a part of all people that wants to experience the satisfaction of observing the rules of social living. The second is that that part of people has to be recognized and nurtured; that is our moral imperative as a society. The third is that being imperfect people in an imperfect world—that will always be the case—individuals will break the rules of social living, but we should never ignore that nor assume unreflectively that we can exempt ourselves from the possibility that we have played a role, however unintended or unrecognized."

End of sermon. May I suggest that Goodman and Lesnick's recent book *The Moral Stake in Education* (2001) would be worthwhile reading for those who wish to go beyond my sermon. Their book is a very creative and probing discussion of the issues as they are manifested and dealt with in schools.

Now let me answer the question I asked at the beginning of the chapter. My answer is in two parts, general and specific. The general statement is that there is an activity or process I have always treasured, that I believe all children and students find stimulating, that when adults experience it they know in John Dewey's terms that they have had an experience, that it is an activity that too soon in life is only occasional (if that), that all students regardless of individual differences are capable of experiencing, *an activity that, generally speaking, is ignored by educators*, to my continuing amazement and disappointment. In brief, what I have learned and come to believe is of little or no significance to others. I find myself, so to speak, out in left field asking myself, Is it possible that I have deluded myself by giving this activity or human characteristic the crucial importance I have? That question kept coming up in my head as I was writing this book. Was I unwilling or unable to face up to the possibility that my biggest mistake was to confuse what was true for me with what I believe to be true for everyone?

The specific and concrete part of the answer is something that only became clear to me in the course of writing this book. More correctly, it was somewhat clear to me before, but I could not bring myself to put it into writing because it might be regarded by others as, at best, presumptuous and, at worst, unbridled solipsism: I believe that all people, especially in their youth, are capable and desirous of experiencing the struggles and joys of learning more about self, others, and the world; of knowing that what you are experiencing and learning has changed and expanded your horizons; that you willingly seek to learn more, to indulge your curiosity, truly to believe that the more you learn the more you have to and are motivated to learn; that the fires powering growth forever stay lit.

I have not learned all I needed to learn or achieved all that I have wanted to achieve. That is a realistically modest statement. In my autobiography (1988) I summarize my career as a series of "goings" from one fog to sunlight to another fog and on and on until today, unlearning and then learning about myself and the world. The kicks came when the sun came out, the fears and struggles came when I was in a foggy period and the fires powering growth seemed to become embers. Then I was confronted with the possibility that I would continue to exist but not to live, and living would mean an absence of kicks, an end to the need to discover something new about myself and the world, the cooling of passion. Falling in love with thinking and learning is like falling in love with another person from whom you *endlessly* hope both to take and to give. To exist without thinking and learning is like existing without loving. (I have been lucky with both forms of love.)

What permits me to say that I want for others what I have wanted for myself? Several things. When I have seen young children come to school for the first time, I have seen them wide-eyed, eager, cautious, sometimes anxious and subdued, with curiosity written over their faces, silently asking themselves questions. They are explorers, as most teachers do not recognize but parents do. I have seen the same children in third and fourth grade, but I would not call them explorers, question askers, expressive kids. They were not unhappy. They did what they were told to do, they were learning. But there was no passion, no visible evidence of lighted fires. I must emphasize that what those children were learning they needed to learn. If I rarely had doubts that the teacher attached great importance to satisfying that need, I very much doubted that the strength of that need in the children was strong.

I did not follow these elementary school children as they went to middle and high school, but there is very credible evidence that as students go from elementary to middle to high school, their interest in and motivation for school learning steadily decreases (Buxton, 1973; Steinberg et al., 1996). Over the decades I have met with scores of middle and high school teachers. Never, but never, did any of these teachers ever doubt the validity of what I have just reported. Each teacher would say that there is, on a percentage basis, a small number of highly motivated students who, as one teacher said, "are a joy to teach." The others, however, are a different story: They show up, many do what they are expected to do but with no discernible enthusiasm, to call them eager beavers for learning would be ludicrous. They are for the most part nice kids who are happy to get a grade of B but are not crushed if it is a C; they are motivated to pass, not to extend themselves even though in terms of family background, resources, and their IQ, they are capable of doing better. *The last point is significant because it was being said by teachers in schools in middle- to upper- social-class communities.*

I observed many of those classrooms, and I have to say that I was appalled. Initially I was just plain bored: Teachers did most of the talking, students rarely asked questions, most of them appeared listless, a few did not seem to be listening or being attentive, but when the bell rang and they exited the room, they all came alive. It was as if puppets had become human. They could talk! But as I learned from spending time in hallways, their talk was not related to school.

Was my consternation justified? Was it any different when I was in public school? If it was different, did that difference play a role in my becoming a passionate learner? If it was not different, how come I became a passionate learner? I began to ask myself those questions and have alluded to parts of an answer in some of my writings. But in the course of writing this self-scrutinizing memoir, I felt compelled to try to organize (or reorganize) an answer. Let me first say that the answer to one of the questions is that, aside from exceptions I shall indicate, the classrooms I had been in as a student were no different than what I have described from my vantage point as an observer. The good old days were not good. In fact, some of those good old days had very adverse consequences for my intellectual development because they extinguished whatever interest I may have had in science, math, and biology. We are living at a time when almost daily the media tell us that the gene for this and the gene for that has been located, and "this" or "that" are usually diseases. Was my disinterest or relative incompetence in math, science, and biology a manifestation of poor quality genes? The fact is that I had a burning interest in these subjects (as does any biologically intact youngster). How are babies made? What is blood, and how is it made? What is temperature, and how does a thermometer work? Why is the sky blue? What makes an airplane stay in the air? Why does a car need gasoline? How come you can hear a person's voice on the telephone even though they are far away? How is rain made? How does the sun give you a sunburn? The questions of children about their bodies and the natural world are many. If, when, and how they are answered depends on whether the person to whom they are directed (1) regards the question as normal curiosity, (2) can give an answer appropriate to the age-maturity of the child, (3) is supportive of the curiosity, and (4) will seek ways to stimulate and capitalize on the child's curiosity. In brief, before I came to school I was more than interested in biology and science generally. You cannot get answers, however true or oversimplified, to questions you do not ask for whatever reasons. In my case the biology questions, I quickly learned, were off-limits; my parents made that all too clear. As for the other science questions, my immigrant parents could not give answers. And as I went through the grades, I got no answers to questions that continue to interest me, if only because I dutifully conformed to the unwritten rule that you only ask questions if you did not understand what the teacher was teaching, and even then you run the risk of being seen as dumb, a risk I and others rarely, if ever, took. When a student learns *only* what others want him to learn, when what puzzles or stirs him in an *intellectual* sense never gets expressed, the staying power of what is learned weakens steadily as time passes. I am not saying that the student has learned little; it may be that the student has learned all he was expected to learn. I am saying that when what is learned remains unrelated to and does not engender and reinforce the desire to learn and explore more, the odds are high that by the time the student has finished school the desire and satisfaction from learning will not be one of his distinguishing characteristics.

There are two reasons I have used my inadequacies with certain subject matter. One is that the current fashion to try to explain these inadequacies in terms of genetics and/or differing patterns of brain function has the effect of glossing over the permutations and combinations of psychological development in the early years. To take one example: It was not so long ago that people nodded in agreement with what William James had said about newborns: Their world was a big, blooming confusion that only after weeks and months could the newborn be capable of making a discriminating response to stimuli in the external world. But then it was demonstrated that *under certain conditions* newborns were capable in a matter of days to respond differentially to the human face. The italicized words are both significant and obvious because it cautions us to recognize that any explanation of why some students have difficulty learning this or that subject matter does not necessarily mean that that difficulty would be observed regardless of any or all previous contexts of learning. Consider the following statements. By their nature (biological and psychological) women cannot responsibly discharge the obligations of voting and participating in the political process. By that same nature women are capable only of being mothers, teachers, secretaries, clerical assistants, or appendages of their husbands. It is ludicrous to expect that a woman could administer a large business. I could go on and on in order to reiterate the point that when conditions are changed, the self-fulfilling prophecy has frequently been proved wrong. In regard to women, let us not forget that how men judged and explained what women would not, could not, or should not do was an explanation with which women long agreed. It took changing conditions over a long period of time for women to change their view of themselves, and for men to change their accustomed view.

Given the current tendency to explain cognitive inadequacies in terms of genes, I should tell the reader that I do not doubt that our genes play a role in human performance and behavior, for good or for bad. But to explain a student's inadequacy in a particular kind of problem solving by his genes or the way his brain is wired assumes that we know all we need to know about how personality and cognitive factors, context, and development become interwoven. That assumption is patent nonsense. Granted we have learned a lot about that interwovenness in early development, but to say that we know all we need to know is an example of rampant oversimplification. Let me give a personal example. It is one I have used in my writings but in the course of writing this self-scrutinizing memoir I realized that I omitted some important facts about my life history, very personal facts quite relevant to how we explain difficulties in learning.

I was at best a low-average student in algebra and a significantly worse one in geometry. On my report cards I would get a *C* or a *D* in algebra; in geometry I got *D* or *F*. All grades in others subjects were *A*. I did not understand algebra, if by understand you mean more than memorizing. I did not understand what the word *algebra* meant, where it came from, where its uses were in the world for me now and in the future. Of course, it was for me a bore, but boredom is one thing and anxious puzzlement quite another thing. I was in a fog, I knew it, I was ashamed of myself, especially since the other students acted as if they understood. The teacher never said a word to me, for which I was grateful because I could not tell her why I was in a fog; I did not know why I was in a fog and/or overwhelmed by anxiety. I could not tell her why I sometimes almost peed in my pants because I felt so alone out in left field. I had never felt that way in school before. In elementary school I had always been a top student, including in arithmetic which was a snap for me; twice I was skipped a year, which meant I entered high school at age twelve. I relate this to emphasize why my inadequacy in algebra and geometry is something I have always wanted to understand, not to label it but to understand it.

I thought I was going to have another such experience with Latin. My cousin Oscar told me Latin was a dead language, but if I ever wanted to go to college, I would not get in unless I knew Latin. For the first month of Latin I was totally bored, not at all anxious, just plain bored. Then, as I explained in Chapter 12, the teacher began to do something for which I have always been grateful. She began to show us how much of English derives from Latin and how to determine from a dictionary whether an English word derived from Latin. I cannot explain why, all I know is that my curiosity was piqued, a dead language had live descendants, Latin had personal meaning for me, I had learned something new, personally meaningful, and usable.

Then came geometry. On the first or second day of class the teacher went to the board, drew two connected lines and said, "That is an obtuse angle." What did *obtuse* mean? What does the word *geometry* mean? Why is he using the word *degree* in ways so strange to me? Why should I be interested in what he was teaching us? What does the word *hypotenuse* mean? Who cares? That course was a total personal and cognitive disaster. Here again the teacher never once sought to discuss my inadequacy with me. I felt totally alone, lost, and stupid. Something was wrong with *me*.

Now I will relate a personal fact: I did not know anything about the "facts of life" until I was in my midteens! I knew nothing about how babies are conceived, how babies emerge from their mothers' womb, that girls do not have a penis, and so forth. I know that what I have just said sounds odd, if not unbelievable, to the modern ear. I said I did not know by which I mean that not until an older, "experienced" friend sensed my ignorance and gave me a short course did I "know." It is inconceivable that I had not been very curious about these matters; I know of no theory which would not make the same claim. I was an irrepressibly question-asking child who had to understand what puzzled him; except for sexuality which was off-limits. I said I did not "know," but later in life when I spent 3 years on the analytic couch, there was no doubt that I had wanted to know and, crucially, when I did not know or understand it, I became anxious. There is a difference between knowing and understanding. For me not understanding something important in my life and for my self-regard is anxiety producing and destabilizing; it is as if I cannot think and cope with the problem. I, so to speak, go to pieces. And that is what happened to me in algebra and geometry. I was in a problem-solving situation in which I was going to be judged, my self-regard was at stake, the teacher was oblivious to my plight, and I did not have the courage to ask questions or talk to the teacher. It was as if I was in a foreign land not knowing the language just as its people did not understand mine, and it was for me a dangerous country. I must emphasize that my response to geometry and algebra was almost instantaneous, a hallmark of the irrational. Readers may not find my explanation plausible. That would not surprise me. Or readers could say that I was an atypical child with an atypical problem. I would not argue with that judgment. In fact, I shall assume that their judgment has merit. What would surprise and disappoint me are several things. The first would be if my atypicality obscured the fact that school learning—whether adequate, inadequate, or worse—is never independent of the personal and cognitive history of students. The second would be if the reader continues to believe that test scores and grades illuminate in any concrete, meaningful way that history. The third is if the reader believes that by their training teachers gain an understanding of the complexity of the issues and are prepared, to some degree at least, to go beyond the surface appearance of students: their performance, attitudes, motivation. The fourth is to ignore or gloss over the fact that teachers, like parents, affect children by what they do and do not do, by what they understand and do not understand. The fifth is that when educators say their goal is to help students realize their potential, they have committed themselves, not only to "teach" them but to understand them as well, and that kind of understanding is precisely what teachers do not get in their preparatory programs.

In college I had to take a math course, which I postponed until my senior year. I approached it with fear, especially because I had come to know the professor in my extracurricular activities and I liked and respected him immensely, and he regarded me highly. That he would change his opinion of me because of my math inadequacies would crush me. But I had no alternative. As I noted in Chapter 12, Richard Henry was the best, creative, understanding, humorous teacher I have ever had. He made math personally meaningful, and he did not water down the substance of the course. And what do I mean by *understanding*? On the first day of class he said (1) that he knew some of us were not looking forward to the class, that we thought we did not have the kind of brain that takes to math, (2) that it was his job to prove us wrong, and (3) that it was our job to tell him in or out of class that we did not understand something and we needed help. This was not empty rhetoric. His openness, spontaneity, personal style and bearing relaxed and stimulated us at the same time. Humorous is the last word that would occur to me as a characteristic of any teacher I had in grade school. It was only a little different in college. Henry was a humorist and as often as not he was the target of his own humor. I learned math, and I deserved the very good grade he gave me.

There are only two teachers in grade school (aside from my Latin teacher) who stirred my interest in learning, more correctly, the joy of learning, not only to get good grades (which I wanted to get) but because their style of teaching forever made me realize that there was a world of knowledge I never knew existed which I wanted to explore and know. They were history teachers. Their classrooms were the only ones in which there was active discussion *among* students and *between* students and teacher about ideas, opinions, and different points of view. Initially, I and the other students were wary of them because they invited and expected us to ask questions about what they had just said or about something in an assigned reading. Having been socialized in classrooms where teachers did the talking and asked questions and our job was to dutifully listen and hope we knew the right answer, we were leery of Miss Stephenson and Mr. Coleman's style of teaching. For example, they would ask, "What do you think about what I just said?" Initially, our silent reaction was, "What do you mean what do we think? If you said it, it must be right, so why ask us what we think?" I'll never forget the incident that broke the ice of protective silence. Mr. Coleman had been relating to us that although the American revolution was fought in the name of individual freedom, witness the Declaration of Independence, the constitution sanctioned slavery and did not give women the right to vote. (Our textbook said little or nothing about this.) "What do you think about that? Why did they write the constitution they did?" Profound silence. And then Izzy Poulton, a budding communist if ever there was one, got up and with trembling voice and hands gave the party anticapitalist line. This was during the Great Depression, and radicals were a dime a dozen. I and some others admired Izzy's courage but resented his anti-American assault. The rest of that class was a free-for-all debate. Mr. Coleman ended the class by saying, "I am glad you are thinking and learning that there is more than one way to explain history." For the rest of that course, slowly but steadily, we were thinking, not regurgitating what the teacher said or what was in our textbook. If we were unable to put our experience into concepts, it only was with the passing of the years that I understood that for these two teachers regurgitation was not synonymous with thinking. Today we hear much about expecting more from students and getting them to be better thinkers. What has already begun to happen is that teachers—often with administrative support if not with a mandate—are teaching to the test, hoping that test scores will rise, indicating learning has occurred and students can think. I predict that the rise, if any, will be small, that it will be a basis for claiming that we are on the right road to improving our schools, and the difference between regurgitation and thinking will continue to go unrecognized and undiscussed.

Mr. Coleman and Miss Stevenson had a standard ploy. If a student expressed an opinion, they asked the class, "What do you think?" Neither of them would say the opinion was justified or unjustified; they would frequently ask, "On what facts are you basing your opinion?" They were two masterful Socratic teachers. They were classes in which we learned a great deal from and about each other, a social context and dynamic orchestrated by two remarkable teachers and thinkers. They expected we could think, that we were not empty mental vessels, that it was their responsibility to get us to believe that *we* had to play a major role in our learning.

What I want for students is what I experienced with the three teachers I have discussed, and by students I mean those with high test scores, middling scores, low scores. And for students like me who are patently inadequate with certain subject matter, I want and expect that teachers will make two kinds of efforts. The first is that they will refrain from assuming that the student simply does not "have it": motivation and cognitive ability. That he is not "with it" is obvious but to assume that not "with it" is synonymous with not "having it" may be grievously wrong and/or the easy way out, short-circuiting the teachers's thinking. Teachers, like physicians, should know and take seriously that there are two kinds of diagnoses: descriptive and etiological. Describing symptoms, interrelating them, and giving them a label is one thing, and a necessary one. But as often as not, perhaps more often than not, the label does not tell you why the condition arose, the etiological factors antecedent to the manifestation of the symptoms. Let me give an example, one of many examples with which I could fill a book. And almost all of the examples would come from my experience as a psychologist in an institution for the mentally retarded.

Anna was a 17-year-old woman whose neighborhood, family, sexual activity, school failures, and an IQ of 70 combined to have her institutionalized. I had tested her and thought her intellectual potential was somewhat better than her IQ suggested but at best her intellectual potential was below normal. The work-placement department placed her in the hospital laboratory for several reasons: she was likeable, compliant, industrious, and trustworthy. Also, the institution's population was growing, the laboratory staff of two was overburdened, and its director was a woman who had great difficulty locomoting because polio had essentially deprived her of use of her legs. Without crutches she could not get around; she needed someone to keep the lab clean and be at her beck and call. After a 2-week trial period she asked to keep Anna on since she had kept the lab spotless and reduced the need for the director to get around the lab. At the end of one year, to my and everyone else's surprise, the following description of Anna's duties was given to me to place in her case folder:

1. Sterilization and chemical cleansing of glassware used in bacteriology and quantitative chemistry
2. Preparation of bacterial media, physiological and chemical solutions used in bacteriology, hematology, and qualitative chemistry
3. Cleansing of volumetric, graduated, and hematological pipettes and special chemical filters
4. Complete urinalysis except for microscopic including qualitative and quantitative sugars, albumin, acetone tests, and specific gravity
5. Streaking and plating of bacterial cultures with aseptic technique
6. Assistance in quantitative blood and tissue chemistry as in total proteins, lipids, sodiums, and potassiums
7. Staining of hematology and bacterial slides
8. Taking stool cultures and finger blood tests alone
9. Keeping daily record of work performed
10. All blood typing (all work is, of course, checked by head of the laboratory)

When I got the description, I called the director to express my surprise and delight, and I was told that Anna was now being instructed in the use of the microscope and that the state's health department had expressed an interest in employing her as a laboratory helper.

How to explain this? I knew that the relationship between Anna and the lab director had become one of mother and daughter. In this isolated institution in the middle of Connecticut's rural nowhere, what happens in one part of the institution quickly became known to those of us in other parts. So I spoke to the hospital staff. Every one of them said that it was as if the lab chief had dedicated herself to demonstrating that despite all that Anna's case folder contained about her deficits, she, the lab chief, had come to believe that Anna had assets, not the least of which was a capacity to love and seek ways to prove she deserved that love. If Anna had been transformed by the lab chief's dedication, it was also the case that Anna had transformed the lab chief's life.

Consider one more example from those days a half century ago when my wife and I played the role of troubleshooter in that institution. If a resident was acting up in ways strange to the cottage staff, they could ask us to talk with the person, as if we possessed some magic we could employ. Louise was one such resident. She was in her twenties but looked like she was 15, she had been institutionalized for most of her life, her mother and two siblings were also in the institution, she had an IQ in the sixties. She was in no way an expressive person but would react negatively and strongly, sometimes explosively, when she felt she was unfairly treated by staff or other residents. I saw her several times, liked her, and thought she was brighter than her test scores, and if she was not placed as a maid in someone's home (a placement then considered the only one for a long-institutionalized female), it would be immoral; she would never "get better." I told Louise that I, like her, wanted her to leave the institution and that to achieve that goal I needed to meet with her regularly to get to know her and help prepare her for placement, which I told her meant I needed to have a better understanding of why she gets into the difficulties she did. I saw her once a week, sometimes more, depending on what happened to cause her to be reprimanded and punished. I saw her over a period of a year, and she was then placed. For my present purposes, I will relate two events. The first involved an altercation with a resident who had called Louise "four eyes" because she wore eyeglasses. Why, I asked her, did she lose control and attack the girl? In the course of the hour Louise would say that you should not call people names or, more characteristically, would remain silent and semisullen. I was puzzled and told her I was, but she was unrevealing. At the end of the hour I said that in light of the relationship we had formed in which we had agreed to be honest with each other, I was both mystified and disappointed. To which Louise replied, looking me squarely in the face, "Because *you* wear glasses."

Louise was placed with a family who, the social worker assured me, was delighted to meet and have Louise. They gave her a tour of the house which had one bedroom downstairs and several upstairs. Louise was to sleep downstairs. Three weeks later Louise was returned to the institution. After her first night there the family came downstairs and found her asleep on the living room couch. She was told she was expected to sleep in her own spacious, well-appointed bedroom. But each morning they found her sleeping on the couch. They very much liked Louise and tried valiantly to get her to understand why she should sleep in her own room. They attributed her lack of understanding to her low IQ. I saw Louise the day after she was returned. I asked her to explain why she had acted as she had. Characteristically, again, she gave no explanation. I tried hard, very hard to get her to give me an explanation, but none was forthcoming. I ended the meeting by saying how badly I felt that the placement had not worked out and I was mystified that she could not or would not tell me what I so much wanted to understand in case another placement could be found. Up to that point she had rarely looked at me and sat with her head down. When I thought that the fruitless meeting was over, she looked at me somewhat angrily and asserted—she did not just "say" it—"If you had slept every night of your life in the same room with 25 other people, *you* would be afraid to sleep alone in a room." I rarely have felt as insensitive, stupid, and mightily instructed.

Let me assure the reader that I do not believe that if you go beyond the surface appearances of all people who have low IQs or who are not retarded but have learning and cognitive deficits, you will discover a potential for learning and for social-interpersonal and self-understanding you never expected of such people. As I said earlier, I am not a mindless opponent of testing because I believe they tell us nothing. Nor do I believe that our genes and other biological characteristics play no role in cognitive development in terms of limitations they may impose. Having said that, I am appalled at how easy it is for people, professional and lay, to offer explanations which assume that we know more than pitifully little about the awesome complexity of the interrelationships among cognitive, personality, and biological development.

Anna and Louise were put into the diagnostic category: familial mental retardation. That category is intended to mean that there is a definite upper limit to what one can expect them to learn and do, and what they can learn and do will occur more slowly than in the case of children with better genetic stock. Let us assume that is true. Even if true, does that explain what Anna learned and did, or what Louise came to understand that I and many other professional staff never understood? Should we ever be satisfied with a one-factor explanation? Is human development and behavior that simple? Are we justified to accept a major inadequacy of a person and, therefore, think and act as if we know how they think and feel, as if it would be irresponsible and wasteful to try to understand them and their inadequacies? When an individual has a cognitive deficit or inadequacy, are we so certain of our diagnosis and what it implies that we are not obliged to seek ways to understand that individual better, to go beyond surface appearances?

If there is anything I regret, it is that during the years I was at the Southbury Training School I did not write up all the instances similar to Anna and Louise. I did write up several cases and in addition three of what I called my diagnostic errors which I am sure the reader would agree are far more dramatic than the Anna and Louise accounts. They were published in the book *Psychology and Mental Retardation* (Sarason, 1985, pp. 31–100). Equally dramatic are several Southbury female, adult residents whom I observed over 2 years in a very special art program by Schaefer-Simmern (1948) and much later discussed in my book *The Challenge of Art to Psychology* (1990a). One factor was common to all of these cases: There was one person who went beyond surface appearances, established a personal bond which no one else had considered appropriate to do, encouraged and supported them to change. Whether the individual had a low IQ, was physically and neurologically impaired, or had a behavior problem—and at least half of these cases had all three features—was, to at least one person, no barrier to capitalizing on assets they thought the individual possessed. The seeds of what I years later called contexts of productive and unproductive learning were planted in me during my Southbury years.

It was not until I left Southbury and began to work in schools that I began to realize, very dimly and slowly, that this common factor had enormous significance for what I was observing about students and teachers, not impaired individuals but intellectually average and above average ones. Few displayed intellectual sparks, let alone creativity or strong motivation to learn. They "learned" with satisfaction (I assume) but not with anything you could call enthusiasm. In inner-city classrooms the assumption of satisfaction from learning was very infrequently observable. Listlessness and boredom were far more frequent.

What about the teachers? In general they were dedicated and hardworking, and impersonal. And by impersonal I mean the way many people characterize their physicians: They are interested in your physical symptoms but not in you; they do not make it easy for you to express feelings, worries, and questions; when they give explanations, you are as likely as not to be confused and feel stupid; they make you feel that time is of the essence to the physician so, please, do not bring up matters on your mind which are not relevant to the bodily symptoms that brought you to his office.

Having spent years in or across the street from a large university medical center, and having a fair number of friends who were physicians, the reader may be surprised when I say that a fair number of physicians would not disagree with my characterization of patient reactions. They give two reasons: The time they can afford to spend with patients is limited, and/or they are not trained to deal with many of the personal, destabilizing problems many patients have.

That is what I mean when I characterize most teachers as impersonal, and I would go so far as to say that that is the way most students see them. This in no way means that students did not respect or like their teacher. What it does mean is that I rarely got the feeling that the relationship between them had any depth; most of class time was spent on "business": learning what the curriculum required. The truly personal element was distinguished by its absence. Indeed, teachers always spontaneously told me that given a class of 20–30 students, it was impossible to give each student the time he or she needed and deserved. Frequently some would say they felt guilty because they knew that some of the students needed a degree of individual attention and understanding they could not provide. No one ever said that their training ill prepared them to give the kind of understanding students needed and deserved. With teachers, as in the case of physicians, time is an issue, a limiting one. But an explanation in terms of time does not in turn explain why I have observed teachers, albeit few in number (again as with physicians), who acted in ways that took individuality seriously, not as rhetoric or an excuse for inaction.

To say that the training of physicians does not prepare them to treat patients with respect, nonperfunctory interest, and relaxed patience will be obvious to anyone who has been in or around medical centers or has been in a position to observe postgraduate intern and residency programs. Similarly, if you, as I have, visited, observed, and discussed preparatory programs for teachers, you are very likely to agree with me that these programs are a charade in terms of how and to what degree they provide education students with what understanding another human being entails. Again, there are exceptions, and all of them were programs for elementary schools. For programs for those who will be teaching middle and high schools, I know of no exception; they are worse than charades. Let me again point out that there is one function that all educators are expected to and do perform for which they got not even 5 seconds of preparation: talking to parents. That makes sense only on the assumption that people who go into teaching have a God-given gift to perform that function: He has provided them the appropriate genes and personality makeup to perform that function.

In the previous chapter I said that until we gain clarity and agreement about the differences between contexts of productive and unproductive learning, the reform movement will bear little fruit. As I said in my book *Letters to a Serious Education President* (1993b), by "differences" I mean that if you observed over a couple of days the two types of contexts, you would not be in doubt that they are different, dramatically so. The reader would be justified in saying, "But that is your opinion." However, if I assume that I would agree the differences are discernible and stark, by what criteria should we judge whether the lives of students in the two contexts subsequently were different not only in level and quality of performance but in their attitudes towards and satisfaction from learning? In other words, will those expected differences be differences that contribute to future compelling differences, if any? Also, in looking ahead, especially in these days of teacher shortages, where are the kinds of teachers you have written about in your books going to come from?"

Those are justified assertions and questions, and they have the unexcelled virtue (for me) of requiring that I express an opinion I should have expressed more directly in my writings; I pulled my punches, I did not want to be perceived as someone who spent his days figuring out whom or what I could next criticize.

It probably is the case that in any research-based discipline the number of research studies that are carefully done and analyzed on what that field clearly deems to be the most important, puzzling problems in need of clarification is not large. Put in another way, most such studies are on problems considered too narrow or tangential or, frankly, piddling in their import. A significant number of these studies reflect the pressures of the publish-or-perish ethos of the university. As many researchers come to learn when they are denied promotion or tenure, you can perish precisely because you published; what they had published was a minor contribution, if that.

The situation in education is very different and very deplorable. For one thing, there is no consensus on what are the most important problems. And by important is meant that if the problem can be solved, even partially, it will have implications for other problems beyond the initial one. It will influence how we interpret or reinterpret other problems. Copernicus, Galileo, Newton, Einstein, Darwin, Hubbel, Crick, and Watson illuminated problems, specific problems that changed conceptions of other problems. When an important problem is clarified, it has an almost unstoppable spread effect. And that spread does not take place because of opinion but because the way the problem was formulated and researched made its implications for other problems quite clear.

Is class size an important problem? Given will and the funding, reducing class size would be no big deal. The important questions are why you consider it an important problem and how you will know whether reducing class size confirms your expectations of outcomes far better than is now the case. The answer to the "why" question is that reducing class size will allow teachers to give more time to the needs of students; teachers will be able to take individuality more seriously than they now can do. The answer is regarded as a glimpse of the obvious. How can you deny that class size is an important problem? As the why question is usually answered, I do not deny it is an important problem. I will later say why I regard class size as a very important problem on the basis of certain considerations not contained or even alluded to by advocates of reduced class size.

What if we took a random sample of teachers who teach classes with 25 students who are comparable in age, grade, home background, and distribution of IQ scores? Half the sample would be urban, and half would be suburban classrooms. Would we be surprised if on conventional tests of school achievement, there was no difference in the distribution of scores or average scores among these classrooms? I shall assume that the reader, like me, would be surprised. Would we be surprised if a small percentage of the classroom scores were either discernibly higher or lower than in all other classrooms? I would not be surprised. (We know that if we sampled schools instead of classrooms, there would be that degree of variation.)

How would we explain why in a small percentage of classrooms the scores are significantly higher or lower than all other classrooms? We could ask the teachers of these classrooms to help us understand why the test scores of their students are so high or low, we could talk to the principal, we could observe these teachers in their classrooms. We would employ these procedures for the obvious reason that we want to determine those characteristics of teachers of high- and low-outcome classrooms which may be playing a role in those outcomes. I have never done such a study, but my experience in schools has led me to several conclusions. First, teachers of low-outcome classrooms know they are in trouble, so to speak, and describe the different things they have done to improve student performance, but to no avail. Some of these teachers will attribute this to characteristics of the students, some will indict the school system which is not sensitive to the needs and suggestions of teachers. Only very infrequently will they criticize their principal, although in indirect ways I felt their assignment of blame included their principal. Few, if any, of these teachers were relaxed, self-confident individuals who enjoyed teaching. They all wanted to be better teachers than they were, but they were not optimistic that they could do better. Nothing in my classroom observation of them led me to regard them as other than inadequate.

With the high-outcome teachers, the story was different. In fact, they had difficulty explaining why their students do so well on a comparative basis. They looked at me as if to say, "What is there to explain?" One teacher said, "I enjoy teaching, I love the kids, my greatest satisfaction is to see them grow, mature, blossom. And do they ever respond when I express my glee that they have learned something that they did not know or could do before." Another teacher said something like the following, "I tell them right off that my job is to help them learn and like to learn. I tell them their job is to learn, and if they have difficulty, I'll help them. And if we both do our jobs, we'll have fun and be happy. Kids are kids, and if they don't take to you, nobody has a good time." Another teacher said, "I love kids, and I want them to love me. I spend most of the first 3 days getting to know them and having them get to know each other. I mean more than what their fathers or mothers do, what they did this past summer, or how many brothers or sisters they have. I want to know what they like to think about and do when they are not in school. Who are their friends, and why do they like them? What is the most interesting thing they have ever read, and why was it so interesting? Over a period of 3 days I learn a lot, and they learn a lot about each other. I also tell them about my husband, my children, my hobbies. In terms of the curriculum, they learn little those early days. I learn a lot."

I cannot refrain from discussing a teacher whose classroom I have never observed. I learned about her from a colleague at the Yale Psycho-Educational Clinic who said that there was a teacher in the school in which he worked whose students got achievement test scores much higher than students in the same grade in the same school. She was, he said, the best teacher he had ever observed. Could he, I asked, be more concrete about why she was so effective? Although I shall paraphrase what he said, what he reported was literally unique so that it may be that my paraphrase is close to a verbatim quote. "Early in the school year she tells her class that she will not always be able to give each student the time she would need in order to get to know them or to help with any problem the student may have. However, although there are days she will not have any free time, on most days she can arrange to have some free time. She will list on the board in alphabetical order the last names of students. Beginning next week the student first on the list will meet with her to talk about *anything* he or she wants to talk about. Not what the teacher wants to talk about or ask, but what the student wants to talk or ask about. When they are meeting, she asks and expects that other students will not bother or look at them but will continue to do what they know they should be doing. 'When your time comes, you too will get all the free time I have on that day. That time is very special to me, and it should be for you.'" And, my colleague assured me, throughout the year the students adhered to the letter and spirit of the bargain. The reader will, I trust, understand why I found this practice unique in my experience.

When I would talk to the principals of these high-outcome teachers, I could count on their smiling or breathing a sigh of relief and saying, "If I had more like her, I'd be in heaven." Every now and then I would ask the principals, "What do you do when you have a poor or subaverage teacher?" Their answers fell into two categories. The first goes like this, "I will make suggestions, go over their lesson plans with them. Sometimes I will sit in their classrooms and observe them, which they usually resent because it makes them anxious. They improve, if they improve at all, minimally." The second most frequent response was: "I did not choose that teacher. She was here before I came, and she has tenure. In fact, previous evaluations of her gave her a satisfactory or even higher rating. I can understand it at the same time I criticize it and have to grin and bear it. When a principal indicates, directly or indirectly, even politely, that a teacher is below par and has to change, not only have you made an enemy but other teachers, not all, get upset. They see me as a threat, as if to say who am I to tell teachers how to teach. I rarely, if ever, get a negative reaction from those who know they are more than adequate because I told them they are."

What does all this have to do with reducing class size? For one thing, it justifies asking the question: Why should one expect a poor teacher with 25 students to be more effective with a class of 15 students? Would you say that a poor physician—regarded as such by his peers—would become a better physician if he or she cut the practice in half? But let us leave aside the clearly poor teachers and ask about a much larger group comprised of teachers whose students do not perform blatantly poorly on tests: On what basis are we justified in assuming that their students regard learning in the way we (I at least) hope they would? I have seen many teachers whose students were passing (in some cases barely so), but whose students by no stretch of the imagination appeared intellectually motivated, challenged, or even interested. Are we to assume that the test scores of these students are cause for satisfaction, that they gave their best and the best was gotten from them? Are we to assume that the absence of any signs of pedagogical creativity or of an interpersonal style of relating to students are unjustifiable causes of concern? That with a smaller class size they would become more creative and challenging teachers? Is the purpose of reducing class size *only* to reduce the number of students who perform poorly or fail, and not to be concerned about whether average students' potential for productive, intellectual growth can be exploited more than it is now? Are we to gloss over the difference between what students are and what they are able to become?

In the research study I sketched above, the best teachers were those whose students performed significantly better than comparable students of other teachers. In my experience, no less impressive than the achievement performance of their students was the pedagogical creativity and interpersonal style of these teachers. I can never forget Mrs. Treadow, a third-grade teacher in a hundred-year-old New Haven ghetto school. When the Psycho-Educational Clinic was established, it was one of the two schools in which we would work. Mrs. Treadow was in her sixties, frail, ailing, and struck me as a sour, quirky person. I did not relish the thought of observing, let alone getting to know her. Ninety-five percent of the students in the school were Black. Mrs. Treadow harbored racial bigotry, which she expressed to me. I had trouble believing what I observed in her classroom. She was as creative a teacher as one will find. She had a closet full of gadgets and academic games, most of which she herself had devised. She made learning more than interesting. In a school rife with student misbehavior, her classroom was a lively, fun place for the students; in the 2 years I worked in that school she never had a discipline problem. In fact, she had no need of me, but I would visit her classroom because it was an oasis of productive learning. Hers was the only classroom in the school in which student achievement test scores were not only above national norms but dramatically so. Despite her racial bigotry, when she entered her classroom, it was as if she were saying, "I don't care who you are, who your parents are, I expect you to meet my standards." In these days when we hear critics say that educators have too low expectations, I do not know whether to laugh or cry. To laugh because it is such empty rhetoric, as if the resolve to expect more magically means you will get more; to cry because I shall never live to see the day when the critics realize, if they ever do, that for expectations to be realized, especially if they are mandated, it requires teachers whose characteristics we know too little about.

I predict that reducing class size will have some desirable consequences but not dramatic ones. I can honestly assure the reader that there is a part of me that wants to believe that the consequences will be greater than I predict. One thing is for sure, where class size is being reduced, there is no research effort to determine why in some smaller classrooms student performance is clearly higher than in other comparable ones. That kind of research has in the past been sparse and what there has been was far from systematic and carefully analyzed, and provides no basis for believing that merely reducing class size will obviously have the consequence its advocates predict.

If I believe that as ordinarily formulated reducing class size is not addressing an important problem, that it is not being implemented in ways that would shed light on other related problems, I believe it is potentially most important for several reasons, one of which is that preparatory programs for teachers and administrators ill prepared their students for the role of teacher as I have discussed in almost all of my writings. The first book I ever wrote on this issue was in 1962, with the title *The Preparation of Teachers: An Unstudied Problem in Education* (Sarason et al., 1962/1986). It was unstudied then, and it is unstudied today. Criticisms of these programs were not then and are not now in short supply, but they do not get to the heart of the matter, in my opinion at least; the questions I have asked and the reservations I have expressed about what one should expect from reduced class size are based on the inadequacies of these preparatory programs. Advocacy for reduced class size has to be seen in relation to these inadequacies, and, if it is not, it will be another example of tunnel vision. There are other reasons that preparatory programs are important, and I have discussed them in some detail in my writings and will not say anything more here except to state that as soon as you conceive of our schools as part of a system that includes far more than a single school or local school district, you begin to understand the crucial importance of the quality of preparatory programs and why reducing class size potentially can be a most fruitful start point for noncosmetic reform efforts. I said earlier that I see no consensus among educators about the two or three problems which, if studied and clarified, would improve educational outcomes. When I have asked that question, the answers can be put into two categories. The first is those answers which are very narrowly conceptualized and their import for other problems hardly discernible, if at all. The second is answers that unreflectively assume that we know enough about the problem to take action, as if careful research is not needed to determine whether the problem as formulated seems to justify widespread implementation. Together the two categories (and they do overlap) explain in part why there is so little research that provides a basis for action, with the result that whatever research has been done on the problems as formulated sheds little or no light on any other problem. I am not saying that some of this research is unworthy or useless, although at the point of a gun I would say that we would not feel robbed if most of this research had never been done. Such a judgment, however, does not apply to that very small fraction of the research which I, at least, think would have more significance if the researcher had related his findings to other problems.

Research is obliged to observe the rules of evidence regardless of whether the researcher is employing a case-history approach or a more formal type of research design requiring statistical analysis. Are my conclusions justified by the data I collected? Are the data I collected in some way incomplete, or am I reading into the data significances I have not demonstrated? Are there conclusions alternative to those I have drawn? These and other kindred questions constitute the scientific obligation of the researcher. We are imperfect organisms; we have difficulty distinguishing between opinion and a fact; we are so enamored with our own point of view that we are unaware that we stated our analyses and presentation to protect our self-regard; we will be crushed if what we have written is ignored or not valued with the esteem we had hoped. What a field judges as good research, basic or applied, is that which has *percolating* consequences for the field because the untoward consequences of the researcher's human imperfections were minimal. By such considerations the quality of research in education is discouraging.

I know there are more than a few researchers who agree with me but who understandably do not want to appear to be demeaning their field. At my age I am past the point where such a concern is relevant. But there is another aspect of this that most of these researchers on the basis of their own experience will not publicly discuss: Whether it is the federal or state government or private foundations, the attitude toward and the funding for educational research is both niggardly and demeaning compared to what they say and fund in other fields. Let me give you the latest example about which I know a good deal. A very well-heeled foundation became aware of a reform effort with inner-city high school students, an effort I regard as remarkable and inspiring. The foundation asked the leaders of this reform effort to apply for funding for that effort to be replicated in a dozen other cities. Their application contained a continuous research evaluation component essentially longitudinal in design. The foundation initially had indicated they expected the replications to cost several millions of dollars. However, before approving the grant, the foundation said they were reducing the grant by an amount which essentially eliminated the research evaluation component. I met with the reform leaders who were joyful that they had been given approval for the replications. I had to overcome a lot of internal resistance before telling them that I thought they should not accept the grant without funds for evaluation without which they would lack the kinds of data that would be credible and compelling. They thought what they accomplished in their city was very important. I thought it was very important. A number of people I respect who had visited the site for 2 or 3 full days thought it was important. But precisely because of their lack of funds, they would be unable to collect the different kinds of data that would be compelling to those who had never visited the site or had a sense of the history and complexity of their reform effort. But with the several millions of dollars dangling before them, they were not about to turn down the grant.

But the point of the story is that this very well-heeled foundation whose officers had no research credentials clearly did not consider evaluation all that important. The founder of the foundation would not have made his billions if his company did not yearly budget many millions of dollars for research and development. I know many more examples when foundations approved reform efforts without ever giving a thought to requiring a thoughtful and comprehensive evaluation even though they were approving an application so vague, fuzzy, and rhetorical that it was obvious that when those reform efforts were ended, we would still be in the realm of opinion. I should also note that the research budget of the federal department of education is truly piddling compared to other departments dealing with major social problems. Why is it that our current and past presidents have been so gung ho for charter schools, each year increasing funding for more of these schools? Is it that they had evidence for such a policy, that research, exploratory or more systematic, had indicated that we knew enough to proceed with more of these schools, that we know how to make them effective? The answer, *of course*, is no. I italicize "of course" because when it comes to education the relationship between power and opinion is the determining factor. No president, or member of the Congress, or governor would ever dream of saying that he or she has heard good things about a drug or treatment program the government should endorse. We have a Food and Drug Administration whose job it is to prohibit marketing a drug to the public unless it has been researched to the point when it is evident that, despite tolerable side effects, the drug does what it purports to do. Charter schools? Vouchers? Reduced class size? A much longer school year? Beginning to teach Head Start children at age 3? Why do we need a research basis for these and other proposals? Isn't it obvious that they will work the way we want them to work? With friends of education like that, educational reform will never lack enemies. Ignorance and good intentions are formidable enemies.

I should hasten to add that I am not asserting that if there were more funding for research, the payoff in results would be discernible. We have learned, I hope, that spending more money on schools does not mean better educational outcomes. There is a difference between saying more money for research and saying more money for better research. And better research means more than adherence to scientific procedure and the rules of evidence. If the problem being studied is narrow or parochial or so globally formulated that you have trouble relating what on earth the researcher is trying to demonstrate, it will have no percolating consequences for the field. If I were Czar of Education, one of the first things I would do would be convene a series of meetings at which participants would present three to five problems and defend why they think they are of crucial importance. And, depending on what comes out of these meetings, I would convene another series of meetings where the participants would discuss criteria for how to judge whether researchers have done scientific justice to problems which a fair number of participants in the first series of meetings had said were important problems. These would be meetings of several day's duration, not 1- or 2-day affairs where each person says his or her piece, and there is no time to confront and hammer out inevitable differences in values, experience, and theoretical orientation. Who should be at these meetings? That is a tough question, and I am not prepared to answer it now except to say that public and private agencies would be invited. *Educational reform is conceptually and procedurally an extraordinarily complex and difficult affair because its main purpose is not to change individuals one by one but to change institutions, be it a single school or school system, and/or relationships between different types of institutions (e.g., colleges and universities).* In educational reform you are always dealing with individuals one-on-one and in small groups for the overarching purpose of changing the institution. Educational reform requires interpersonal skill, patience, a high degree of frustration tolerance, a lengthy time perspective, and more. I would hope—hope does spring eternal in me—that the funding agencies would begin to appreciate better the awesome task the educational reformer confronts and why research evaluation is crucially necessary. I have met too many in public officialdom and foundations who do not know how much they do not know about schools and what changing them entails. Not only do they not know how much they do not know, but what they do know is 95% wrong. Lastly, they do not like to be told they are ignorant. After all, they do control the purse strings, and being supplicants, the educational reformer and researcher cannot run the risk of alienating them.

Readers do not need me to tell them something they know well: Changing the quality of American schools is awesomely complicated both on the conceptual and action levels. I have long argued that the major source of difficulty has been the failure to flush out and scrutinize the unverbalized axioms undergirding the organization and behavioral and programmatic regularities of schools. Axioms are silent because they are regarded as obviously true, so much so that we do not have to examine and challenge them. We literally "pay them no mind." Just as it was axiomatic in pre-Copernican days that the earth was the center of our universe, there are axioms in regard to education which I and many before me have said required challenge. In this and my previous books I have said that the conventional view of school learning was wrong and counterproductive. And I have discussed my deep conviction that the starting point for a challenge to the conventional view is preparatory programs for educators: the selection and training of educators. Drastically changing these programs confronts you with the problem of institutional change. These programs are embedded in a larger institution: colleges and universities not noted for their willingness to change. And that is certainly true in regard to the relationship between departments or schools of education and our institutions of higher learning. I have discussed this in some detail in my book *American Psychology and Schools: A Critique* (2001). The attitude of universities to schools of education varies from ambivalence, at best, to a downright demeaning attitude, at worst; they tolerate, they do not respect their schools of education, although there is less than a handful where those attitudes are less apparent. Even in those few universities a significant number of their faculty would not be heartbroken if the school of education was reduced by half or more, or even eliminated (as in the case at Yale which I discuss in my last book).

This is in part why I have never expected that preparatory programs would do other than change cosmetically. But it would be unfair to hide my opinion that some who direct preparatory programs would like to change noncosmetically. Nevertheless, if they were to seek the kinds of changes for which I have argued, they would get nowhere because the changes would require resources the university decision makers and academic power elites would reject out of hand. I bring this up in order to emphasize a point that took me too many years to recognize despite its obviousness: When you try to reform one part of the educational system, you soon find that there are drastic limitations on what you can achieve because of other parts of the systems which have their own vested interests and traditions. I do not know of any educational reformer who has not come to the same conclusion. Why did it take me so long to reach that conclusion? For one thing, I made a mistake reflected in the title of my 1971 book *The Culture of the School and the Problem of Change*: I was riveting on encapsulated classrooms in encapsulated schools and was not taking seriously that the school is part of a large system comprised of universities, unions, state departments of education, legislatures, governors, and parents. How and why any part becomes relevant to a reform depends on its vested interest. It is far from a coordinated system; it is a system with adversarial features. It was not until that book was republished in 1996 as *Revisiting "The Culture of the School and the Problem of Change"* that I tried to make amends. But there was another reason I had not taken the obvious seriously: I did not want to face up to its implications—that reform would be cosmetic because of the existing system. That was and is an overwhelming thought, a discouraging one because no part of the system recognizes the nature of the system.

What has to happen for that recognition to gain currency? Take the following examples from the post–World War II era:

1. It took the Great Depression for the public radically to change its conception of the responsibility of the federal government toward the economic welfare of the people.

2. It took the experience in World War II to require the federal government to become the major player in the support of research by creating the National Institutes of Health and later the National Science Foundation.

3. For most of our national history the federal government essentially played no role (and was expected to play no role) in support of education. Because cities and states lacked the resources to deal with the economic and demographic changes that came in the wake of World War II, the federal government changed its traditional role in regard to education.

4. The medical, psychological, familial, economic plight of increasing numbers of old people had been a serious concern of Presidents Franklin Roosevelt and Harry Truman, but nothing happened because of opposition on the basis that government should not intrude in such matters. The passage of the Medicare and Medicaid legislation in 1965 reflected how much had changed in attitude about the responsibilities of the federal government, especially as in this case the states lacked resources.

5. The United States did not join the League of Nations after World War I, but it played the major leadership in creating the United Nations, a barometer of how isolationist sentiments had been overcome by the realization that, like it or not, the United States had global responsibilities which it could ignore at its peril.

It took catastrophes for these sea-swell changes to occur, and there is no reason to believe that these changes will be reversed. That is by way of saying that what heretofore had been considered axiomatic was challenged by unwanted events which threatened the social fabric.

In regard to educational reform there is one extraordinarily relevant example which I did not mention. I refer to the 1954 Supreme Court desegregation decision. It was more than a decision about schools. At its root it was a moral decision having enormous implications for how Whites and Blacks should regard each other and work and live together in venues other than schools. For those implications to become appropriately manifested would require more than money and legislation, both of which are obviously important but in no way mean that long-standing attitudes will change. Even among those who greeted the 1954 desegregation with relief and enthusiasm were people who were unprepared for how strongly they felt when, so to speak, their oxen were being gored by those who proposed policies and programs requiring them to change their thinking and planning about their children. Schools are more segregated today than in 1954; that would never have been predicted by supporters of the decisions, let alone the Supreme Court justices who said that desegregation should take place "with deliberate speed." Yes, the Court's decision was about schools, but if anything is clear a half century later, it is that an important social problem influences and in turn is influenced by related problems, a relationship we tend to ignore when we focus on the single problem of most interest to us. That kind of conceptual tunnel vision has been characteristic of the efforts of the educational reform movement.

What will it take for the educational community and people generally to recognize and challenge long-standing assumptions of how learning is conceived and directed in most American classrooms, and to comprehend the differences between contexts of productive and unproductive differences? Researching those differences is the most basic problem. I have expressed and tried to describe what those differences are. I would not argue with the reader familiar with my writings who concludes that I have not conceptualized or described those differences comprehensively or compellingly. The only response I have to such an opinion is itself an opinion I came to after long thought and experience which, needless to say, does not transmute my opinion into validated fact. What I can say is that it is an opinion I came to long ago, and it permitted me then to go on published record that the educational reform movement would have pitifully few accomplishments to show for its efforts, that what would best describe that movement is the saying that the more things have changed, the more they have remained the same. I have my moments when I question the strength of my conviction that the differences between contexts of productive and unproductive learning is the basic starting point which will allow us to see what we call our educational system in a more realistic way. You may say I am being presumptuous. But there is one opinion about which I am the opposite of presumptuous: I cannot say how, why, or when our complicated world will require people to give up counterproductive conceptions of learning and schooling.

Chapter 14

Ending with Starting Points

Many years ago I had a long talk with a colleague, John Dollard, who was a sociologist by training, became a psychoanalyst, an anthropologist, and a psychologist. Wrapped up and integrated in his head was a formidable knowledge of the social sciences. In the last two decades of his life he and Neal Miller were very influential in the effort to integrate learning theory and psychoanalytic theory. I was in awe of John for two landmark books he had written in the 1930s: *Criteria for the Life History* (1935) and *Caste and Class in a Southern Town* (1937). From its title you might think that his first book was written for social workers. You could not be more wrong because that book was a devastating analysis and critique of an American social psychology riveted on the individual and scandalously superficial in its conception of context and culture. His second book is based on his anthropological-sociological field study of a southern town, a study that foreshadowed the later clear recognition of the fabric of the race problem in America: its personal, interpersonal, sexual, religious, political, and economic components. I regard both books as classics, which is why in my writings I refer to and implore readers to read those two books. I may be the only psychologist in the post–World War II era who refers to them. I have no reason to believe that my efforts to persuade have had any effect whatsoever. The concepts of context and culture have a high frequency in the psychological literature, but they lack the substance John Dollard attempted to convey; they are signifiers that their users want to be seen as holistic thinkers, not narrow ones. That intention is laudable but not when it lacks substance or operational clarity. Although I have tried to avoid using these concepts in a vague, global, and empty way, I have not always succeeded. I, like most everyone else, find it all too easy to use these concepts as if we know what we concretely mean. When you read Dollard's two books, you have little doubt that you know what he means.

The meeting with John was initiated by me because I had been harboring a puzzlement which only he could clarify but which would require me to express my deep reservations about what he and Neal Miller were doing to wed learning and psychoanalytic theory. The question I put to him was this: Given what you wrote in earlier years, why did you become so interested in a learning theory which was based on rats running mazes? To my surprise the answer came quickly and clearly. Paraphrased, it went this way:[1] "However you define culture, it points to, describes, and provides a rationale for practices and behavior in different contexts as well as the life span of singular importance to its people. Culture is an indoctrinating, educational process. The neonate is not born with a culture but catapulted into one, the purpose of which is to shape the organism to become 'cultured.' That shaping is done by adults, the source of continuity of the culture. If you ask them why they think and act as they do, you get a standard response, so to speak, the culture's 'party line.' If you ask the growing child why he thinks and does what he does in the circumscribed contexts which the culture has deemed important, his answer will almost always involve the perception of the expectation of others which he endeavors to satisfy or, if he does not, there will be penalties. How the adults think and act, how the growing child thinks and acts, can be recorded and described. But there is something missing, and it is the details of the process whereby the individual acquires the ability and motivation to make those discriminations, to give meaning to them, and to respond to them in the expected manner so that he is perceived by others as 'one of us.' Concepts like assimilation and accommodation beg the question. Of what are these concepts comprised? How do the cognitive capacities of people and the features of their external surround get connected? Cultures differ, but the ways in which these connections get made and change do not differ because the culture is different. How does one type of connection get connected to and intertwined with other connections in ways that give the individual (and those who know him) the sense that he is an organized identity? *What is the process which serves as the glue that makes for an organized entity?* What I came late to recognize is that it is the complexity and efficiency of the dynamics of the learning process that is the glue we need to explain how the individual becomes acculturated. It is my belief that learning theory and the research to which it has given rise will contribute mightily to our understanding of the force of culture and why and how cultures change. It is easy to say people learn, but that has little or no explanatory power. Learning theory is the attempt to illuminate how and what people learn in the contexts a culture deems important. A learning theory is a way of indicating far better than we now can do those processes that mediate and organize relationships between what is inside and outside the individual."

----

1. I taped the 90-minute conversation and played it numerous times, but when I moved offices in 1970, I was unable to find it again. The conversation took 90 minutes because John had known and was known by all of the greats in pre–World War II social science, and he regaled me with juicy stories about them, and on and on it went.

I refrained from telling John that what he had said in no way explained why he thought that rat-based learning theory and research—a very dominant area for decades in psychology—could explain the culture-context problems he had so brilliantly written about. As I said earlier, it was an answer to that puzzling question that I had hoped to get. What John had told me only confirmed what I already concluded: the process, mechanisms, and substance of learning were crucial for understanding human behavior. Learning is, among other things, about change, not only changes we can see and record but changes implied by such concepts as attitudes, self-concept, striving, aspirations, levels and objects of curiosity, and so forth. From day one of our lives, and especially in our early years, we undergo change. We know that our outside world plays a role in change, just as we know that individuals differ dramatically in how they are shaped by that world and, no less important, how they impact on that world. We experience a variety of contexts that have structure no less than we as individuals have structure. How do these structures transact with each other?

There was one metaphor John employed in our conversation that I have never forgotten, and that was when he said that the concept of learning was the "glue"—the missing glue—for comprehending how and why internal and external structures become seamlessly organized into a whole. I completely agreed with John at the same time I thought it tragic that he thought that the glue he sought would be provided by studying the maze running of rats.

What does my conversation with John have to do with educational reform? For one thing, although American psychology recognized the centrality of learning theory for comprehending human development and its vicissitudes, it went about it in ways that guaranteed a drastic limitation on the significance of learning theory and research for contexts of human learning. It was an example of identifying an important problem and then essentially trivializing it. Why American psychology took the direction it did, I have discussed in my 2001 book *American Psychology and Schools: A Critique*; I must refer the reader to that book. Nevertheless, despite my saying what I did about trivializing, the learning researchers did confirm the obvious: The degree of motivation of the rat (by restricting, varying food intake) made a difference in the speed of learning, a finding which, however obvious, has enormous practical implications for classroom learning. The learning researchers had no interest in the relationship between motivation and learning in classrooms. Were the educators interested in that relationship? To that question the educators would have answered, "of course." *But from those early decades up until today, if you sit and observe the modal American classroom (especially in middle and high schools), you will be very hard put to explain why most students do not manifest observable indicators of motivation*. I know there are classrooms where students are "alive," active, goal-oriented, and interested in what they are doing. There are always, thank God, exceptions: they are not boring, stultifying, uninteresting places to their students. But they are just that: exceptions. But what if we focused our attention on teachers? What is his or her apparent "theory" about when and how to motivate students, and what kinds of student behavior motivates a response? The questions are many, but I find it remarkable that there have been so few studies on barometers of teacher and student motivation. Like motherhood and patriotism, we say we are in favor of motivation. If, as I have, you press people to say what they mean by motivation, by far the most frequent answer, after a somewhat long reaction time, is that the more motivated the student and teacher, the more learning takes place, and faster. That answer states a goal; it has no practical import. The learning researchers could tell us what they mean by motivation and could demonstrate how variations in its strength have this or that consequence for learning in rats. But motivation in humans is far more complex than in rats, and a maze is a far more simple context for rats than the classroom context is for students. Indeed, the learning researchers preferred rats and mazes because they were controllable in a scientific sense. Classrooms are complicated social psychological affairs, but that was not and is not an excuse to avoid studying it in a classroom. It reminds me of the joke about the drunk who is on his hands and knees searching for something he had lost. When a passerby asked where the drunk thought he had lost the object, the drunk pointed down the darkened street. The passerby asked why, therefore, was he looking for it where he was, to which the drunk replied, "Because there is more light here."

Any noncosmetic educational reform has, if not an explicit then an implicit, conception of why motivation will change in the classroom context as a function of the reform. For example, we hear much today about stating and adhering to high rigorous academic standards and greater expectations of what students can learn. No student will be promoted if he falls below standards, and a school with a record of many students who fail will be given two to three years to improve or be closed. This is what I call the shape-up-or-ship-out policy and conception of how to increase motivation in students and teachers. The history of the adoption of that policy leaves no doubt that it was an explicit criticism of educators who were seen as watering down standards and not motivating students to do better, and glossing over unacceptable behavior. Educators have looked upon this as another chapter in the scapegoating of educators, as if teachers had lacked the motivation to produce better educational outcomes. A majority of the states adopted the policy, and with much fanfare and self-satisfaction. There have been two major results. Teachers resent what they regard as scapegoating, but they resent even more the pressure and anxiety they feel to "teach to the test," i.e., to devote more time to what will be on the test, thereby reducing time to subject matter that will not be on the test. The other result has been that the number of students who in the first year of the new policy fell below the new standards was far greater than anticipated. So what have they done? They have lowered the standards and extended the time schools will have to meet the new and lowered standards.

I predicted these results primarily on two grounds. The first was that when policy makers adopt a new policy intended to change the behavior of those far below them in the hierarchy of status, power, and independence, and when that new policy is an implicit or explicit criticism of them, the empirical evidence does not permit you to bet the ranch that the goals of the new policy will be achieved. You can bet the ranch that the consequences will be destabilizing. Destabilization is not inherently sinful; it can be a temporary condition, a precursor to a more productive one, but only if the local implementers are motivated to think and act in ways consistent with the new policy. I am not aware of any evidence that shape-up or ship-out ultimatums have their intended motivating effects. That they may change the motivational picture is very likely, but that in no way means that the changes are those intended by the new policy, especially if the new policy has called into question the motivation, goals, even competence of those most affected by the new policy. I consider it ironic in the extreme that the new standards-expectations policy rests on the near identical conception of learning and motivation of many rat-based learning theories of the stimulus-response variety: You change the policy (stimulus) so as to change the learning context and motivation and the intended goal (response) will be demonstrated. The conception has the virtue of simplicity and the vice of mindless oversimplification. Perhaps a less pejorative way of putting it is wrapped up in Mencken's caveat that for every major social problem there is a simple answer that is wrong.

The second ground for my prediction is a conclusion which has a good deal of face validity: When in an individual or in a society a problem has been intractable to solution or amelioration, it is very likely that the diagnosis of the problem is wrong or very incomplete. That certainly has been the case with educational reform in the past 50 years. In fact, the awareness of intractability of schools to reform and the recognition of how high the societal stakes are have engendered increased frustration, anxiety, and desperation; a situation not conducive either to clear thinking or self-examination. For example, when you listen to what the top policy makers of the higher standards–greater expectations–rigorous testing policy say, their diagnosis is that the problem is the people in the trenches, not the policy makers whose previous prescriptions were feckless, wrong, or both.

Policy makers may have never been in the trenches or were there years ago and have forgotten what its features were; they are absentee landlords who are playing a game of policy chess, no less stalemated than the players who came before them. Is there something missing we have overlooked, something no less missing in our diagnosis than it is in the thinking of those in the trenches? The policy makers do not, cannot ask and pursue those questions. The universe of alternatives they consider is pathetically restricted. Euclid assumed, and for two and a half millennia everyone else assumed, that parallel lines will not meet. Einstein demonstrated under what conditions Euclid's assumptions would be wrong. Einstein did not do that by himself; in the intervening centuries a scientific culture had developed in which alternatives to conventional wisdom (in Kuhn's words "normal science") could and should be considered. There were no sacred cows, or if there were, they stood a good chance of losing their sanctity.

It was not until I had been working in schools for a number of years that I was emboldened to say that there was one problem that if not recognized, clarified, and taken seriously insured that educational reform would continue to be a series of failures. What emboldened me was that what experience had forced me to conclude was what others have said long before I came into this world. I was a Johnny-come-lately. The problem was this: What are the differences between contexts of productive and unproductive learning? When you pose that question, you do not short-circuit thinking by considerations of measurement, initially at least. You start with the question, What do we or should we mean by productive learning? If we mean *x*, what does that say about what we should be able to see and record in a classroom? What are its near-term consequences? Long term? What are the indices of motivation for learning we will have to develop? When we say productive learning, we mean that what is now being learned will sustain and/or increase motivation for learning in the near and long term. How will we best determine that? I ask these questions—and I could ask a lot more—as a way of saying that we start with the basics. What do we mean by learning? Willy-nilly children learn, but we are not satisfied with that because we believe, indeed our rhetoric insists, that schools must achieve several goals: (a) to mine, exploit, sustain the motivation to learn; (b) to learn those skills and that knowledge that make the world, past and present, meaningfully comprehensible; (c) to instill the sense of personal competence and social responsibility. That does not describe willy-nilly learning in which chance is a dominant factor. It begins, and only begins, to describe what we think we mean by productive. William James, always the pragmatist, said the litmus of the efficacy of what we do is its "cash value": how much of what we wanted to achieve we have achieved. The cash value of educational reform is written in red ink.

What do we mean by learning? What do we mean by productive? Those are not questions being asked by a carping critic. I have yet to meet or hear anybody who is opposed to productive learning. In all but a few instances the gulf between the policies they advocate and the results their actions produce exposes the emptiness of their rhetoric. Indeed, when they become aware of the failures of their policies, they are incapable of entertaining the possibility that their understanding of productive learning has no substance, and so they continue to come up with a new policy or diagnosis, again confirming the adage that the more things change the more they remain the same. In my conversation with John Dollard, he said that neurotic behavior is stupid behavior because the person keeps making the same mistakes in his or her thinking and actions. *He was not using the concept of stupid as an antonym to intelligent.* What we loosely call neurotics includes a very large number of "intelligent" people who have accomplished much in life, *except in regard to the problem that has brought them to a psychotherapist.* Educational policy makers are also intelligent in the conventional sense, but they are no less stupid than the clients John was characterizing. Readers may regard what I have just said as harsh, impolite, uncalled for, and ad hominem. May I point out that in no way am I disrespectful of their intentions to repair a serious problem. No policy maker has ever solicited my opinions about what they are doing and planning, let alone told me that they are discouraged and disillusioned by their past failures of reform. Some of them may have read some of what I have written, but I have never heard from any of them. Readers would be completely wrong if they concluded that these words are being written by a frustrated, depressed old man whose howls are not taken seriously and so in desperation he resorts to a final howl, to name-calling. Certainly I am old and I admit being frustrated, but frustration stems not from considerations of the personalities or intentions of those I criticize; they are as a group decent, public spirited, and committed to making a bad situation better. My frustration derives from the obvious fact that the significances I attach to a concept of productive learning are so unassimilable by policy makers as well as by the bulk of people in the educational community.

Why do I persist? Because I think I am right just as some who came long before me believed they were right. But it is not a matter of simple belief. What has continued to inspire me is when I have had the luck and/or the opportunity to observe and study instances where they took seriously the task of differentiating between contexts of productive and unproductive contexts of learning, and they took appropriate actions. And in almost all instances they demonstrated, I would say proved, that the cash value of their accomplishment was considerable, despite the facts that they were not working with privileged populations; that the demands on their time, energy, and creativity were enormous; and that they were viewed by others in the school system with apathy, disinterest, or disdain. The number of these exceptions-to-the-rule instances is very small, but I have reason to believe from what I have read or heard about that there are more. Even so, the number of exceptions is truly minuscule. Nevertheless, these exceptions confirm me in my belief that becoming clear about the differences between contexts of productive and unproductive learning is the most important starting point for educational reform. I should also point out that none of these exceptions was stimulated by me and my writings but by individuals who took John Dewey seriously. So let me turn now to a recent best-selling book in education, a remarkable book both for what it does and does not say. I tend to agree with a fair amount of what the author documents and says, although the conclusions she presents are empty rhetoric, a restoration of policy that is failing and will continue to fail. What she does not talk about is the most important problem. Dianne Ravitch is a deservedly respected educational historian, and the reader will gain much from reading her book. I regret having to criticize the book as I shall now do. The book's title is *Left Back: A Century of Failed School Reforms* (2000). It has been that kind of a century! In her introduction Ravitch states clearly and succinctly the tenor and goal of the book:

> Though American educators, parents, and policy makers living through . . . [the] disputes . . . [of] the 1980s and 1990s doubtless thought they were pioneers, in fact these issues have a long history. They have been debated for the past century. The great educational issues of the twentieth century in the United States centered on the questions of who was to be educated and what they were to learn: What are schools for and what should they aim to do? What is it that schools must do? As the stakes attached to education grew higher, parents' anxiety about their children's schooling grew as well; as the cost of education escalated, public officials insisted on surer evidence that the schools were succeeding in their most important tasks. (p. 14)

That the different reform efforts were intended to overthrow what their advocates perceived as stifling and unrealistic traditionalism cannot be doubted as the ringing rhetoric of those reform advocates proclaimed loud and clear. To the reader who is unfamiliar with the history of reform in the twentieth century, Ravitch's account is reason enough to buy the book. There is another reason for that advice: She makes it clear that at the beginning of that century the emergence of "educational experts" and the massive problems schools confronted because of waves of immigration set the stage on which the reformers could begin to exert influence on changing the old order. And in more than a few instances the reformers (really ideologues) were part of or sympathetic to the forecasts of the eugenic movement, which looked upon the masses of immigrants (especially those from Mediterranean countries and eastern Europe) as no less than a disaster for America. That is why tracking in schools mushroomed. And that is also why the early reformers considered it preposterous that the immigrants should be burdened with a curriculum that would have no utility whatsoever in the lives the likes of them would lead. And the emerging field of psychology played a very willing role in devising intelligence tests that could be used to sort the wheat from the chaff, spearheaded by psychologists enamored with eugenics. The Great Depression gave rise to new direction for reform, and the same happened in the sizzling turmoil of the 1960s.

From her detailed account of twentieth-century-reform failures, Ravitch concludes, rightly so, that "without firm adherence to the goal of intellectual development, schools lost their sense of purpose."

> By succumbing to the demands for industrial education in the early years of the century, they subjugated their programs to the needs of industry. In their attempts to be "socially efficient," educational leaders told themselves that they were responsible for guiding social change, forgetting that they were responsible for improving the lives of many individual children, each of whom was precious to someone. The widespread use of mental testing served to propagate the belief that students' innate ability counted for more than their disciplined effort. The testers persuaded principals, teachers, and parents that the tests could accurately and conclusively identify children's native capacities, thus relieving schools of their responsibility to teach all children and to awaken new interests by varying methods and materials.
>
> Intellectual development was further undermined by the child-centered advocates of the 1920s, who tried to eliminate an orderly curriculum and external standards and to make schools as much like "living" as possible, free of lessons, tests, marks, competition, textbooks, and lectures. Their conscious effort to build curricula around children's interests instead of intellectually challenging studies implied not only anti-intellectualism but a huge disadvantage for children of poor and immigrant families, because (as Dewey noted) children's interests are conditioned by what they already know and have previously been exposed to. (p. 460)

No reform movement takes place in a social vacuum; it is a reaction against a perceived unsatisfactory state of affairs and powered by a vision of a more desirable state of affairs. However different educational reform efforts have been in their purposes and rationales, they begin with an answer to one question: What are people capable of learning and becoming? Ravich does not attempt to answer that question in any detailed fashion, but she is crystal clear that she is morally and intellectually opposed to any answer that prematurely and arbitrarily assumes that certain individuals and groups cannot learn and develop. In short, she is outraged (not too strong a word) by reform movements blind to the illogicalities of self-fulfilling prophecies: you start by assuming a group is incapable, you take actions consistent with that assumption, and then you congratulate yourself for demonstrating that indeed they are incapable. Ravitch does not assert that all people are equally capable of learning *x*, *y*, or *z* or capable of engaging in this or that career. Equality of opportunity to learn does not guarantee equality in outcomes, but that in no way justifies dramatically and prematurely narrowing, watering down, let alone closing off opportunities to learn and become.[2] There is an underlying educational morality here: We should feel sincerely (not ritualistically or rhetorically) obliged to provide opportunities to acquire knowledge, skills, and ways of critical thinking crucial to becoming a productive and independent citizen. This is an obligation we "owe" all students, whether college bound or not. As a colleague once said to me, "The student who is not college bound may not have a so-called first-rate mind, but he can be, and we better be damned sure he will be, a first-rate person and citizen. I am not impressed with the number of first-rate minds who are first-rate people and citizens."

I have made it clear where I stand in regard to current proclamations and policies about the wondrous consequences we should expect from stating and adhering to high standards of academic performance, greater expectations that students can meet those standards, and careful and systematic evaluation of student performance. As I write these words, it is already apparent to the educational and political establishment that this approach is not having its intended consequences, that standards will have to be scaled down, that evaluating student performance by the usual kinds of tests is deceptively simple and straightforward, and that there is no basis whatsoever for saying that students are more highly motivated to learn than they were before. I am not opposed to standards, I am not opposed to evaluation of student performance, and, of course, I am not opposed to increasing student motivation to learn. I am opposed to proclaiming goals as if proclamations of educational virtue are tantamount to their realization, as if realization is a matter of engineering, as if between proclamation and

---

2. If I am very sensitive to the excesses of self-fulfilling prophecy, it is because of the years that I lived and worked with mentally retarded individuals. By the time I left I had been forced to unlearn what I had been taught about low test scores and problem solving. For example, if your neighbor's child chokes your dog to death, and that child has an IQ of 170, you will not conclude that the child's action is a consequence of having a high IQ. However, if that child had an IQ of 50, you are likely to conclude that he did what he did because of his low IQ. My years at the Southbury Training School was one continuous seminar on the dynamics of the self-fulfilling prophecy.

realization we need not worry that errors of omission and commission of long standing will defeat our intentions.

Up until the last chapter of her book, my sole reservation was that Ravitch was building a case supportive of today's "high standards" approach to educational reform. My reservation derived not only from her obvious antipathy to (if not outrage at) the degree to which the intellectual purpose of schooling had been watered down, crowded out by fads and fashions antithetical to extending intellectual horizons. What I found puzzling is that a book with the subtitle "A Century of Failed School Reform" never deals with the questions, What is meant by learning? What is meant by productive learning? Are the failures of school reform, any school reform, to be judged primarily by the subject matter the reform emphasizes? When it is said that a student has *learned* a subject matter, is that the same as saying that the student knows how to *think* about it? For example, Ravitch is no partisan of "a harsh regime of memorization and recitation" (p. 462). Why is she not a partisan; on what conception of productive learning does her opposition rest? Clearly, she has a conception of unproductive learning: a classroom in which students memorize what they are told to memorize and recite whatever they have been told to recite, as if they are puppets whose actions are solely determined by a master puppeteer. But Ravitch tells us nothing about what a context of productive learning should or might look like. Permit me to be concrete (and repetitious). The data are clear that in the modal American classroom students ask very few questions, teachers ask a plethora of questions. Is that regularity irrelevant to your conception of productive learning? Is it not likely that it is part of an explanation for why interest in learning and subject matter goes steadily downhill as students go from elementary to middle to high school?

The initial problem in educational reform is not one of subject matter but rather gaining clarity and consensus about the distinguishing features between contexts of productive and unproductive learning. If that problem is ignored or glossed over, what will follow (what *has* followed) will be as effective as when you put the cart before the horse. However, if you take the problem seriously, you may soon conclude that you have to deal with questions as frustrating as they are obvious and illuminating. For example, the classroom context has a cast of many discrete student learners, discrete learners organized and treated as a single group, the teacher, and a script (curriculum). In his seminal book *The Classroom Crucible* (1991) Pauly has well described how psychologically, interpersonally, and socially complicated the classroom context is and, therefore, how it suffuses the learning of everyone. In fact, Pauly's major point is that there is a predictable disconnect between a school policy and what happens in a classroom. Policy makers like to believe that once they have proclaimed a new policy intended to influence what goes on in a classroom, teachers will understand, accept, and appropriately implement that policy. Generally speaking, and to indulge in understatement, teachers look upon policy makers with unarticulated derision; they regard them as adversaries.

The point here is that if you take what I call the initial problem seriously, you will be making an egregious mistake if you assume that your words, oral or written, will be appropriately understood, accepted, and implemented by classroom teachers. By virtue of their training and experience, policy makers are fated to confuse hope and good intentions and outcomes. In the land of the blind, the one-eyed astigmatic man is king. As I have emphasized before, the preparation of teachers is almost totally antithetical to the letter and spirit of a context of productive learning. I trust that the reader will understand why I contend that if you seriously pursue the differences between contexts of productive and unproductive learning, you will begin to see that classroom learning is embedded in and influenced by contexts beyond the classroom, the individual school, and the school system, and I am here directing attention to colleges and universities which prepare educators. There are no villains in this story. The problem would be less difficult if there were villains. The problem has been that in the twentieth century those who have been in the corridors of educational power, policy, and influence have been unable to recognize and confront what I consider to be a basic starting point and question: What do we know about the differences between contexts of productive and unproductive learning, and what do we have to begin to do over the years to capitalize on that knowledge?

Ravitch does not pose that question, and I may be unfair in having hoped that she would pose it. She is a historian, and a very admirable one, who has written in a very clear and instructive way about a century's failure to reform schools. She has exposed the sources and contexts of different reform efforts, never hiding her position, which I share, that the intellectual skills, knowledge, and horizons of several generations of students were negatively affected. Until her last chapter Ravitch's critique is devastating. In her final chapter she points to the direction we should go:

> *It is no simple matter to demarcate the divide between what is called progressive education and what is called traditional education.* Neither term can be easily defined. The meaning of both terms has shifted over time, and there is a tendency to react to one or the other of them as "good" or "bad" depending on one's experiences and preferences. Both sides have had their virtues and defects, depending on circumstances. . . .
>
> Despite the heated controversies of the past century, there is surely an area of commonality between the best impulses of progressivism and traditionalism. (p. 462; emphasis in original)

I find her words very unconvincing. She is correct in saying that labels like progressivism and traditionalism are hard to define; they are rallying cries, not usable concepts. Neither movement was nor is without merit. Unfortunately, what both movements have in common is the failure to put flesh on the bones of a concept of productive learning. That concept is not an "impulse," nor should it, as in the case of labels like progressivism and traditionalism, be employed as an empty badge of honor, a signal that one is on the side of the angels. I have tried in these pages and previous writings to describe in concrete terms features of the concept that observers can identify. William James and John Dewey identified some of those features more than a century ago although neither of them provided a coherent, organized account of how these features interrelate. I do not pretend that I have gone beyond them except for trying to describe and clarify how the culture of the school makes the creation and sustaining of contexts of productive learning *both for students and teachers* an astonishingly infrequent occurrence.

Ravitch is a historian and I am a psychologist, and that may well account for the different judgments we make about a century of failed school reform and how and why we should regard the future as each of us does: I am far more pessimistic than she is. Why? Generally speaking, historians tend to deal with the thinkers and doers of the past, the "movers and shakers" in the arena of theory and ideology, individuals who left a written record of what they were for and against and who the historian assumes had varying but significant impact on those they regarded as their constituencies. That is to say, it is assumed they reflected the experiences and opinions of those constituencies or sought to influence them, or both; in the competition for acceptance of their beliefs some "won," others "lost." It is one of Ravitch's major contributions that she identifies and discusses those who "lost" but whose point of view turned out to be prophetic, and by prophetic Ravitch explicitly means that she agrees that they should have been heeded and if we do not now heed them, the future will be a carbon copy of the past.

There is a limitation to such histories, and it inheres in the fact that, generally speaking, the constituencies of historians are other historians and/or nonhistorians who are in positions of power to take actions consistent with the conclusions of the historians. Those actions, usually in the form of new policies, are intended to effect a change in a much larger group who, so to speak, are on the "front lines." Concretely, and in relation to educational reform, Ravitch gives us a very instructive account of what the movers and shakers said but nothing about how the mass of teachers felt about and responded to the messages and policies directed at them. One can safely assume that the reactions of teachers were not monolithic. Did a few, some, or most of them change what they did in their classrooms, or did they roll with the punch without changing their style of teaching? Was the content of the curriculum change appropriately understood and implemented by teachers? Given a century of educational-philosophical controversy and failed or misguided efforts of school reform, can we attribute what happened only to the theories and ideologies of the movers and shakers who operated on the level of theory and social beliefs, who wrote, lectured, taught, and assumed that teachers were like puppets who were willing and able to conform to the wishes of the intellectually elevated puppeteers? Did the battle the traditionalists were losing to the progressives (and others) in no way relate to the pedagogy of traditionalist teachers? Similarly, were the failures of the progressives independent of how teachers comprehended the pedagogical implications of the theorists of progressive education? Ravitch has done an excellent job of clarifying some of the unfortunate consequences of the different reform movements, but her explanation is incomplete to the extent that her criticisms address only the theories and ideologies of the proponents of these movements and say little or nothing about why it was expected that teachers would comprehend and appropriately change their pedagogy. It is not my intention here to criticize either the proponents of reform or the teachers but rather to note and emphasize a disconnect that has long been a characteristic of educational reform movements: changes in theory or policy have surprisingly little influence on what happens in a classroom if only because the policy changers assume that what they say, communicate, or write will be appropriately comprehended by teachers, as if both sides understand each other. If that disconnect was not clearly recognized in the first half of the twentieth century, it should have been in the second half as the disasters of the curriculum reform movement of the 1950s and 1960s unfolded. But it was not recognized then, and it is not recognized now as a crucial problem by Ravitch in regard to her proposal that we seek to wed the best aspects of traditionalism and progressivism. I am very much in favor of such a marriage if by marriage you mean a commitment to a partnership in which both parties understand each other and willingly confront the practical problems they predictably will encounter. Too many marriages end in divorce because hope and good intentions are frail reeds for dealing with the realities of individual change, let alone institutional and professional change.

The problem I have raised here is extraordinarily complicated and neither in these pages or in previous writings have I dealt with it in a comprehensive manner. But in matters of educational reform you have to choose a starting point, and I have been clear that my starting point is the selection and training of educators; not only teachers but administrators as well. It is a starting point Abraham Flexner chose in 1910 when asked to come up with a plan to reform a very inadequate system of medical education, a system that was not a system but a congeries of disconnected parts in which most medical schools were not connected to universities or hospitals, practice was hardly informed by research, and selection to a medical school was by criteria which were scandalously low and inadequate. Flexner concluded that unless and until medical education was radically transformed in terms of selection, content, and purpose, there was no hope for improvement of the quality of practice and the prevention of disease. He came up with a plan that truly transformed the medical arena. We would do well to try to benefit from his vision and courage as we move into a new century, which I fear will be a rerun of what Ravitch has described about the twentieth century.

Starting points are just that: starting points. My starting point derives from several considerations, but the most important one is that a starting point be one which will have percolating consequences rather than local or circumscribed ones. We are not in the position to deal simultaneously with all or even most of the important problems. We have to make a choice which holds out the promise of reducing the strength of other problems. You could call it the "falling dominos" approach: If you get to first base in regard to problem A, then problem B becomes less knotty as a problem. If my starting point is not convincing to the reader, I can only say that of all starting points others have proposed, none makes anything like a case that it will have percolating consequences for schools generally. Are we to be content with each of us tending our own garden zealously, protecting it against external baleful influences or, worse yet, giving up the garden because the rewards are minimal, temporary, or a source of burnout? By what kind of cost-benefit analysis should starting points be judged?

Chapter 15

The Continuity Value

In the last few years I found myself calling into question something I had said and emphasized in my previous writings. It was not that what I had emphasized was wrong but rather incomplete in a basic way that caused me to think differently about purposes of educational reform. I was not and still am not secure in judging this (for me) new line of reasoning. But this is a self-scrutinizing memoir, and I decided that I should discuss it here. That readers may disagree with what I shall say or conclude that I am not as clear or logical a thinker as I should be is no basis for not telling this aspect of my self-scrutinizing "story." So I ask the reader patiently to indulge me as my thinking unfolds.

If you were forced to choose between passing on to your children your genes or your values, which would you choose? There are societies in which many of their people have children for economic reasons in order to insure that in old age parents will have sources of support; genes cannot support you, children brought up prepared to take care of infirm parents can support you. These parents may know how children are "made," but they are not making a choice; having children is instrumental for inculcating personal-familial values as guarantors against the consequences of infirmity. Newborns who are females are less valued than males; female neonates may in fact be killed. These are actions and attitudes expressive of individual, clan, tribal values intended to insure continuity of those values over coming generations. Genes are hardly in the picture, if at all.

In our society in recent decades there have been far more parents who seek to adopt a child than there are available children. In fact, they literally scan the nations of the world where they allow adoption by foreigners of different races and ethnicities. These parents give little thought, if any, to the genealogy of the children they seek to adopt. Yes, they do want some minimal assurance that the child is basically healthy or if the child is sickly (or currently ill), he or she can be made healthy, physically normal. Why do they seek to adopt? The answer is a complicated one, but one crucial part of it is that like most parents of biological offspring, they want to give their children that kind of mixture of love, nurturance, instruction, and opportunities that allows a parent to conclude they have cause to be satisfied and proud of the kind of person the child became. And person means far more than occupation and income, even celebrity. It does not mean a person who knows the cost of everything and the value of nothing. He or she is a person whose actions and values transcend narrow self-interest and contribute to the improvement and continuity of family, and the local, state, or national community. The goal of living has meaning in action and thought beyond individual self-interest.

The most instructive and inspiring doctoral dissertation I ever supervised was about 20 families who had adopted severely mentally retarded and/or neurologically or physically handicapped children. Some of these parents already had two or more normal children. What these parents had in common was a set of values, usually religiously derived, which obligated them to embrace these children, to do for them what no one else was prepared to do. Obligated is really not the right word because these parents did not see themselves as martyrs; they were doing what they felt was simply the right thing to do.

Although parents may not clearly articulate it, or articulate it at all, over time they judge themselves and their children by what I shall call the "continuity value": However different my child may be from me in interests and goals, how well has he internalized values I consider essential in governing personal and societal relationships and obligations? That question does get articulated, however vaguely, as the child leaves the geographical orbit of the home and has to deal with a very complicated world in which there is a host of conflicting values. For example, the now legendary 1960s were marked by generational conflict about many things, not the least of which concerned the values which should inform thinking and actions. It was a clash in the present, but it was in a truly basic way a clash between different perceptions and, therefore, judgments of history: familial, institutional, and national. For the first time for many parents what their rebellious offspring was advocating and doing made them, the parents, aware that they held values, moral and political, very much related to an established order of things they believed was rooted in history. That, of course, is where they were in agreement with their children, except that the latter were espousing a new set of values and advocating a change in the established order of things.

I referred to the sizzling sixties as a way to state several conclusions. The first is that in explanation of our individual lives or of the life of a country, history is always a crucial variable. Second, the life history of the individual and of his or her country are interrelated in subtle and obvious ways, which is why a French person and an American one are so different in so many ways. Yes, they are similar in many ways, but those similarities pale in consequences compared to differences. Third, a major function of history is to shed light on the interconnectedness of individual and national life: how and why values and goals are learned, change, transform, even wither away, or are lost to memory; history is about change. Fourth, and related to the third, history, individual or national, is about means and ends, how each to small or large degree affects the other; ends are valued goals, they are justification for what we want to accomplish in the future, which is why we warn ourselves and are warned by others to choose means that will be appropriate to our valued goals. Fifth, history is always a revisiting of the past using the lens of the present; if history is about change, by its very nature history changes. Sixth, how we think about and deal with change in the present depends to a very significant degree on how well we know, if we know at all, that as individuals and nations we are rooted in history. Fish swim in water and do not know it; too many people do not know they swim in history.

I said earlier that parents want their children to reflect the continuity value: There are certain values parents consider desirable and basic which they hope their children have internalized and will in the future pass on to their children. Generally speaking, when forced to define those values they state them in ways that are so vague or abstract as to provide no direction whatever to what they should or might mean for concrete action. It is when parents observe their children, especially young ones, acting in a way that is at variance with their values that parents begin to understand that internalizing a value is not a consequence of having heard the parent state it, that internalization is a complicated process embedded in or associated with concrete situations and feelings. It is not attained or learned in one trial. And what complicates the process is when the young child cannot comprehend the "justice" of the value the parent espouses and the child expresses mystification and anger and asks the why questions: Why can't I do what I did or am doing? Why are you unfair? There are parents who make short shrift of the reactions of the child. There are other parents who will try to explain concretely why what the child did has unacceptable consequences, how if everyone did what they wanted to do, there would be a lot of unhappy people. I can assure the reader that I know that (1) rearing a child is awesomely complicated and consequential and (2) that what textbooks say does not prepare you for what you should concretely think and do about the concrete actions your concrete child in a very concrete situation has said or done. I do not say this only on the basis of personal experience. I have known world-renowned developmental psychologists who have said what I just said. As one of these colleagues said to me—it was the late William Kessen—and I paraphrase, "The hardest thing for a parent to do in rearing a child is to respect the child's feelings and actions. And respect means you try to understand his actions from his perspective and on that basis decide where you stand the best chance to get to first base in altering his thinking and actions. If the parent is one who has to hit home runs, that parent is contributing to the future income of psychotherapists. But even if you respect the child's thinking and actions and you are successful 50% of the time, you still are 20% above the parental average." I will never forget when decades ago Kessen was told that his wife had given birth to triplets, thus making for a family with five children!

For Kessen, respect was a treasured value which did not necessarily mean that in child rearing it took precedence over other values. What he did mean was that when parents discharge their obligations to inculcate values they deem essential for the kind of child they want him or her to be, respecting the child's perspective is the basis for altering behavior, not mindlessly accepting or ignoring it. *It is a child-centered value only if you mean (as you should) that acting in accord with that value, you want to decrease the child's egocentricity, to broaden and deepen his understanding of self, others, and the world. The internalization process is one in which both parent and child are learners.* That is why many parents will say that the mistakes they made with their first child they tried not to repeat with their second child.

How do parents define a mistake? That is a question parents like not to think about and like even less to talk about. I am not referring to mistakes that have very temporary consequences because the parents quickly realized that in some way they wrongly understood their "subject matter": their child's response or actions. If such mistakes are legion, they nevertheless underline the importance of knowing your "subject matter." What I am referring to are mistakes the parents consider, rightly or wrongly, to have had long-term consequences both for parents and child. These are not one-time mistakes but rather a semicontinuous series of the same mistake that the parents now consider to have in some way produced in the child characteristics at variance with the parents' hopes and fantasies. The parents define the mistake in terms of history: What happened in the past influenced the future. And for parents, the most troublesome of these mistakes has to do with the continuity value: The child does not or may not hold, express, or implement the interpersonal and social values highly prized by the parent.

Parents, of course, vary both in the substance of the continuity value and the clarity with which they articulate it. However they vary, their continuity value over time almost always undergoes change and in a particular direction: They begin to see their child in the context of a societal present and past, more specifically, a societal change which may undermine their grown child's ability to think and act appropriately in accord with their continuity value. Let me give a concrete example.

It was in 1956 and I was conducting a research program on test anxiety in elementary school children. One of the things I was doing was interviewing the parents, almost always mothers, of high- and low-test-anxious children. One of those mothers was Mrs. Cochrane whose daughter, Lesley, I had observed in the classroom. Mrs. Cochrane was college educated, 35 years old, and had taught in an elementary school for 4 years before Lesley was born. Lesley was 10 years of age. (The resemblance between mother and daughter was striking.) The interview format was semistructured. Mrs. C. was articulate, thoughtful, forthright, and self-confident in a nondogmatic way. Toward the end of the interview was this question: Parents have a picture of what they would like their children to be when they are grown. What is your picture? Here is what she said, paraphrased:

> [She laughs.] Like a lot of parents I can answer by saying that I want her to be able to do what she decides to do. Lesley is bright, as you probably know, and she is very creative. I can't think of any line of work in which she would not succeed if that is what she decided to do. We will be supportive. [She laughs again.] Of course I want her to be happy, financially comfortable, to feel fulfilled, and recognized for her accomplishments. [A somber look appears.] But you know what? When I think of the world we live in, some of the craziness that goes on, the pressures, the competitiveness, the frustrations it can produce, the things you cannot control, I worry about Lesley. She is a decent, good, strong kid, but will that be enough? When I start thinking that way, I sort of lower my sights that she will be the kind of person who respects others and in turn is respected by them for what she is as a person. I don't know how else to say it. I want her to be what I consider to be a good person and citizen and to pass on that goodness to her children. [She laughs.] I do not understand why I said that is lowering my sights. I should have said that I was raising my sights.

I interviewed many parents, but the interview with Mrs. C. was the only one that remained clearly in my memory for almost a half century. I often wondered why. One reason may be that I am a worrier and what she said was grist for my neurotic mill; my daughter, Julie, was 2 years old at the time, and I was already indulging my proclivity to worry about which illnesses or accidents could befall her! And it was when I was thinking about this chapter that what Mrs. Cochrane said popped into my head.

Parents are teachers, by which I mean that both have "subject matter" they want their students to assimilate because they deem it important for the children's future roles as working and productive individuals as well as responsible citizens. And both have the task and obligation to employ a pedagogy appropriate to the task. And by "appropriate," I mean that they are expected to take into account that the child (= student) is a developing, changing, striving organism who has to be understood in order for the child to learn. It is what I like to call the "you have to crawl before you walk" principle. They know that children are not clay, impersonally to be molded and manipulated, that teaching is not a cut-and-dried, cookbook process, that teaching subject matter requires what can be legitimately called personal artistry. What and why a child learns is never independent of the kind of person the teacher or parent is. That is something parents learn about classroom teachers when their child starts formal schooling or even is enrolled in a nursery school. And, of course, that is something teachers learn about the parents of their pupils. Parents do not thank God for all the teachers their child has had, just as teachers do not thank God for all the parents of their pupils. The categories of teacher and parent, like that of pupil, contain a range of psychological variations that is as bewildering as it is obvious.

If the roles of parent and classroom teacher are highly similar—in principle, purpose, and content—and there is more I could have discussed—there are differences; they are differences more in degree than in principle. For example, a teacher may have 20–30 or more pupils close in age; parents may have several but of greater variation in age, more like a one-room schoolhouse. The parents have a more intimate relationship with their "students" than the classroom teacher has with his or hers, and the parents know their child in ways and situations about which the teacher knows nothing. (As I learned early on, the picture I got from observing children in a classroom or from talking to their teachers, and the picture I got from parents could be very different, frequently dramatically so.) But there is one difference that is a very big difference. The teacher has students for one year, and his or her goal is to get the students to a particular level of educational achievement by the end of that year; the students are then passed on to other teachers. Compared to the time perspective of the teacher, that of the parents concerns a long, indefinite future, ending only with parental death. It can, sadly, end with the child's premature death, which then causes the parents to mourn, among other things, a future in which the child would have become the kind of person the parents wanted him or her to become.

I have no data which confirms my opinion that by the time their child finishes formal schooling (including college) and enters the "real" world, the continuity values are near or at the top of their scale of values. To my knowledge, that opinion has not been studied in the longitudinal manner the opinion requires. As luck would have it, I write these words the day after I saw the movie *Almost Famous* in which that opinion is extraordinarily well depicted. The film takes place in the turbulent sixties when generational conflict was so frequent and troublesome. That film reminded me of the earlier film *Dirty Dancing*, which had the same theme in the same time period. Anyone like me who lived through that period will have no doubt that my opinion is a tenable one. I know that anecdote and film have (as they should) questionable status in the court of scientific evidence, but I have to say that I can fill a book, a sizeable one, about families from that period right up until today whose greatest concern was or is centered on the continuity value: Will my child stay true to the values I tried to inculcate, the personal and social values I tried to inculcate in him or her? Work or career is one thing but personal and social values are another, and for parents the latter becomes over time a greater cause for worry than the former. It is not that work and career became less important but that the continuity value has vastly increased in saliency.

Generally speaking, parents do not think about the continuity value in political-historical terms except in times of turbulent social change. Is there anyone who would not characterize the post–World War II era as one of dramatic social change? For example, take the Supreme Court's 1954 school desegregation decision. There were millions of people who in the abstract had longed for that decision and greeted it enthusiastically but who when confronted with its practical implications, such as bussing, were troubled by what it could mean for their children's future, personally and otherwise. There were also millions of people who had long looked at racial mixing of any sort as a catastrophe for them and their children; they were not in doubt that their continuity value would be undermined to their and their children's detriment. For the millions who were for or against the desegregation decision, the continuity value could no longer be seen as only a family matter but rather as a consequence of national, political, legal history. They became aware that, like it or not, their continuity value had taken on a strength and complexity they had not anticipated.

But that is an old story in America. What about the millions of immigrants who in the nineteenth century and the early decades of the twentieth came in waves to these shores? Countless sociological tracts, films, plays, and novels have been written about immigrant children adjusting to new ways, values, and lifestyles quite at variance with those of their parents who struggled and fought against the widening gulf between parent and child, who saw only discontinuity in values. That their children may have been successful by American standards was small solace or substitute for the continuity of their old-world values and life styles. Immigrant parents learned very quickly and concretely what they knew abstractly before: America was not the "old country." America projected itself as a new, powerful, opportunity-laden, superior country with distinctive values not least of which was rugged individualism, striving, personal responsibility, and pride in country. If parents of immigrant children had any doubts about those values they were erased when their children began schooling. Bear in mind that most of these children knew either little or no English: The problem of bilingualism has a very long history in American education. And let us not forget that teachers were sincerely patriotic and sincerely saw it as their responsibility to make these immigrant children into Americans and that meant making them as different from their parents as possible. When you read accounts of teaching in those early decades, you probably would agree with me that a primary goal was to tame and socialize immigrant children. Inevitably it contributed to a discontinuity in values between parent and child. Those were days when concepts of individuality and the ethos of multiculturalism were not in the educational picture; they were alien concepts.

If parents take the continuity value seriously, it is when social change becomes apparent that parents are forced to recognize that their continuity value had taken history for granted. That is to say, they had not been aware that that value assumed a kind of political, societal status quo; there had been a general national consensus—which does not mean unanimity—about values contained in its founding documents and in subsequent legislative and judicial findings. In one or another way these values gave direction and protection to personal freedom in order to insure the continuity of those values over time. Put in another way, those documents deliberately made it extraordinarily difficult to change those values in any way. Sustaining those values was of overarching importance. Fatefully, however, those values were made inapplicable to slaves. One could argue on the basis of the historical record that if the antislavery states had insisted on the eradication of slavery, there would have been no United States. The pro- and antislavery states had irreconcilable continuity values. I need not elaborate about what it has meant to subsequent American society.

The Declaration of Independence was a statement about history, "human history," in the near and distant past. It was a statement about "self-evident" values or truths the rebelling colonies should honor and perpetuate if they were to avoid the mistakes of the past. When a decade or so later the Bill of Rights was appended to the Constitution, it was to concretize those values, increasing the chances that they would be a bulwark against discontinuity of those values. Continuity and discontinuity of those values were center stage in the thinking of the leaders and people of those times. Like parents they had a hierarchy of values, but at the top was the continuity of those values. History books, especially those used in schools, tend not to note or emphasize the degree of anxiety the founding fathers had about how well the continuity value would be honored in practice. You could say that they viewed the Bill of Rights as a kind of Ten Commandments without which a democratic society would not long continue. Again like parents, they were less concerned about the continuity value in their immediate present and more about a future in which there would be challenges of diverse sorts from diverse sources to the continuity value. I cannot refrain from saying that it was as if they regarded the new nation as parents view their newborns: Will they honor and act consistently with values the parents (= founding fathers) tried to instill in them. As I said earlier, the salience of the continuity value in parents becomes increasingly important to them as their offspring leave childhood and later the family. That degree of saliency and importance was what the founding fathers experienced at the birth of the newly born nation. They could not afford to wait for their child to grow up by which time the game might be over. They were a wondrous lot! Let us listen to what one of them said:

> There must doubtless be an unhappy influence on the manners of our people produced by the existence of slavery among us. The whole commerce between master and slave is a perpetual exercise of the most boisterous passions, the most unremitting depotism on the one part, and degrading submissions on the other. Our children see this and learn to imitate it. . . . The parent storms, the child looks on, catches the lineaments of wrath, puts on the same airs in the circle of smaller slaves, gives a loose to the worst of passions, and thus nursed, educated, and daily exercised in tyranny, cannot but be stamped by it with odious peculiarities. The man must be a prodigy who can retain his manners and morals undepraved by such circumstances. And with what execration should the statesman be loaded who, permitting one half the citizens to trample on the rights of the other, transforms those into despots, and these into enemies, destroys the morals of the one part and the *amor patriae* of the other. . . . With the morals of the people, their industry is also destroyed. For in a warm climate no man will labor for himself who can make another labor for him. . . . And can the liberties of a nation be thought secure when we have removed their only firm basis, a conviction in the minds of the people that these liberties are of the gift of God? That they are not to be violated but with His wrath? Indeed I tremble for my country when I reflect that God is just; that his justice cannot sleep forever; that considering numbers, nature and natural means only, a revolution of the wheel of fortune, an exchange of situation, is among possible events; that it may become probable by supernatural interference. The Almighty has no attribute which can take side with us in such a contest.

That is as good an example of the force and strength of the continuity value as one can find. The man who wrote it could not have done so when he was a young man. He was by today's understanding and standards a racist, indubitably so. But he came to realize—still holding some of his racist proposals—that sustaining the psychological dynamics of the master-slave relationship endangered the continuity of the values contained in its founding documents. The man was Thomas Jefferson. Ironically, he was also the first education president in our history, for reasons I detail in my book *Presidential Leadership and Educational Failure* (1998b). Indeed I regard him as the *only serious* education president in our history. He understood why a free country had to instill in coming generations understanding and respect for the values for which the nation had striven.

With that long prologue I can now discuss why I have come to conclude that something I have emphasized in much of my writings is very insufficient and unconnected to the continuity value. In skeleton style here is why I emphasized what I regarded as the overarching purpose of schooling.

1. If, like the poet Yeats, you regard education not as a process for filling empty buckets but rather lighting fires, then the modal classroom is a context of unproductive learning and not one of productive learning.

2. There is good evidence that as students go from elementary to middle to high school their interest in learning steadily decreases. That evidence does not include my personal observations as much as what many scores of middle and high school teachers have told me. Part of that evidence does rest on research clearly indicating that in the modal classroom students ask a pitifully small number of questions and teachers ask fantastically more. I assume (hope) the reader does not believe that not asking questions is a sign of interest.

3. The overarching purpose of schooling should be that when students graduate high school, they want to continue to learn *more* about self, others, and the world. Put in another way, reinforcing and sustaining *wanting to learn* in students is the most important criterion by which we should judge a school. There is a difference—a vast psychological difference—between wanting to learn and feeling compelled to learn. *The subject matter which parents, the larger society, and the school agree students should master is not the issue; the issue is that subject matter not be taught in ways that extinguish interest in it and cause students to put it in the file-and-forget category from which they perceive no need for retrieval.*

So why do I now believe that formulation is seriously incomplete? Asking that question led me to ask another question of great concern to young people before and during school: the substance of one's sense of personal identity. Admittedly, the concept of the sense of personal identity is a complicated and fuzzy one hard to define and study. It does not refer to visible and palpable things, it changes over time, and it has diverse sources of which we are dimly aware or not aware at all. Why am I not like other people? Why do I value some things and people and devalue others?

What is there about me that some people like and that makes them want to be my friends, while others seem to dislike me and avoid or reject me? What is there about me I wish I could change, and what is there about me I will never want to change? Why do my parents not understand me and yet keep saying they love me? Why do my friends and a lot of other people have more self-confidence than I do? What kind of a person would I like to be or become? If people knew what I often think about or imagine, would they think I am a nut?

Then there is a question which is not central to the development and formation of the personal sense of identity. It is more a question than a declaration that many students—far too many students—articulate to themselves and to each other: "Why do I have to learn what in school we are told we have to learn? It is so boring, it is like taking a terrible medicine that you do not need because you are not sick." And that kind of reaction implies a sense of identity that places school learning low on the list of important values. That was not true when eager, open-eyed, and curious, they started school. They have remained curious but not about school learning. It is events and people outside of school, not inside it, with whom they identify. In fact, the small number of students who appear to like and flourish in school are judged by their classmates in derogatory terms.

Teachers of middle and high school students will understand and agree with what I have said. Indeed, what I have said is based not only on my personal experiences and observations but on what scores of teachers have told me over the decades. (There are exceptions, of course, but they are *exceptions*.) Their explanations of what they see center on what they would term *adolescent turmoil*, the years of rebellion, conflicts about the sense of personal identity, the "who am I?" question. Teachers assume, they certainly hope, students are going through a "phase," which will be followed by another phase in which the crises of personal identity have subsided and the student comes to terms with the complex realities of the larger society. I have never met a teacher whose explanation included a criticism of how subject matter was taught and why. That is not surprising because teachers' own sense of personal-professional identity—derived as it is from his or her own schooling, formal preparation for teaching, and then socialization in the culture of the school—makes criticism of the usual pedagogy an alien thought. And, it should be stressed, that pedagogy is what the larger society increasingly has come to require, even demand, and it does so not only because of dissatisfaction with the academic performance of students as that is measured by tests, but also because of puzzlement and even anxiety about youth whose values, life styles, and disinterest in participating in matters of public or civic affairs (voting, for example) are seen as threats to societal and political values and traditions of long standing.

I am not passing judgment here. I am reporting what I hear being said on radio, TV, the mass media, journals of social commentary and criticism by people of widely varying political, philosophical, and religious affiliations, and occupations.

I also like to listen to radio talk shows because what passes for expression of point of view on TV I find utterly boring. (A notable exception is the morning C-Span *Washington Journal* where the host is studiously neutral and the callers who, after identifying whether they are Democrats, Republicans, or Independents, express their views about issues of the day.) On the radio talk shows the host is explicitly liberal or conservative, and each, of course, draws largely listeners with similar perspectives. On the conservative shows most callers perceive the youth of today as hedonistic, demeaning of American traditions, blurring the line between right and wrong, and victims of parental work and lifestyle. What is surprising about the liberal talk shows is that a fair number of the callers do not basically disagree with the conservative callers, although they differ in how this state of affairs came about and is being sustained by public policies: domination of the force of religion, too easy access to abortion, and mass media depicting unbridled violence. So, for example, some conservative callers say, "Guns don't kill, people do," and gun control is no answer. Some liberal callers retort that easy purchase of guns make it easier for youth and others to give overt expression to violent fantasies.

All that I have said above was what the nation was discussing for at least 2 months after the killings in Columbine High School in 1999. No one, liberal or conservative, denied the assertion that the youth of today were, generally speaking, a troubled and troublesome cohort whose attitudes and behavior did not bode well for the societal future. Not long after Columbine there were other killings in schools. People were appalled when they learned about the frequency of criminal violence in schools (student to student, student to teachers). This was taking place at a time when schools were vehemently being criticized for having lowered academic standards, for having expected too little from students, for promoting students who should have been kept back. *Columbine and the call for higher standards was a confluence of the concern for the continuity value on a national level and the individual parental level.* And it is worthy of emphasis that it is when children are graduated from high school and go off to college or work that parents' interest and concern about the continuity value sharply escalate.

The more I observed the social scene and reviewed my past writings from a self-scrutinizing stance, I found myself asking and struggling with three questions. Is it sufficient or justified to say that the overarching purpose of schooling is to instill, reinforce, and sustain in students the desire to want to continue to learn more about self, others, and the world? Is it not as or even more important that students assimilate and hold values that over a lifetime are part of a sense of personal and societal-historical identity? Are those aspects—and they are only aspects, not the whole content—that should be regarded as indispensable to the overarching purpose of schooling I previously had asserted? And that question forced on me the realization that to want to know more about self, others, and the world they live in, students had to have a historical perspective that has put its imprimatur on them in countless ways, the most important of which centers on the continuity value, a value in which personal and societal values are seamlessly combined. If that is correct, a further question arises: What do we want students to understand about the continuity value in America as they experience and judge it in the present? And by "understand" I mean that their living present inevitably includes an awareness and respect for a salient past that should be continued in the future or if the judgment is to reject that past, it is a considered judgment, not one taken lightly because of the pressures and heat of the present. Either way, history informs the judgment. It is one thing to know in the abstract that we are products of a national past, a past we hardly think about or comprehend in regard to values informing our actions, goals, and relationships. It is quite another thing to be aware that the past is in or should be in our psychological bloodstream because inevitably, whether we know it or not, we are conduits of the continuity value even when we believe that in this or that respect we must depart from or change the direction of that value.

Let me now concretize what I have been saying. I shall use two examples. I could have used many more to illustrate why I have come to believe that the continuity value is no less important—perhaps from the societal standpoint more important—than the overarching purpose of schooling I have previously held. I restrict myself to two examples because if they are not clear and persuasive (to some degree, at least) there is no point in giving more examples. Many people in the present and past give the continuity value the importance I now do but their writings rarely and concretely center on how it should suffuse what is taught in and goes on in a classroom.

The first example will seem very remote from a classroom. *It is about an event that has occurred only once in the history of countries.* I refer to the fact that during World War II a national election was held in the United States. Governments typically had either canceled elections or were overthrown during war time. We had the typical presidential and congressional campaign, all the hype, hoopla, rhetoric, accusations, and fanfare—all of this during a truly global war the outcome of which no one, but no one, doubted was fateful for this country and the world. And that is an understatement.

How and for what purpose can that event be capitalized on, say, in a history course in high school. What if we, as we should, start by asking students, What might be the significances of that singular event? I have never taught high school students, but I have on several occasions asked that question of individual or a small group of high school students. Their reaction was a mixture of puzzlement and wariness—puzzlement because they did not know how to reply, and wariness because they suspected I was setting them up to expose their ignorance about something they should know. Aside from one student who said, "A law is a law and you have to obey it," the singular event had no special significance to them. Subsequent to these students, and after I mulled over their puzzlement and wariness, I asked a student the same question and got a similar response, after which I said the following: "Have you heard of Wilt Chamberlain, the great professional basketball player? (He did, so I went on.) He is the only professional basketball player who scored 100 points in a game. He was above 7 feet in height, very strong, very agile. There are and have been other players as tall, strong, and agile, but none has come close to that unusual performance. It was and still is what we call a singular event. How can we explain it? And that is the same question I asked about the national election during World War II. How do we explain it? What can we learn from it?"

I did not expect the student to answer the question in regard to Wilt Chamberlain, nor did I want him to think that the two events were comparable in principle or importance. I said to him, "Comparing Wilt and the election is like comparing apples and oranges, they taste and are very different to us." I was quite aware that my choice for comparison was not a felicitous one, but it popped into my mind because, I think, of my very limited goal in some way to explain to the student that however strange the question and I were to him (and both were very strange to him), I had a purpose in asking the question. Here is what I said to him: "When something truly unusual happens to us or another person, or in the life of a country, it not only gets our attention but we also try to explain it. But why do we try to explain it? Because of the fact that it is so unusual, that it obviously contrasts to the way things usually are, we feel we should try to understand why it happened to us, or another person, or a country. Something in us tells us we would learn something important we didn't know before."

I do not defend how I handled that interaction. And I would not defend myself against the criticism that I had asked questions I assumed the student, like the others, would not know how to answer. But I had a strong need to test that assumption. I was not a teacher. I was a strange person asking strange questions. You could say that I was indulging my needs at their expense. Enough of mea culpas!

But what if I were their history teacher asking the question about the election during World War II? What understanding would I (or the reader) want students to assimilate? Let us not be detained by the very thorny problem of the pedagogy we might employ that would make the issues personally meaningful and important to students. Here are some of the aspects of what I mean by *understanding*.

1. This country is based on a written constitution implicitly and explicitly containing values—statements about what is right or wrong, permissible and impermissible—about individual and governmental actions and purposes. There are values and there are values, but there are two that suffuse the Constitution. The first is the protection of individual rights and liberty against governmental actions that would restrict or nullify those rights and personal freedom. That protection was axiomatically the highest value. When Patrick Henry said, "Give me liberty or give me death," it was not empty rhetoric or bombastic, mindless patriotism about the colonists' war against England. What he said was what colonists thought, except of course for the minority who were loyal to Great Britain. The Constitution reflects that value.

2. The other of the two values centered on continuity. It is not an exaggeration to say that this value was associated in the minds of those in the Constitutional Convention. Would this newborn country stay true to the letter and spirit of the Constitution? There were external enemies, to be sure, but a greater source of concern was the people themselves. Would they be divided and corrupted by factions seeking power? Would self-appointed demagogues attract and seduce sufficient numbers of people to make them tyrants? Democracy was an experiment vesting power in the people; would they be wise and strong enough to stay true to the responsibilities given them in the Constitution? There is a provision in the Constitution for amending the Constitution, but it deliberately makes it a peaceful but difficult process that takes time and debate. *The continuity value was never to be taken lightly.*

3. There is no provision in the Constitution for canceling or postponing an election. To do so was tantamount to subverting totally the "we the people" ethos by unconstitutional means, by undemocratic means. What is remarkable about the election is that practically no one even suggested postponement. *Of course you have the election. Not to have it would be unthinkable. It would also be illegal. We have to express our opinions by voting. Continuity with our past is essential.*

4. What I regard as the most courageous act by a President in the twentieth century occurred during the Korean War when President Truman removed General MacArthur from his post. MacArthur had long served

his country; he was respected and revered, an icon to the general public. He also had a galactic-sized ego and did not take kindly to any interference with his plans and goals. At some point in the Korean War President Truman and his advisors placed restrictions on how MacArthur could conduct the war. MacArthur was furious and by public statement and well-placed leaks he made it known that the President was preventing a victorious end to the war. It was an instance in which a military man was rebelling against his commander-in-chief, the president. President Truman was one of the most historically minded presidents we have had. He knew that MacArthur by his actions was challenging, rebelling against civilian control over the military. He also knew that by firing MacArthur he, the president, would, so to speak, be tarred and feathered by a large part of the citizenry. (He was in fact excoriated. MacArthur was given a huge ticker tape parade down New York's Fifth Avenue. He also was invited by Congress to address it, and he did so in a way that could have earned him honorary status in Actors Equity.) The continuity value was in the President's psychological bloodstream, more correctly, in his political superego together with the Constitution. Today he is applauded for that action and many others.

5. Truman took office after President Roosevelt's death. FDR had been elected four successive times. Several years later Congress and the states approved a constitutional amendment limiting a president to two terms. That amendment very clearly reflected the founding fathers' concern about the possibility that executive power could in the hands of a power-hungry president subvert the continuity value. Again the continuity value played a decisive role. (That value is also in the picture in states which have set term limits, or have tried to set limits, to those in elective office.)

6. The Civil War was at its roots about slavery. But the immediate cause was a legal-constitutional one: Did the Constitution grant states the right to secede from the union? That question, of course, derived from two polar opposite views about the continuity value. The South sought to depart from that value, the North did not. There previously had been bitter struggles about slavery, and several compromises had been reached. But there came a time when the South said, "No more compromises; we will go our own way and that requires secession; the union as it is will not and should not continue."

Why do I regard it as of bedrock importance for students to begin to understand the continuity value? There are two reasons, and they frequently are experienced as one. The first is that as individuals they have been or will be confronted with pressures, internal or external, to question or to depart from the continuity values they hold. It may be in regard to family, peer groups, sex, drugs, the law, career, and school learning. No one can escape the fact that he or she possesses a continuity value. They may not articulate it or think about it until something happens that forces them to be aware of it, at which point it becomes salient, a troubling salience because they know that departing from their continuity value may or will have untoward consequences. So, for example, there was a time not so many decades ago when parents felt obliged—or felt pressured to feel obliged—not to seek a divorce because the discontinuities in its wake would have untoward consequences for their children. Divorce laws made getting a divorce very difficult. Marital conflicts should be resolved by sacrifice and compromise for the sake of the children; breakup of or "secession from the union" should not be an option. The story today is a radically different one, which some people regard with favor and others as a societal catastrophe, just as in our Civil War the South viewed secession in one way, and the North, in another way. I know no one who denies that divorce has negative consequences for children. The question today is how many children are scarred by divorce, and the nature and duration of the scarring. The research evidence does not provide the clearest of answers, but it goes in a direction comforting to no one. My friend and colleague, Murray Levine, would classify divorce as an instance of problem creation through problem solution. That always happens when there is a departure from the continuity value.

The second reason I attach great importance to the continuity value speaks to a feature of our sense of personal identity we think about infrequently, or take for granted until (again) something happens. I refer to the fact that we are Americans, not only because we are born here or through naturalization became an American citizen, but because we are shaped in diverse witting and unwitting ways to think and act in distinctively American ways. The millions of people who came and come to these shores are not in doubt from day one that Americans are distinctively different in obvious and subtle ways from the people in their native country. Similarly, the millions of American tourists who have gone abroad for the first time are not in doubt that Americans are not Frenchmen, Russians, Chinese, Kenyans, Egyptians, and so forth. Americans are not unique human beings; they are just different, but it is a difference that makes a huge difference for our sense of personal identity and, therefore, how much we know about and regard the continuity value.

War, unfortunately, is the clearest instance when the continuity value of individuals and their country intersect. America has been in a number of wars when that intersection occurred without conflict. The one exception was the Vietnam War and the consequences of the conflict between the continuity value of individuals and the government still reverberate today. A country, a religion, a tribe does not have to decide the centrality of the continuity of its and their members. It is, so to speak, "natural." And it devises a variety of means to instill that value in their members, and one of those means today is the requirement of states that American history be taught. That these courses are taught in an abysmally stultifying way, that they turn students off rather than on, that history has no personal relationship to personal identity, that to be ignorant of national history robs individuals of the means to make considered judgments about public issues involving the continuity value, that history is not a collection of facts soon forgotten but rather about facts only understood in their relation to processes and values—all this and more influences the sense of personal identity.[1]

Finally, let me now state something I did not state or intend to say or imply. *The continuity value is not an argument for mindless or passive conformity.* It is an argument that asserts that as individuals and a country we are and will be confronted with issues challenging the substance of this or that aspect of the continuity value and, therefore, should oblige us to know the substance and justification of the continuity value as it is posed in particular circumstances. The continuity value is not about whim or feeling, but about ideas, processes, direction, and vision, departures from which should never be taken lightly. *That does not mean that those departures should not be taken but rather that they be taken on the basis of an understanding of past experiential-historical considerations.* The continuity value is not a red light for departures but rather an amber one during which you decide whether when the green light appears you will turn left in the direction of the continuity value or turn right to depart from it. That may not be a felicitous way of saying it, but I trust the reader gets the point. When Jefferson wrote in the Declaration of Independence that when a people are tyrannized by government they have a right to overthrow it, he was recognizing the more general and obvious point that the continuity value should be no bar to considered departures from it. That is or should be true in the life of an individual as well as in that of his or her country.

Stating or holding a continuity value is one thing, acting consistently and appropriately in regard to it is another matter. When the continuity value is defended or employed illogically or inappropriately, there will always be some people who will recognize the defense for what it is and

---

1. I could argue at length, but not with any claim to expertise, that every subject should be taught from a historical perspective. For example, the history of science is a series of productive discontinuities. But it is also a history in which one feature has remained constant and is drummed into would-be scientists: The scientist is obliged by the scientific community to be as scrupulously dispassionate as possible in conducting his studies and reporting them to others both for judgment and replication. His or her sense of personal identity should reflect that value or morality so treasured by the scientific community. Not to respect that value is a secular sin.

will seek to right matters, not by departing from it but by pointing out that the continuity value is not being honored. That was the case with slavery, women's rights, and more in our national history. That is why I have said many times in my writings that there are two different histories you can write about this country: One is about this country's glories in being consistent with the basic values embedded in the Constitution, and one is about the blatant ways it subverted the letter and spirit of those values. Only in recent years have the history books used in schools begun (very gingerly and unsatisfactorily) to deal with the seamy side of national history, as if a more balanced and truthful account would diminish in young minds their respect for this country's traditions. The fact is—and I consider it a fact— that in the individual lives of high school students there are times when they want to be but are not faithful to the substance of continuity values in which they truly believe. (The Catholic confessional booth and the confession by Jews of their sins on Yom Kippur are examples.) In individual and national life and history the complexity and challenges to the continuity value cannot be avoided but neither should those histories be seen as unrelated. And that brings me to my second example of why I have come to regard the continuity value as so basic in schooling. It is an illustration about which I can be much more brief than I was with the first one.

In the course of engaging in the self-scrutinizing process and coming to regard the continuity value no less important than wanting to continue to learn, I realized that in my 1971 book *The Culture of the School and the Problem of Change* I failed to do justice to a particular concept in a particular place; more correctly, the seeds giving rise to the present chapter were in that book, but they remained just that: seeds that did not sprout in my thinking.[2] I refer to the concept of the constitution of the classroom. The classroom, I said, like any other group organized and sustained over time has, formally or informally, a constitution which governs relationships and actions of the group's members. I pointed out that the classroom is a place where the constitution is written, so to speak, by the teacher because he or she is the classroom's executive, legislative, and judiciary branches. The students are silent or passive in regard to constitution writing. The teacher is the benevolent despot. The noun *despot* may not sit well with some readers, but I use that noun because one of the defining features of a despot is that they make all decisions and do not take kindly to challenges to their power and authority. Teachers are, generally speaking, nice, decent people who seek to further

---

2. Even when that book was reissued by Teachers College Press as *Revisiting "The Culture of the School and the Problem of Change"* (1996), and I added a hundred pages to the book, I did not elaborate on the constitution of the classroom even though I emphasized issues of power more than before.

the intellectual and personal growth of their students, but they are totally unaware that they do as they do by the defining stance of a despot, however benevolent: They make all the decisions about the governance rules of the classroom, ultimate power resides in one person. That is not the case because teachers have in a most conscious sense decided to adopt such a role. By virtue of the teachers' own school experience, what they have been taught in preparatory programs, what they observe in the school where they begin their career, what the larger society expects and supports, parental expectations—all of this does not cause teachers to question their stance in regard to power, authority, and decision making. For teachers that is the way things are and should be. Why question what is right, natural, or proper?

That stance makes no sense unless you assume several things. The first is that students, all students, have no interest in participating in some way in the formation of the constitution of the classroom. The second is that they are too immature and inexperienced to participate in some way in such an activity. The third is what I call the "If you gave them an inch, they will ask for a mile" expectation. Students have to be told what the constitution is, and it is the responsibility of the teacher to instill in students a sense of responsibility to the laws and spirit of that constitution and in accordance with an underlying continuity value that must be protected if students are to learn what society says they should learn. To do things otherwise, to depart from that continuity value, is to produce disorder, even chaos.

I assume that readers will agree that by the time a child starts formal schooling he or she has had a good deal of experience with issues of power and authority. You can say that for parents one of the most troublesome and inevitable—and I use that word advisedly—tasks in rearing children centers on power and authority issues. There are issues about feeding and eating, preventing actions dangerous to physical safety, toilet training, how to relate to and play with other children, and so forth. And if there is more than one child in the family, and/or if grandparents live with the family, issues of power and authority can become very complicated.

In the first 2 years or so, the child expresses his or her reactions to power and authority largely by crying and body language. Expression changes when the child begins to use language to challenge in some way parental suggestions and dictates. The frequency of "no" and "why" and "I don't want to" increases. The frequency, force, and consequences of these challenges depends in large part on parental style and values. Neither the child nor the parent chooses their temperaments, and when there is a mismatch in the temperaments between parent and child, the consequences can range from the unremarkable to something like total war. For the child and parent, the child's transition from a near total egocentricity to one of trying to comprehend the actions and feelings of the other guarantees that issues of power and authority will be in the picture. Death and taxes are by no means the only inevitabilities we experience!

Humans, especially preschoolers, are question-asking organisms. And, I would contend, by the time the child starts formal schooling, the child's rate of question asking (publicly or privately) reaches its peak, not because that is the way humans are, so to speak, "programmed" but because classrooms are not conducive to children's asking questions. For a period of 2 years I spent several hundred hours in kindergartens and first and second grades. Teachers asked questions, scads of them. Children asked pitifully few. There are few if any parents of these children who would say that their child's question-asking behavior at home dropped once the child started formal schooling.

I am belaboring what I consider to be obvious: Children come to school full of questions about what they might expect and hope for. Ninety-nine percent of those questions do not get asked, although many of them will get asked at home. Children find themselves in a classroom where the constitution governing that classroom has already been written by the teacher. And parents play a role, in that most of them have already told their children to do what the teacher tells them to do. Teachers do not tell children not to ask questions. But by their manner and what they say—and this might be done in a calm, friendly, even loving way—the children are not in doubt about who has sole power and authority and what the rules of the game are to which the child must conform. Why these rules are what they are is not to be questioned because they are rules intended to help children learn. Teacher knows best.

So what is there to criticize? Am I suggesting that teachers should not have ultimate power and authority about the classroom constitution? Definitely not. Am I suggesting that teachers should be aware and respectful of the fact that children may be very interested in why the rules are what they are, that children, as they will move up the grades, will be the opposite of neutral about the classroom constitution? And if in the earliest grades children do not appear interested in the significances of the "why" of the constitution, should it not be the educational obligation of the teachers to stimulate such interest so that the child begins, however dimly or inchoately, to recognize that he or she has a vested interest in constitutional matters, that it is an interest that carries with it obligations? My answer to these questions is, definitely yes. I do not dispute the ultimate decision-making authority of the teacher, and I am not one who overestimates the wisdom or knowledge of students. But I do dispute the antieducational exercise of power and authority that is not preceded by an open discussion in which students feel safe to express opinions. And, of course, discussion is never to be confused with a lecture or a sermon or a noblesse oblige, ritualistic teacher stance. I am talking about a teacher sincerely listening and trying to understand what is in the minds of the children. The teacher, no less than the students, is learning and in the process beginning to think about how to respond in ways that is not a criticism or put down or, worse yet, ignoring what students have said because he or she wants quickly to get to the point where "real learning" begins. The students may be first graders, but they are quite capable of knowing when someone is seriously listening to their opinions and suggestions. Not a few students learned that in regard to their parents.

I have never taught in a public school. For half a century—that is longer than if I said 50 years—I taught college undergraduates and graduate students. On more than a few occasions I was challenged on constitutional issues. In the beginning years I was an anxious and insecure teacher who could not conceive of engaging students about why I organized the course as I did, about why I would grade as I would, about why I frowned on students who came late or left early, why I expected class and term papers to be handed in on time and not a day later, and why students who never made a comment or asked a question would not be given the top grade for the course even if I gave them an A on the final exam. I was playing the role in a way all but one or two of my university professors played with what seemed to me the height of self-confidence. I was a newly minted assistant professor, and given my insecurity, I played the role experience had "taught" me. It took me a while to begin to relax, to begin to realize that the students were reasonable people and I was treating them as potential threats to my way of thinking and decision making. Gradually, teaching became more interesting and enjoyable for me, and the same was, I believe, true for the students.

Let me illustrate aspects of the above by an experience from the early 1970s. It occurred a couple of weeks after the killing of student demonstrators at Kent State University, which was fresh in the minds of the nation, and the murder trial of Bobby Seale and other Black Panther militants was about to begin in New Haven. The governor had ordered the National Guard to the city. Yale students were expressing all kinds of criticisms about how the university was run in ways that were insensitive to the opinions of students who had no voice whatsoever in decision making. Keep in mind that Yale was physically *in* New Haven but not *of* an economically impoverished, population-declining New Haven and was surrounded on two sides by Black ghettos; and the protests against the Vietnam War were daily fare. Many students boycotted classes, and some parents came to New Haven to take their students home. For one (perhaps two?) days the university canceled classes to facilitate meetings between students and faculty, forums for airing points of view and suggestions for change. I trust the reader gets the picture of conflict, turmoil, and the potential for physical violence.

I attended one of those meetings which was held at the Psycho-Educational Clinic. Although it would be correct to say that the students clearly and vigorously expressed their views, there was no doubt their suggestions were meant as demands. I agreed with a few of their suggestions, especially those concerning Yale's aloofness from New Haven and its many problems, most especially its inadequate, deteriorating school system. But as the meeting continued, I found myself getting angry about suggestions for adding certain kinds of courses and changing requirements for what constitutes a major, criticisms of the failure of faculty to represent all relevant points of view, and, certainly not least in importance, demands that students should have a voice in matters of educational policy, such as the selection of new faculty and the need for new programs students deemed relevant to their interests and social, economic, racial, and equity values of paramount concern to them.

Why did I bristle? The short answer is that a fair number of the things required an obvious departure by Yale from its long-standing conception of its continuity value, adherence to which had made it a great university. But that short answer really does not explain my bristling reaction which was in response to the fact that students had not thought through the possible consequences of what they wanted. Their hearts were in the right place, but what emanated from their hearts was, I felt, poorly connected to their minds. It was not because they were young and immature. Yes, they were young, but very bright and very knowledgeable about what was happening in the world. And they were not immature if only because they were grappling with societal problems that people older than they also were trying to understand and ameliorate. Rather it was because Yale (and other Yales of the world) had never bothered to explain to students the substance and sources of its continuity value, and why it treasured its continuity value.[3] And if it did not bother, it was because of two assumptions: Students were not interested and, besides, it was none of their business. That, of course, is precisely the stance of teachers in grade school in regard to the classroom constitution.

Uncharacteristically (!), I did not say much at the meeting. A fair number of the students knew I was not a political reactionary seeking to preserve the status quo. The clinic and its faculty were known as activists very

---

3. For 5 years before I retired I asked graduate students in my seminars to write and describe the process, step-by-step, the university employs (and why) in selecting new faculty. Their ignorance was profound and totally ahistorical. Hiring new faculty is the process which illuminates par excellence, the significances attached to the continuity value. The importance of the rationale for the continuity value is known and understood, albeit in varying degrees, by faculty. But how, when, and where can students begin to understand the continuity value in the university? That is a rhetorical question.

much involved with underserved populations in the city, which is why some students I did not know chose to come to the clinic and not other meeting venues. In any event, toward the close of the meeting I decided that there was one point I wanted to, had to, make even though it was critical of what I felt was basic to their stance.

> I agree with some of the criticisms you have made of the university. But when you criticize faculty about course content and kindred matters, I am puzzled about how to respond in ways that I feel you have not.
>
> Everyone in this room can talk a long time about the garbage that radio and TV networks offer us. So imagine that we have made appointments to meet with the networks' executives to express our outrage. We meet with Paley at CBS, Sarnoff at NBC, and Goldenson at ABC, and we ask loud and clear, "How do you justify the garbage you offer to the public?" And do you know what their answer will be? Their answer will be, "That is what people tell us they want. If we offered them what they do not want or are not interested in, our bottom line would be written in red ink and we would be out on our ears."
>
> Are you telling the faculty to give you what you want? Is that your conception of the obligations of a professor? Is a professor someone who asks students what they are interested in so he can give them what they want, the way the networks' executives responded to us?

Whenever I replay that experience I know I was posing the issue too starkly, that the issue was not either-or. But like everyone else in the meeting, I was not as thoughtful or calm and collected as I might have been. (That is an explanation, not an excuse.) What I am trying to say is that if Yale became a place where faculty were obliged to satisfy what students want, Yale would no longer be the university it is and has been. Of course, faculty should be more than interested in what students want and expect, and should give time to finding that out, which too many faculty do not do. There may not be a meeting of the minds, but when push comes to shove, the professor owes it to the students to explain why he or she can or cannot accede to what students want. A professor is someone who has something to profess. That is why he or she was hired. I continue to be amazed how little understanding students have of the professor's role and obligations, just as I am amazed how many professors never think it important to explore what students want and expect. And by explore I do not mean an effort reflecting the stance of a king benevolently and ritualistically giving his subjects an opportunity to address him. You explore because there are things you do not know that you feel you need to know, and exploration is your way of finding out about those things. There will be surprises ahead from which you will learn important things, surprises which may cause you in some ways to rethink how you reach your goal; your goal is a constant, the means to reach it are not. In matters educational there is not one, and only one, way to reach your goal. To believe otherwise is to ignore the obvious and to indulge arrogance.

Now back to the school classroom. *There is no feature and/or problem of individual, social, and group life outside of the classroom that is not at some point a feature of life in the classroom and school.* When I have said this to numerous groups or individuals and asked if anyone could think of an exception, no one was able to come up with one. (Perhaps there are exceptions, but by virtue of being exceptions, they prove the rule; rules are not laws.) I have in these pages concentrated on two features. The first is the continuity value: the classroom is a place required by the larger society to stimulate and oversee in students the acquisition of subject matter and skills that contribute to their becoming productive individuals and *responsible citizens.* I italicize "responsible citizens" to make the obvious point that classrooms make no sense unless one understands that society has a continuity value that says, so to speak, "We are a society that has a past in which certain values were so highly prized that they gave rise to a Constitution by which we are governed today and seek to continue in the present and future. Therefore, schools are places where young people will come to understand those values and Constitution so that they will voluntarily seek to honor, protect, and obey them. The liberties the past has given are those that students today will pass on to those who come after. Vigilance is the price of liberty and continuity."

Those are nice words with which people will agree. They sound patriotic, a word one does not hear often today and one that to some people means a mindless conformity to a past in the service of an ignorance of past departures from the continuity value. That has sometimes been the case. Ironically, however, these critics are ignorant of past history. In our national history there have always been disputes about what is or is not patriotic, but the Civil War aside, the continuity value was not in the picture and disputes were somehow worked out by constitutionally appropriate means.[4]

---

4. This book was written weeks before the Twin Towers tragedy of September 11, 2001. It is little short of amazing how that event made the continuity value salient for the entire country, a value many had not previously thought about or may even have disparaged. The awareness of the importance of continuity was similar to that when Pearl Harbor was bombed, President Franklin D. Roosevelt died suddenly, and President John F. Kennedy was assassinated. And by importance I mean that there are values which we come to see as truly overarching.

What I have said about patriotism is not a digression but central to the importance I attach to the continuity value and the teaching of history. The continuity value has been forged by challenges to it, sometimes rightly so, sometimes not. Even after the Civil War and after many unfavorable judicial decisions, it took almost 90 years for the Supreme Court to render its desegregation decision in 1954. By declaring segregated schools unconstitutional the Court was prohibiting a process—discontinuing a practice— and reaffirming a continuity value about freedom, liberty, and equal opportunity. That is why most people, whether they were for or against, knew in their heart of hearts that the decision was putting flesh on the bones of a continuity value too long misinterpreted, ignored, dishonored.

So, educationally speaking, what does this mean for the classroom? What do we want students to learn and understand about American history? Why? My answer to the why question derives from what I said earlier: The classroom and school contain the major features of social-political life which led to the contents of the country's Constitution, which subsequently altered or amended that Constitution and remain obvious and even controversial today. These are features of family living as well as of classroom and school life. There are features centering on rights, rules, governance, goals, and values. They are features which in the early school years students do not know how to articulate and are not helped or encouraged to think about and articulate. But to anyone knowledgeable about middle and high school students, those features become, however publicly unarticulated, sources of resentment, complaint, or even rebellion, or a passive conformity that is skin deep, or, worst of all, a decreased interest in or motivation to learn. From the standpoint of students, most but not all students, school is a kind of boot camp run by sergeants whose job it is to tame and socialize them to conform to army life. What students think and feel is not what the sergeants were hired to understand; they were hired to socialize students in groups of battalion size in schools containing upwards of several thousand students, which has the consequence of insuring personal anonymity. Students talk among themselves about the school and school personnel in ways only the more imaginative teachers can intuit, and even then with difficulty. From the standpoint of students there are pitifully few opportunities or forums to express their thinking, feelings, points of view, opinions. *Having said that, however, let me assure the reader that I am not suggesting that students and school personnel can ever reach the point when they feel they fully understand each other and there are no unbridgeable gulfs that divide them, if only because of differences in power and authority, differences I do not dispute.*

I am asserting (not suggesting) several things. First, the gulf today is inexcusably wide and deep. Second, that gulf is antieducational in that subject matter becomes a collection of facts that has no personal meaning for students, facts which are perceived by students as occupants of a museum of historical relics which do not connect with life in the classroom and school. Third, life in the classroom and school can be conceptualized, presented, discussed, and debated in ways that make the past part of a living present. There is a difference, a vast one, between knowledge and knowing. Knowledge is factual, independent of the knower, "out there." Knowing is a product of a lived experience which becomes part of your psychological bloodstream; you "own" it in a truly personal way. You do not "own" facts, you inherit them in a purely impersonal way. Fourth, nobody advocates for an anarchic classroom, everybody is in favor of explicit rules for governance; but we have yet to take seriously that when constitutions are unilaterally formulated and mandated and justified neither by discussion nor past experience with constitution building, the people (= students) over time will resent their being left out of the process. The slogan of the American colonists was, "Taxation without representation is tyranny." Students, especially those in middle and high schools, feel unrepresented.

Readers may ask, "How should this be done? Are teachers trained to handle such an approach with the willingness, sensitivity, patience it requires? Will they not encounter problems, challenges, and God knows what else young people can come up with?" To the first question I readily admit that I am not prepared to say how it might be done. It was not until I began to think about writing this self-scrutinizing memoir that I realized how superficially and briefly I had examined the constitution of the classroom, any classroom in any subject matter. I did not understand that wrapped up in the constitutional issue are the most important features of group living, of the rationale for and the tensions between obligations and governance, of the importance of respect for the continuity value which, I feel compelled to say again, does not mean an unthinking, slavish conformity to the status quo.

To the other two questions I have to say, as I have said about many things, that the preparation of educators is for all practical purposes almost totally inadequate, and if I were totally candid, I would strike out the word almost. That, I must emphasize, is not a criticism of teachers; that would be an instance of blaming the victim. It is a criticism of colleges and universities which have preparatory programs. These programs have never taken seriously John Dewey's statement that schooling is not a preparation for life but life itself.

Ironically, there has long been one group that should be most sympathetic to what I have said about how students are perceived in regard to the constitutional issue: teachers. Anyone who is even semifamiliar with the history of education up to and including today will know that teachers are viewed by their administrative superiors (and boards of education) as without competence to participate in the *discussion* of educational policy. Please note that I did not say *formation* of educational policy because by law the ultimate decision makers are not teachers. But the law does not prohibit *participation* in some meaningful, nonritualistic way by teachers. So it is not surprising that teachers look up at the hierarchy—teachers are at the bottom of it—and on the basis of their experience judge them as uncomprehending, unilateral, insensitive, capricious, demeaning, impersonal, aloof, masters of all they survey and yet ignorant about what is going on, uninterested in what teachers think and feel, and mindless protectors of a continuity value they do not and cannot reexamine. Unfortunately, there is nothing in preparatory programs, and certainly nothing in the way schools are organized and administered, to make it possible for teachers to feel kinship with students. As for administrators, I would be rendered speechless if they agreed with what I have said about students, teachers, and their kinship.

The classroom is not a democratic setting if by democratic you mean that those who comprise it have voting power to approve or disapprove the actions of its sole leader, let alone to remove them. As I have said, I do not suggest that students be given voting power. But if by democratic you mean the spirit (not the letter) of the democratic ethos, then the classroom should reflect that spirit. Will there be problems, challenges, and disputes? Of course. If there is anything predictable from the democratic ethos and spirit, it is that it brings to the fore expressions about governance and experience of it. Winston Churchill once quipped that democracy is the worst of all forms of governance except for all other forms. What that quip reflects is the importance Churchill gave to the continuity value in regard to the right of people to be heard. No one understood this better than the founding fathers. They knew they were going into uncharted seas; most of them were fearful about people acting responsibly with the rights accorded them; they feared the rise of parties, divisiveness, and narrow partisanship. They literally prayed that their societal experiment and all that it represented would have continuity value and not be aborted or distorted. They were wrong, of course, about parties, divisiveness, and narrow partisanship, about which the United States takes second place to no other country. And yet the hopes and dreams they had for the new country managed to withstand the messiness, threats and departures from the continuity value (slavery, women's rights, an undemocratic electoral process for members of Congress, and so forth). That is a history every student should know, but more important in my opinion is that major features of that history can be experienced in the classroom in a way that makes for knowing and not only impersonal knowledge.

I have no concrete program for how to do it. I had no such program when I first wrote about the constitution of the classroom in 1971, and I do not have one now. I could dream up such a program. Indeed, in the course of writing this book all kinds of possibilities entered my mind. But I long ago realized that if I wanted truly to understand the practical problems my ideas would encounter and have a basis for believing I was moving in the right direction, I, not somebody else, had to try out, to implement, those ideas. One of the few things Karl Marx said that deserves remembrance is that if you want to understand the world, try changing it. At my age I do not have the energy to deal with such complicated problems on the levels of action. So I am left with thinking, reviewing, and writing. I am grateful for that even though the brute fact is that nothing I have written that I think is important in regard to educational reform has changed anything. I am also grateful that a fair number of people have read my writings with approval. Authors need and write for the choir, and although that choir may be small, authors thank God for big favors. And for me it is a very big favor!

References

Aiken, W. A. (1942). *The story of the eight year study with conclusions and recommendations*. New York: HarperCollins.

Alinsky, S. D. (1946). *Reveille for radicals*. Chicago: University of Chicago Press.

Alinsky, S. D. (1971). *Rules for radicals: A practical primer for realistic radicals*. New York: Vintage.

Bensman, D. (1987). *Quality education in the inner city*. New York: Center for Collaborative Education.

Bensman, D. (2000). *Central Park East and its graduates*. New York: Teachers College Press.

Brouillette, L. (2002). *Charter schools: Lessons in school reform*. Mahwah, NJ: Erlbaum.

Buxton, C. (1973). *Adolescents in schools*. New Haven, CT: Yale University Press.

Dollard, J. (1935). *Criteria for the life history*. New Haven, CT: Yale University Press.

Dollard, J. (1937). *Caste and class in a Southern town*. New Haven, CT: Yale University Press.

Flexner, A. (1910). *Medical education in the United States and Canada: A report to the Carnegie Foundation for the Advancement of Teaching*. Washington, DC: Carnegie Foundation for the Advancement of Teaching. (Reprinted in 1960)

Gerstner, L., & Thompson, T. (2000, December 7). The problem ain't the kids. *New York Times*.

Gladwin, T., & Sarason, S. (1953). *Truk: Man in paradise*. New York: Wenner-Gren Foundation.

Goodman, J., & Lesnick, H. (2001). *The moral stake in education*. New York: Longman.

Heckman, P. (1995). *The courage to change*. Newbury Park, CA: Corwin Press.

Hill, D. (2000, August/September). Punching out. *Teacher*.

Horwitt, S. D. (1992). *Let them call me rebel: Saul Alinsky—His life and legacy*. New York: Vintage.

James, W. (1900). *Talks to teachers and to students*. New York: Holt.

Kammerand-Campbell, S. (1989). *Doc: The story of Dennis Littky and his fight for a better school*. Chicago: Contemporary Books.

Levine, E. (2001). *One kid at a time: Big lessons from a small school*. New York: Teachers College Press.

Mayhew, K. C., & Edwards, A. C. (1966). *The Dewey school*. New York: Atherton Press.

Merrifield, J. (2001). *The school choice wars*. Lanham, MD: Scarecrow Press.

Monterra, V. (1996). *Bridging the gap: A case study of the home-school-community relationship at the Ochoa Elementary School*. Unpublished doctoral dissertation, College of Education, University of Arizona, Tucson.

Pauly, E. (1991). *The classroom crucible: What really works, what doesn't and why.* New York: Basic Books.

Ravitch, D. (2000). *Left back: A century of failed school reforms.* New York: Simon & Schuster.

Sarason, E. K., & Sarason, S. B. (1969). Some observations on the teaching of the New Math. In Yale University Psycho-Educational Clinic, *Collected papers and studies* (S. B. Sarason & F. Kaplan, Eds.). Boston: Massachusetts State Department of Mental Health.

Sarason, S. B. (1971). *The culture of the school and the problem of change.* Boston: Allyn & Bacon. (Reprinted in 1996 by Teachers College Press in *Revisiting "The culture of the school and the problem of change."*)

Sarason, S. B. (1972). *The creation of settings and the future societies.* San Francisco: Jossey-Bass.

Sarason, S. B. (1976). The unfortunate fate of Alfred Binet and school psychology. *Teachers College Record, 77,* 579–592.

Sarason, S. B. (1983). *Schooling in America: Scapegoat and salvation.* New York: Free Press.

Sarason, S. B. (1985). *Psychology and mental retardation.* Austin, TX: Pro-Ed.

Sarason, S. B. (1988). *The making of an American psychologist.* San Francisco: Jossey-Bass.

Sarason, S. B. (1990a). *The challenge of art to psychology.* New Haven, CT: Yale University Press.

Sarason, S. B. (1990b). *The predictable failure of educational reform.* San Francisco: Jossey-Bass.

Sarason, S. B. (1993a). *The case for change: Rethinking the preparation of educators.* San Francisco: Jossey-Bass.

Sarason, S. B. (1993b). *Letters to a serious education president.* Newbury Park, CA: Corwin Press.

Sarason, S. B. (1993c). *You are thinking of teaching?* San Francisco: Jossey-Bass.

Sarason, S. B. (1995). *Parental involvement and the political principle.* San Francisco: Jossey-Bass.

Sarason, S. B. (1996). *Revisiting "The culture of the school and the problem of change."* New York: Teachers College Press.

Sarason, S. B. (1997). *How schools might be governed and why.* New York: Teachers College Press.

Sarason, S. B. (1998a). *Charter schools: Another flawed educational reform?* New York: Teachers College Press.

Sarason, S. B. (1998b). *Political leadership and educational failure.* San Francisco: Jossey-Bass.

Sarason, S. B. (1999). *Teaching as a performing art.* New York: Teachers College Press.

Sarason, S. B. (2001). *American psychology and schools: A critique.* New York: Teachers College Press.

Sarason, S. B., Davidson, K., & Blatt, B. (1986). *The preparation of teachers: An unstudied problem in education.* Cambridge, MA: Brookline Books. (Original work published in 1962)

Sarason, S. B., Levine, M., Goldenberg, I., Cherlin, D., & Bennett, E. (1966). *Psychology in community settings*. New York: Wiley.

Sarason, S. B., et al. (1977). *Human services and resource networks*. San Francisco: Jossey-Bass.

Sarason, S. B., & Klaber, M. (1985). The school as a social situation. *Annual Review of Psychology, 36*, 115–140.

Sarason, S. B., & Lorentz, E. M. (1989). *The challenge of the resource exchange network*. San Francisco: Jossey-Bass.

Sarason, S. B., & Lorentz, E. M. (1992). *Crossing boundaries*. San Francisco: Jossey-Bass.

Schaefer-Simmern, H. W. (1948). *The unfolding of artistic activity*. Berkeley: University of California Press.

Schumacher, E. F. (1973). *Small is beautiful: Economics as if people mattered*. New York: Harper & Row.

Sen, A. (1998). *Development as freedom*. New York: Knopf.

Shirley, D. (1997). *Community organizing for urban school reform*. Austin: University of Texas Press.

Skinner, B. F. (1962). *Walden two*. New York: MacMillan.

Steinberg, L. D., et al. (1996). *Beyond the classroom*. New York: Simon & Schuster.

Susskind, E. (1969). Questioning and curiosity in the elementary school classroom. Unpublished doctoral dissertation, Yale University, New Haven, CT.

Tanner, L. (1997). *Dewey's laboratory school: Lessons for today*. New York: Teachers College Press.

Traub, J. (2000, January 16). What no school can do. *New York Times Magazine*.

Vlahakis, R., et al. (1978). *Kids who care*. Oakdale, NY: Dowling College Press.

Wertheimer, M. (1945). *Productive thinking*. New York: Harpers.

Wilson, K., & Daviss, B. (1994). *Redesigning education*. New York: Teachers College Press.

Index

About the Author

Seymour B. Sarason is professor of psychology emeritus in the Department of Psychology and at the Institution for Social and Policy Studies of Yale University. In 1962 he founded and directed the Yale Psycho-Educational Clinic, one of the first research and training sites in community psychology. Fields in which he has made special contributions include mental retardation, culture and personality, projective techniques, teacher training, anxiety in children, and school reform. His numerous books and articles reflect his broad interests.

Dr. Sarason received his Ph.D. degree from Clark University in 1942 and holds honorary doctorates from Syracuse University, Queens College, Rhode Island College, and Lewis and Clark College. He has received awards from the American Psychological Association and the American Association on Mental Deficiency.